PRAISE FOR RICHARD HEYMAN'S PREVIOUS *HOW TO SAY IT®* TITLE

How to Say It® to Teens

"Heartfelt and genuinely practical advice . . . Parents wary of addressing difficult topics (contraception, curfews, peer pressure) with their teens will find plenty of tips, including specific questions to jump-start conversations, words to employ and phrases to avoid . . . Parents seeking the 'right' words will be grateful for Heyman's forthright approach and encouraging tone . . . [*How to Say It® to Teens*] will find a wide and grateful readership."
—*Publishers Weekly*

How to Say It to Boys

Communicating with Boys
to Help Them Become the Best Men
They Can Be

RICHARD HEYMAN, ED.D.

PRENTICE HALL PRESS

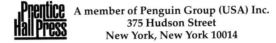 A member of Penguin Group (USA) Inc.
375 Hudson Street
New York, New York 10014

Prentice Hall Press edition: May 2003

Library of Congress Cataloging-in-Publication Data

Heyman, Richard D.
    How to say it to boys / Richard Heyman.
        p.   cm.
    Includes bibliographical references and index.
    ISBN 0-7352-0368-7
    1. Boys—Life skills guides.   2. Boys—Conduct of life.   3. Teenage boys—Life
skills guides.   4. Conduct of life.   I. Parenting.   II. Parent and child.
HQ775 .H57   2003   2003042923
305.23—dc21

Printed in the United States of America

10   9   8   7   6   5   4   3

CONTENTS

PART ONE

Baby Boys and Toddlers (0–2 years)

PART TWO

Preschool Boys (3–5 years)

PART THREE
Young Schoolboys (6–8 years)

PART FOUR
Older Schoolboys (9–12 years)

PART FIVE
Young Teenage Boys (13–15 years)

PART SIX

Older Teenage Boys (16–18 years)

ACKNOWLEDGMENTS

To Laura Williams for giving me the benefit of her experience.

To Donna Crawford for putting me on to some wonderful sources of information.

To Don Braid and Sydney Sharpe for always being there.

To Dylan Zack for being a young boy who I could learn from.

To Hunter Graves and Jonah Heyman for being infant boys just when I needed some.

To Adam Heyman, Peter and Amanda Graves, and David and Sarah Heyman for being the parents of Dylan, Hunter and Jonah.

To Phoebe Heyman for her tolerance, inspiration, intelligence, help and love.

To Tom Power, my editor at Prentice Hall, for his friendship and for the opportunities he gave me.

To Jennifer Hirshlag, my copyeditor at Penguin, for her close and intelligent reading of my manuscript and for her invaluable suggestions.

To Tiffany Kukec, my book designer, for perfectly catching its mood and message.

To Sheila Curry Oakes, my editor at Penguin, for taking me in from the cold and helping me to do my best.

To Patricia and Mike Snell, my agents, for their unfailing support, encouragement and work on my behalf.

PREFACE

◆

Until I researched and wrote this book I had no idea how much the differences between boys and girls were biological rather than social. I was a firm believer in the power of socialization. And I still am. But now I realize that boys and girls are hardwired to be what they are to a much greater extent than I ever thought. Biology ensures that boys and girls are different.

A good starting point for talking about the important differences between boys and girls is to look at the power of the male hormone, testosterone. Boys aren't just *taught* to be different. The differences are there from the start. Approximately six to seven weeks after conception a male fetus forms testes from embrionic "ovotestes." These must produce enough testosterone for a fetus to continue to develop as an anatomical male, or it will develop anatomically as female, even if it is genetically male.

Testosterone is so powerful that it can also dramatically affect the female body. For example, I recently read about a woman who undertook sex change therapy after decades of feeling, for whatever reason, that she was really a male in a female body. As a young girl at school this woman always played the boy roles. In playing house she was always the husband. To her friends she seemed to combine the toughness of a boy and the vulnerability of a girl.

As an adult, after living this dual life for many years, she decided to begin the medical transformation from female to male. Part of the process involved testosterone therapy, a series of male hormone injections, 200 milligrams every two weeks, which yielded powerful results.

Over the next few years this female came to look and act like a male. "He" developed "broad, triangulated shoulders, a square jaw and a voice that's midrange bass and continuing to drop." His shirt size increased, his waist size decreased, and his hairline receded by an inch and a half. Other physical changes were just as remarkable. His nose became bigger, his eyebrows heavier, and his shoe size larger. He started to shave every day and grew chest hair. His arms and legs became more muscular from his work as a carpenter, and far more male than female in their look and size.

He changed socially as well. As a male he became more confident since his ability to do his carpentry job was never questioned, whereas as a female he was always asked for references. He started to move like a man and he learned "guy talk." His emotions, too, began to change. Crying did not come easily, anymore. The tears, he said, got stuck in his chest.

There seems to be no question that male body chemistry, in particular, testosterone, causes many of the boy/girl differences. While not all of these differences mean you have to communicate differently to boys than to girls, some do. In this book I have tried to show how these boy/girl differences translate into specific communication practices for you to use with your boys.

How to Use This Book

I have designed this book to be dipped into when you need it, rather than something to be read from cover to cover. When you have a question about how to talk to your boy about some important topic, or how to communicate with your baby boy who is just beginning his life, you can find suggestions in this book. This book is a beginning, not an end. It tries to point you in the right direction so that you can start talking about subjects that are easy, or difficult.

I have used the introduction to give you a good summary of the latest research findings on the differences between boys and girls and what importance they have for communicating with your son in ways that best suit his male nature. I have given you a number of communication principles to help you in all your interactions with him.

The book has six parts, each covering an important age group for boys: 0–2, 3–5, 6–8, 9–12, 13–15, and 16–18. Each part contains fifteen chapters, each covering a different topic of importance to parents and boys, totaling ninety topics in all. In each chapter I introduce the topic in a context, which may or may not be the right one for your own situation, but which will give you a good idea of what I'm talking about. I then discuss some of the most important things to consider when you're talking to your boy about this topic. I present three things that I think you must do in communicating on the subject. I then suggest what you may want to say and do about the topic and what you may *not* want to say and do, as well as some words, phrases, or actions to use or avoid.

You are free to use my suggestions, or not, to agree with my point of view, or not. The most important thing is for you to realize that your boy needs your attention, your love, your listening to him, your sympathetic understanding, and your being there for him always.

At the end of the book I have listed a number of resources that I found invaluable in my research on boys. I recommend them all to you as excellent further reading on the topic. They will all contribute to a better understanding of those wild, willful, and lovely creatures we call our boys.

INTRODUCTION
BOYS AND GIRLS: DIFFERENCES
THAT MAKE A DIFFERENCE

My lovely living boy,
My hope, my hap, my love, my life, my joy.

—Guillaume de Salluste, Seigneur de Bartas

My fair son!
My joy, my food, my all the world.

—William Shakespeare

After centuries of neglect and oppression, much of which continues to this day, our world is rightly preoccupied with the needs of girls. However, the women's movement, with its justifiable emphasis on righting centuries of injustice toward girls and women, has threatened to make boys the forgotten gender. We must continue attending to the special needs of girls, but we must also do the same for boys. Boys, as much as girls, need special treatment and consideration because boys are different from girls, and these differences create their own unique problems and opportunities.

Christina Hoff Sommers, a strong advocate for giving boys as much careful attention as girls, points out in her stimulating book *The War Against Boys* the startling statistics on boys' performance compared to girls in critical areas of school, learning disabilities, and antisocial behavior. Here is what she discovered:

- Boys, more than girls, say they are less committed to school.
- Boys don't read as many books as girls.

- Boys' writing skills are far below those of girls'.
- Boys don't score as well as girls on tests of ability in art and music.
- Boys are more likely to be suspended from school.
- Boys are more likely to be held back in school and to drop out prematurely.
- Boys are three times more likely than girls to be in special education programs.
- Boys are four times more likely than girls to be diagnosed with ADHD (attention deficit hyperactivity disorder).
- Boys are more likely to be involved in crime, to drink alcohol, and to take drugs.
- Boys are more successful than girls at committing suicide, even though more girls make the attempt.
- As of 1996, 25 percent more girls than boys went to college and this difference is projected to increase by one-third by 2007.

Depressing, isn't it? Let me add to your depression with some data from Michael Gurian's bestseller, *The Good Son*.

- 90 percent of those who commit violent acts are male.
- 90 percent of children arrested for crimes are boys.
- 90 percent of those in jail are male.
- 80 percent of drug addicts and alcoholics are young males.
- 90 percent of the approximately three million children taking Ritalin (a drug that treats ADHD) are boys.
- 90 percent of males who get a teenage girl pregnant abandon her.
- 90 percent of the discipline problems in school are boys.
- Boys constitute the majority of child abuse victims.

These figures make it crystal clear that our boys need serious help and attention in their struggle to be successful in today's world.

How to Say It to Boys focuses on special ways, which take into account genetic and social characteristics, to talk and interact with your son to help him become a competent, successful, loving, and beloved boy and man. To do this I have translated the research on gender differences into specific principles and practices for communicating with boys. Whether it be your boy's need for more physical space than his sister, his higher level of male physicality, his male aggressiveness and risk-taking, or his need for both security and independence at the same time, I will help you make sense of the differences by suggesting the particular words and phrases you should use in talking to your son.

"It's a boy!"

You've just had a baby. How wonderful! The first thing the doctor says, even before she counts the fingers and toes and the nurse weighs and measures the child, is: "It's a boy!" or, "It's a girl!" That is what everyone wants to know.

Why do we want to know the gender? Because it makes a difference—not in how much we love our baby but in how we start thinking about him, or her. The images come to mind of how they will look as they grow up, the clothes they'll wear, the games they'll play, the toys they'll want, the problems they'll have, the sports they'll play, the interests they'll have, and the careers they'll choose.

Boys and girls are made differently. Boys vary more than girls in virtually every aspect of their growth and development. In size, fine motor skills, social development, behavior, and school performance, the variability among boys will be greater than that among girls. The time it takes for boys to acquire self-control, to learn to handle frustration, and to adapt to the demands of a school classroom, varies more than with girls.

While in the womb, the male and female brains develop differently. The right brain dominates in males and the left brain in females. The enriched right brain of the male contributes to enhanced spatial ability, the enriched left brain of the female to enhanced language-related skills. Brain chemistry seems to stimulate aggressive and impulsive behavior in males, and inhibit it in females.

Here is a summary of the brain differences that make boys boys and girls girls— each gender so different from the other in many important ways.

BRAIN SIMILARITIES AND DIFFERENCES	EFFECTS
1. Emotional processing area larger in males.	1. *Boys tend to be more aggressive than girls.*
2. Nerve bundles in central nervous system develop earlier in females.	2. *Girls talk in sentences earlier than boys.*
3. Brain sequences that control movement engage faster in males.	3. *Boys respond faster to attention demands.*
4. Speech processing areas more active in females.	4. *Girls have better verbal skills.*
5. Connections between brain parts stronger in females.	5. *Girls have better language and fine motor skills, and are more intuitive.*

BRAIN SIMILARITIES AND DIFFERENCES	**EFFECTS**
6. Connection between spinal cord and brain more direct in males.	**6.** *Boys respond faster to physical crises.*
7. Brain part controlling high intellectual functions and memory and interpretation of sensory input thicker on right side in males and on left side in females.	**7.** *Boys are better at depth perception, direction, and three dimensionality.*
8. Brain part controlling consciousness, voluntary actions, and thinking used in greater part by females.	**8.** *Girls are better at multitasking.*
9. Connection between brain hemispheres larger in females.	**9.** *Girls are better at using both brain hemispheres.*
10. Estrogen, the female sex hormone that causes the female cycle and shapes female brain present in much greater volume in females, but also present in males.	**10.** *Girls tend to be less aggressive, competitive, self-assertive, and self-reliant. Defense mechanisms, projection, self-deception, and denial better developed in females.*
11. Brain part that helps speech, thinking, emotions, and skilled movement seems more active in females.	**11.** *Girls are more skilled in verbal communication.*
12. Memory storage area much larger in females.	**12.** *Girls have large memory storage capacity.*
13. Area controlling heartbeat, breathing, temperature, and sexual differences significantly denser in males.	**13.** *Boys have a greater sex drive.*
14. Left hemisphere, more developed in females, controls all aspects of language processing, including reading, writing, math, thoughts and memory, and self-image.	**14.** *Girls are better at talking and listening, and language-based learning.*
15. Neurotransmitters, which deliver brain messages, differently distributed between males and females.	**15.** *Boys and girls tend to process data differently.*

BRAIN SIMILARITIES AND DIFFERENCES	EFFECTS
16. Brain part that "sees" and interprets visual images different in males and females.	**16.** *Boys see better in brighter light, girls in lower light.*
17. Brain part that interprets bodily sensations—pain, pressure, temperature, and touch—more active in females.	**17.** *Girls have more sensitivity to tactile sensation.*
18. Hormonal secretions that affect growth, metabolism, and other glandular activity seem stronger in connecting fight-or-flight data between glands in males.	**18.** *Boys make faster fight-or-flight decisions.*
19. Right hemisphere, used for abstract problems, more developed in males.	**19.** *Boys are better at spatial relationships.*
20. Differences between males and females in sensory receptors and transformers.	**20.** *Boys and girls show consistent differences in ability to discern and integrate information.*
21. Memory storage area shows stronger neuron connections in females.	**21.** *Girls have better short-term memory for random information. Girls are superior in language-using tasks.*
22. Testosterone, the male sex hormone, greater presence in males than females.	**22.** *Boys are more aggressive, competitive, self-assertive, and self-reliant.*
23. Brain part that regulates emotions and processes sensory input works faster in females, especially during menstruation.	**23.** *Girls experience greater stress and activity in this part of the brain, especially during menstruation.*
24. Brain area that connects thought and language seems more active in females.	**24.** *Girls tend to have better communication skills than boys.*

(I have derived this summary of brain differences from the excellent work of Michael Gurian in his book *Boys and Girls Learn Differently!, pp. 20–26.*)

Communicating with Boys

I have attempted to translate these differences between boys and girls into specific principles and practices. The way you talk to your boys should reflect the fact that boys develop differently physically and mentally and don't always see or understand the world in the same way as girls. Boys need more help with language skills and less help with gross motor skills. Boys need to be free to be aggressive and competitive, but they need your help in making their aggressive and competitive instincts work for them, not against them.

Here are twelve principles that come out of the "maleness" of boys. You can use them to guide what you say and how you say it.

Everyday Communication Practices for Every Parent of Every Boy at Every Age:

1. **Love** your boy in every way and show it in what you say and do.
2. **Accept** your boy for whom he is, not for whom you want him to be.
3. **Listen** to your boy whenever he talks, giving him your undivided attention.
4. **Teach** your boy the things you know will help him become a loving and beloved man.
5. **Praise** your boy whenever he attempts something good, new, or challenging, even if he doesn't succeed.
6. **Reward** your boy for trying to do the right thing.
7. **Encourage** your boy to become self-reliant.
8. **Follow** wherever your boy leads you so you can be there for him.
9. **Lead** your boy by setting a good example for him in every aspect of life.
10. **Understand** what your boy says and does on his own terms.
11. **Know** your boy as the individual he is.
12. **Hug** your boy at least once every day.

Now is the time to learn how to make sure you communicate with your boy in the best possible way, from the moment he is born until he is as much a friend as a son to you.

These principles translate into the following list of practical, everyday ways of communicating with your boy as he grows from infancy to adulthood. Refer to this list to help you decide on what to say and do as you watch your boy grow and change each day.

Sixty Important Communication Practices with Boys at Different Stages of Their Lives

Baby Boys and Toddlers (0–2 years)
1. Communicate by hugging your boy and saying you love him.
2. Communicate by touching and stroking your boy.
3. Communicate by talking to your boy lovingly, laughingly, matter-of-factly, or sternly, as the situation requires.
4. Communicate by singing to your boy.

5. Communicate by dancing with your boy in your arms.
6. Communicate by smiling at your boy.
7. Communicate by reading to your boy.
8. Communicate by bathing your boy.
9. Communicate by nursing/feeding your boy.
10. Communicate by listening to your boy.

PRESCHOOL BOYS (3–5 YEARS)
1. Communicate by hugging your boy and saying you love him.
2. Communicate by giving your boy the space he needs to run around and play.
3. Communicate by reading exciting stories filled with action, to your boy.
4. Communicate by listening to your boy's stories.
5. Communicate by understanding your boy's need to roughhouse and compete.
6. Communicate by praising your boy for all his accomplishments.
7. Communicate by giving your boy the objects and things he loves to play with.
8. Communicate by recognizing that your boy may choose to use dolls to fight and play war games.
9. Communicate by patiently helping your boy learn to use words and sentences.
10. Communicate by accepting your boy's short attention span and lack of empathy for you and his playmates.

YOUNG SCHOOLBOYS (6–8 YEARS)
1. Communicate by hugging your boy and saying you love him.
2. Communicate by reading to your boy often and helping him with his reading.
3. Communicate by giving your boy a firm set of rules for behavior at home and at school.
4. Communicate by encouraging your boy in his interest in sports.
5. Communicate by encouraging your boy in his interest in the arts.
6. Communicate by explaining to your boy your reasons for doing and saying things.
7. Communicate by encouraging him to talk to you.
8. Communicate by never being too busy to listen.
9. Communicate by playing games together or watching television together.
10. Communicate by playing music and singing songs together or any other activity that you both enjoy

OLDER SCHOOLBOYS (9–12 YEARS)
1. Communicate by hugging your boy and saying you love him.
2. Communicate by acknowledging the beginning of your boy's hormonal changes.

3. Communicate by encouraging your boy to follow his natural inclination to explore and experiment with things.
4. Communicate by showing your boy how to settle differences without fighting.
5. Communicate by encouraging your boy to develop his skills at games and sports.
6. Communicate by letting your boy be in charge of some details when you are on a trip.
7. Communicate by giving your boy extra help with his reading and language skills at home and school.
8. Communicate by recognizing your boy's need to control more of his life.
9. Communicate by encouraging your boy's interests in music and the arts.
10. Communicate by asking your boy to organize family activities.

YOUNG TEENAGE BOYS (13–15 YEARS)

1. Communicate by hugging your boy and saying you love him.
2. Communicate by acknowledging your boy's puberty.
3. Communicate by helping your boy control and channel his aggressive feelings in a positive direction.
4. Communicate regularly with your boy about his schoolwork and offer help where needed.
5. Communicate your continued pleasure when your boy succeeds at games, sports, and building things and taking them apart.
6. Communicate by being involved with your boy's interests at school, and knowing his teachers and the school administrators.
7. Communicate by being actively interested in your boy's friends in and out of school.
8. Communicate with your boy by discussing the biological and safety aspects of sex.
9. Communicate by listening to your boy talk about his life, his interests, his fears, and his successes and failures.
10. Communicate by trading stories with your boy about his life and yours.

OLDER TEENAGE BOYS (16–18 YEARS)

1. Communicate by hugging your boy and saying you love him.
2. Communicate by letting your boy talk to you about possible careers.
3. Communicate by helping your boy pursue his interests and passions.
4. Communicate by praising your boy for his abilities and his strengths.
5. Communicate by encouraging your boy to make the most of his talents and his appearance.

6. Communicate by being involved in your boy's circle of friends, knowing that his peers socially accept him.
7. Communicate by giving your boy clear rules about curfews, party-going, and drugs and drinking.
8. Communicate by helping your boy channel his anger and aggressive impulses in productive directions.
9. Communicate by knowing where your boy stands with his group of friends.
10. Communicate by talking to your boy about any noticeable changes to his habits and appetite, or the disappearance of valuable possessions like watches, skateboards, audio systems, or electronic games.

In the many sections and chapters of this book that follow, I will help you apply these principles and practices to communicating with your boy about a wide range of important topics and events in his life. Use my suggestions as a guide. Use what makes sense to you and don't use what doesn't make sense. Use what you agree with and ignore what you disagree with. But, above all, reflect on what you and your boy need to do to make your communication relationship the best it can possibly be.

The Communication Ethic

In my book *How to Say It to Teens* I introduced parents to five critical principles that I believe provide the best foundation for communicating with children. I called these principles the *communication ethic*. I want to end this introduction by restating these five principles because I believe they are even more important for communicating with boys than with girls.

PRINCIPLE ONE: BE INVOLVED
Boys are aggressive, adventurous, and risk-takers. They need their independence, but also the security of your attention to them even when they seem to reject it. Pay attention to your boy's life at every age. Know his likes and dislikes, his strengths and weaknesses, his talents and abilities, his friends and enemies. Know his tastes in music, movies, games, boys, and girls. Spend time with him talking, playing, or just walking in silence. Ask him questions about himself and share things about your life with him. Look into his eyes when he talks to you because his eyes are the windows of his soul.

PRINCIPLE TWO: MAKE LOVE THE CONTEXT
Boys need your love as much as girls, even if they seem to reject it and their actions often make them more difficult to love than girls. So it's important for your boy to know that you love him unconditionally. Show him you love him, tell him you love him, let

your whole being express that love for him. Never withhold that love, or threaten to take it away no matter what he does. Lose your temper with him, be angry with him, scold him, discipline him, give him rules and values to live by, but do it all with love for him in your heart.

PRINCIPLE THREE: LISTEN MORE THAN TALK

Boys are less verbal than girls. Encourage your boy to talk to you by showing him that you're always ready, willing, and anxious to listen. Give him your full attention when he talks. You can show him you're listening and understanding by saying the right thing when it's your turn, by nodding, smiling, laughing, frowning, or being serious as he talks. Your instincts are to tell him what you think he needs to know to do the right thing—you want to teach him and to do that you will preach at him. But remember that good communication goes two ways. Let him talk while you listen. The more you listen the more he'll tell you. The more he tells you the better you'll know him. The better you know him the easier it will be for you to do the right thing for him.

PRINCIPLE FOUR: WITHHOLD JUDGMENT

Boys take more risks and get into far more trouble than girls. They need you to confide in. If you want your boy to talk to you about the really important things in his life, as well as the unimportant things, then be a good reactor. We all decide what we'll tell others by guessing at how they'll react. We'll tell people who have good reactions much more than people who have bad reactions. Don't give your boy a knee-jerk reaction to things he tells you, even if they are unpleasant things. If you do, your boy will put you out of the loop. He'll only tell you things he knows you like to hear. He will not share really important things with you when he really needs your help and support because he will be afraid of your reaction. So give things time to settle, learn all the facts and all the angles, listen to all sides of the story before you act or react. Your boy will love you for it, and he'll share almost everything in his life with you.

PRINCIPLE FIVE: NEVER GIVE UP

Boys are trouble—some more than others—but most boys are much more trouble than most girls. You and your boy may argue, fight, disagree, and not even talk to one another. But no matter what happens, never give up on your boy. If you give up you have lost him. If you never give up you may still lose him, but there is always that chance that some day he will realize that you have always been there for him. He will love you for it and he will come back to you. And you will be made whole again.

PART 1

Baby Boys and Toddlers

(0–2 years)

BATH TIME

◆

You and your baby boy have had a busy day and the evening meal is done. It's time to bathe your boy and get him ready for bed. This is a wonderful opportunity for communicating with him. He has always loved his bath and as he grows older and can sit up for himself, you and he can play with the water and toys. It's a wonderful, intimate moment for the two of you as you wash his body and hair, then slowly rinse him off with a wet cloth, being careful not to let any soap get in his eyes. When he's had enough, you pick him up and towel him dry, then put on a fresh diaper and pajamas.

Things to Consider

Most babies love physical contact, according to Dr. Eli H. Newberger, author of *The Men They Will Become.* You need to touch your baby boy as much as you would touch your baby girl. Affectionate strokes can help your baby boy sleep, reduce his irritability, and increase his weight. Use bath time as you would any other intimate moment with your boy. It is another opportunity for you to communicate your love and concern for him. Your boy will enjoy his bath as long as the water is neither too hot nor too cool, and you are there to make him safe. He will play with the water and with his toys. He will even play with himself. It is perfectly normal, so don't discourage him from doing it.

Communicate your love for your boy through your gentle touch as you wash him, and later as you dry him off. Communicate your love with your kisses all over his body. Let him enjoy his nakedness. Help him play and explore with his bath toys.

Your boy will want to actively move around in the bath. Your job is to communicate safety and security while he does this. Never leave him alone in the bath. Always remain at his side, supporting him when he can't support himself, keeping him from slipping or falling. Remember that babies can drown in as little as one inch of water. Gently remind your boy about things he mustn't do in the bath because they are dangerous, like touching the hot water tap or standing up. This will help introduce him to the importance of rules.

Bathing gives you the chance to communicate love, caring, games, safety, concern, pleasure, fun, and the importance of cleanliness. Enjoy it!

Three Things You Must Do

1. Talk to your boy.
2. Praise your boy.
3. Love your boy.

Things to Say and Do

Make bath time a happy time for you and your boy. Say such things as:

- Bath time!
- What fun. It's time for your bath.
- Let's go play in the bath.
- Where's rubber ducky (or whatever your boy's favorite toy is)?

Tell your boy what each step is at bath time as a way of talking to him and teaching him about the things you do together. Say such things as:

- Now's the time to get you clean and comfortable.
- Let's get these clothes off.
- Is the water just right?
- In you go.
- You can play for a while.
- Let's get you clean.
- Time to come out.

Make your boy feel totally secure in the bath. Say such things as:

- I'll help you stand up, but you must be very careful not to slip.
- Mustn't touch that tap. It's very hot and not good for boys.
- I'll hold you while I soap you up and rinse you off.
- I'll stay right here to keep you safe.

Words, Phrases, and Actions to Use

Communicate verbally and nonverbally by saying and doing the following things:

- I love you.
- What a big boy.

- What a good boy.
- Be careful.
- Hug your boy.
- Kiss your boy.
- Wash your boy with great care and attention.

Things Not to Say and Do

Don't teach your boy to associate bathing with unpleasantness. Don't say such things as:

- You dirty little boy.
- All you do is poop and pee. You'll never be clean.
- I'm sick and tired of trying to keep you clean.
- Stop fussing. You have to have a bath.

Never leave your boy alone in the bath. Don't say such things as:

- You be careful. I have to leave you alone for a minute.
- I'll be right back.

Words, Phrases, and Actions to Avoid

- Sit still, you silly boy.
- Don't be a sissy.
- Stop it right now.
- Why can't you do what you're told?
- Don't move.
- Don't expect your boy to sit still.
- Never hit or shake your boy.
- Don't yell or scream at your boy.

BEDTIME

◆

It is 7:30, bedtime for your little boy. He may fuss and cry, but you have tried to establish a routine with him for meals, play, and sleep as he has grown from being an infant to being a wonderful little boy who has just learned to walk and has begun to talk. You know that he always cries at bedtime because that seems to be in his personality. You make sure that his diaper is clean and that he is tucked in for the night. After reading to him from his favorite book you stroke him as you softly sing him a lullaby.

Things to Consider

You want to develop routines with your boy once he has passed his first three months of life. Bedtime is one of the most important routines you can have. It is good for your boy and for you because it helps him learn discipline and promises you some time for yourself. Boys will differ on how they behave when you put them to bed. You must take account of who your boy is, but you must still communicate firmness and resolve.

Your bedtime routine tells your boy that this is the normal time for him to go to sleep, by himself. Even if you've been letting your boy sleep in your bed part of the night, there comes a time in the first year of his life, when you must teach him to sleep on his own. Bedtime is a wonderful time to bond with your boy with stories, soft singing, holding, kissing and stroking, to make him feel loved and safe, and to prepare him for the moment when you make sure he's comfortable and you leave the room. You can spend those moments having little conversations with him even though they will be very one-sided at first.

It's important that dad shares in this bedtime ritual and uses this opportunity to communicate his love. Even today, moms spend more time with their babies than dads. So this is a time when dad can make up for missing a large part of his son's daily life.

Bedtime for your boy gives you the chance to communicate love in many different ways.

Three Things You Must Do

1. Develop routines with your boy.
2. Give your boy lots of physical contact.
3. Read to your boy at bedtime.

Things to Say and Do

For baby boys and toddlers bedtime separation can be an unhappy time. When it's time for him to go to bed say such things as:

- It's bedtime. Time for your favorite story.
- Before was the time for playing. Now is the time for sleeping. Let's go do this together.
- I love you very much. You need lots of sleep to grow big and strong.
- Time for boys to go to bed. Let's do it together.

Make bedtime a happy time for good communication. Say such things as:

- Bedtime and story time.
- What story do you want to hear tonight? (Then tell his favorite story.)
- Tonight I'm going to tell you a story about you when you were a very tiny baby. (Even very young boys love hearing stories about themselves.)
- Let's sing our little song.

Just before turning off the light and leaving the room say such things as:

- I love you.
- I'll be just downstairs/down the hall/in the next room.
- Sleep well, my darling.
- You're such a good boy.

Some things to do:

- Carry your boy to bed.
- Hug him tightly.
- Stroke him as he lies there.
- Kiss him after the story and the lullaby.
- Tuck him in and kiss him goodnight.

If your boy cries or fusses after being put to bed, let him go on for fifteen minutes. Then, if he hasn't stopped, go in and pick him up, hold him and stroke him, and kiss him for fifteen minutes. Then put him down again. Repeat if necessary. He should learn after a few days of this routine that bedtime is time to go to sleep.

Words, Phrases, and Actions to Use

- ... love ...
- ... darling ...
- Bedtime, my darling.
- Story time.
- Sleepy time.
- All boys like you go to bed now.
- Give me a big hug.
- Give me a big kiss.
- Let's sing a song.

Things Not to Say and Do

Don't say or do anything to make your boy feel unloved or insecure simply because he resists going to bed or going to sleep. Don't say such things as:

- If you don't go to sleep I won't love you anymore.
- You're going to bed whether you like it or not.
- If you don't shut up I'm going to leave you.
- Quiet, you stupid kid.
- Just shut up.

Don't tell your boy he's no good or bad for not wanting to go to bed or to sleep. Don't say such things as:

- You're a rotten kid.
- You're a bad, bad boy for not going to sleep.
- Only bad boys don't do what their mommy/daddy tells them.

Never physically abuse your boy for not going to sleep. Never do such things as:

- Spanking your baby boy.
- Shaking your baby boy.
- Hurting your baby boy in any way.

Words, Phrases, and Actions to Avoid

- Bad boy.
- You're a rotten kid.
- I don't love you.
- Nobody loves you.
- I'm leaving.
- Now you're going to be punished.
- I'll make you sorry.

CRYING

◆

Your boy is crying. You're not sure why. He is only two months old. Perhaps he's hungry? You try nursing/feeding to see if that works. All the time you're talking to him, asking him what's wrong, knowing that he can't possibly tell you. Your only way of knowing is through the experience of knowing your boy and his habits and personality, which you learn through trial and error. Your main concern is finding out what's wrong and fixing it so he will stop crying.

Things to Consider

Dr. Eli H. Newberger in *The Men They Will Become* tells parents of a "crying curve." It goes up and down in the following way: "twenty-two minutes of crying each day for the first three weeks of life on average for infants in industrialized societies; thirty-four minutes per day from then until the beginning of the third month; and down to fourteen minutes per day by the beginning of the fourth month." What's more, evenings seem to be a favorite time.

Your boy will cry to tell you he is hungry, wet or poopy, physically uncomfortable, and upset. It's amazing how well you learn to understand your boy's crying. As you well know, it's his most effective way to communicate with you for his first months of life.

Don't feel you have to respond to his every cry. But if he doesn't stop soon pick him up and try to figure out the problem while you comfort him by stroking and talking to him in a soothing voice.

If your baby's crying becomes too much for you, put him down and find someone to help—a spouse or relative, a neighbor, a friend, your doctor, a parents' help line, or even a friend or relative in another city who you can reach by phone. Don't be ashamed to admit that you need help with his crying if that's what it takes to keep him safe.

Never shake or strike your baby boy. Baby boys suffer much more abuse by shaking than baby girls do.

When your toddler cries in anger or to get attention, sympathize with his crying, but don't let him manipulate you by it. Tell him that crying is not the best way to solve his problem. Once again, never strike or shake him. Be firm so that he learns your rules.

The bottom line is to know your boy, what makes him cry, and know yourself, how it affects you. When your boy cries it gives you a chance to communicate love, understanding, sympathy, firmness, rules, comfort, caring, and discipline.

Three Things You Must Do

1. Accept your baby boy's crying as his chief way of communicating.
2. Learn what your boy's different cries mean.
3. Never shake or strike your boy. Get help to cope with persistent crying if you need it.

Things to Say and Do

A baby boy who is crying needs you to figure out why. Communicate your love for him by saying such things as:

- What's wrong, darling?
- Poor baby, what's the matter?
- Don't cry, darling. I'll find out what's wrong.

A toddler who is crying needs you to comfort him and to get him to tell or show you what's wrong if you can't figure it out. Say such things as:

- Poor little boy, tell me what's wrong?
- Show me the problem.
- Are you hungry?
- Does something hurt?
- Did you hurt yourself?

A toddler throwing a tantrum should be comforted and then told how best to solve the problem that caused it. Say such things as:

- Let me hold you tight.
- What's wrong?
- Let me see if I can solve the problem.
- Mommy can't let you do this.
- This is not the best way to solve the problem; let's try something else.

If your boy's crying is driving you to violence against your boy, do one or more of the following:

- Put your baby down.
- Find help.
- Find or call your spouse.
- Call a friend or relative.
- Call your neighbor.
- Call your doctor or the hospital emergency ward.
- Call a friend or relative in another city.

Words, Phrases, and Actions to Use

- I love you.
- What's wrong?
- How can I help?
- Can you tell me what's wrong?
- Does it hurt?
- Let me hold you.
- I'll kiss it better.
- Check his diaper.
- Look for signs of physical pain.
- Sing him a song.
- Hold him tight if he'll let you.

Things Not to Say and Do

Most baby boys and toddlers cry for good reason. Don't say such things as:

- Big boys don't cry.
- Stop crying, right now.
- If you don't stop I'll leave.
- You're crying for nothing.

Don't let a toddler's tantrum get the best of you. Don't say or do such things as:

- Okay, I give in. What do you want?
- If you don't stop I'll hit you.
- Don't hit him or shake him.
- Don't feel you have failed as a parent if you sometimes let your baby boy cry.

Don't say such things as:

- I'm a rotten mom/dad.
- I just don't think I can cope anymore. (If you really feel this then seek professional help.)

- I hate what that boy has done to me.
- I can't fight him anymore. He wins.

Words, Phrases, or Actions to Avoid

- You're a rotten kid.
- You stupid little boy.
- I hate him when he cries.
- I can't stand it any longer.
- I'll show him who's boss.
- If you don't stop right now you'll be sorry.
- Never hit your baby boy or toddler.
- *Never shake your baby boy or toddler.*

DON'T DO THAT

◆

Your boy has grown so quickly from being a tiny baby whom you could hold in one hand to being a little man who has learned how to crawl, stand, walk, hop, and run, sort of. He climbs up and down stairs and over obstacles, and loves the swing, slide, and seesaw. As a boy he loves to open and close drawers, cupboards, boxes, and doors. You're constantly watching him, always knowing where he is and what he's doing, worried that he will hurt himself. You seem to be saying "Don't do that!" more than anything else you say to him. You don't like doing that, but his safety comes first.

Things to Consider

Once your boy can move around by himself, he begins the stage of development that I like to call the "What happens if I do this?" stage. He's learning about the world, about himself, about what he can and cannot do, about what he can and cannot control, and about the consequences of his actions. This learning is essential, but it can be very dangerous.

You have to teach your boy the dangers, while allowing him to experiment and explore. Each moment you need to make a choice between the risks and rewards of letting him do something. Even if you've child-proofed your home you still can't make it completely safe for him. But that's life. What you can do is watch him and protect him against major catastrophes while accepting the fact that learning about life means taking risks and sometimes getting hurt. Your job is to make sure that he never does anything that would seriously hurt him. The most important thing is to be consistent with your do's and don'ts.

Your boy needs lots of space. He needs to explore, be active, be aggressive, and practice his gross motor skills, and learn to develop his fine motor skills. Your boy, compared to most girls, is likely to move more and faster, be more active, creep more, climb more, pull himself up more, and show more interest in objects and manipulating them. He doesn't listen as well, perhaps partly because boys don't hear as well. He is less compliant and more defiant. He is more easily frustrated and he gets angry easier.

That's why you will find yourself saying, more often than you'd like to, "Don't do that!" Saying this gives you the chance to communicate love, concern, rules, discipline, empathy, and an understanding of your boy's masculine needs.

Three Things You Must Do

1. Say "Don't do that!" whenever it's necessary, and be consistent.

2. Tell your boy why he mustn't do that.

3. Don't say "Don't do that!" more than you need to, but be consistent.

Things to Say and Do

Most important, stop your boy from hurting himself. Say such things as:

- Be careful. That can hurt you.
- Boys can't do that until they are five (or whatever age you choose).
- That's very dangerous. Let me show you what can happen.
- I'm watching you.

When you stop your boy from doing something and he protests, say such things as:

- I know you're angry, but I love you so much I don't want you to get hurt.
- Let's find something else for you to do.

If you don't want to say "Don't do that," you can help your boy do whatever it is, safely. Say such things as:

- Let me help you.
- You can't do that alone. But I can do it with you.

Don't hesitate to be firm in telling your boy that something isn't allowed. Say such things as:

- I don't want you to do that. It's too dangerous.
- That's not allowed because it can hurt you.
- You know you're not allowed to do that.

If your boy pretends he doesn't hear you or gets angry and cries when you say "Don't do that," say such things as:

- I know you hear me. You have to listen to me.
- Don't pretend you don't hear. You mustn't do that.

- You can cry, but you still can't do that.
- I'm sorry, but those are the rules.

When necessary, physically remove your boy from temptation.

Words, Phrases, and Actions to Use

- No!
- You know that's not allowed.
- Be careful.
- I'll help.
- Don't touch.
- Boys have to be _____ years old to do that.
- Are you upset?
- What else would you like to do?
- Tell me all about it.
- Seal off the dangerous areas of the home with gates of one sort or another so he can't get into trouble.

Things Not to Say and Do

Your boy may not listen to you. Even if he ignores you, don't get angry. Don't say such things as:

- You're a naughty little boy.
- If you don't stop I'm going away.
- Go ahead and hurt yourself, see if I care.
- I don't love you anymore.

Even if your boy disobeys:

- Never hit your boy.
- Never shake your boy.
- Never leave your boy alone in the home.
- Never frighten your boy.
- Never let your boy hurt himself.
- Never trust your boy to do the safe thing without monitoring his behavior.

Words, Phrases, and Actions to Avoid

- You miserable little snot.
- You're an evil boy.
- I'm going to hit you for that.
- I'm leaving you.

- Hitting.
- Shaking.
- Beating.

DRESSING AND UNDRESSING

◆

Your little boy is so dependent on you. You must do almost everything for him in the first six months of life and then many things until he is at least two. One of the most tiring jobs, especially if you live in a cold climate, is dressing and undressing him. But it can also be one of the nicest jobs when you use it to communicate your limitless love for him. You think about how innocent he is as you pick out the clothes he must wear and slowly put them on. It's wonderful when he is around a year old and you see him trying to help you. He knows his shoes go on his feet, even if he can't manage them himself, and he knows how to put his arms in sleeves and his legs in trousers, if he feels like it. If you started him early enough, he will even wear a hat without fussing. But watch out for those socks. He'll pull them off every chance he gets!

Things to Consider

In the first two years of life your totally helpless little baby changes into a self-possessed, walking, talking, demanding little boy with an incredible range of skills and understanding and a growing desire and ability to control his own world. He has gone from being unable to do anything but eat and sleep and pee and poop to being able to have lots of opinions about things, including what he wears and especially what he doesn't want to wear. Even by age two he's much better at taking things off than putting them on. (I think of that as the second law of boyo-dynamics—boys will move from a state of dress to a state of undress unless prevented from doing so.)

The way you dress and undress your boy can communicate much of how you feel about him. You will try to dress him appropriately, not overdressing him in warm weather or underdressing him in cold. You'll show your concern for him by always having clean clothes to put on him when he gets dirty. The clothes needn't be new, or fashionable, or even the right size, as long as they are not so small that they'll hurt him or so large that they're dangerous.

Dressing and undressing your boy gives you the chance to communicate love, caring, cooperation, self-control, names of articles of clothing, words for putting on and taking off clothes, and how to develop gross and fine motor skills.

Three Things You Must Do

1. Talk to your boy as you put on and take off his clothes.
2. Be patient as he tries to help, and praise him for being helpful.
3. Stay calm when he gets his clean clothes dirty.

Things to Say and Do

As you get your boy out of bed in the morning, change his diaper, and clean him up, you can prepare him for getting dressed by saying such things as:

- Now, my lovely little boy, time to get dressed.
- Will you help me put your clothes on?
- What do you want to wear today?

If he fusses when you're trying to dress him, as many little boys do, don't get angry. Hold him firmly, speak firmly, and say such things as:

- Please hold still while I dress you.
- As soon as we get you dressed you can play.
- You can help me do this faster by holding still.

Make getting dressed a game by focusing your attention on each action. Say such things as:

- Now let's put your arm in here. Where's your hand, where's your hand?
- Now I'm going to pull this over your head. Here we go. Where's _____? (insert your little boy's name)
- First we put one leg in. Then we put the other leg in.
- Or, sing a song about it to your boy. Make up the words and melody yourself, or use a melody you already know like the tune from "Merrily we roll along," "Here we go Luby Loo," or "Frere Jacques." Always use your boy's name in the song; it needn't rhyme or make sense—only you and your boy will hear it.

Encourage your boy to try things himself and praise him when he does. Say such things as:

- Okay, now you try it.
- Put your arm in the sleeve.
- Put your foot in the pants leg.
- Put your head in.
- What a clever boy.
- What a good boy.

You can say and do the same thing in reverse as you're undressing him or changing him.

Words, Phrases, and Actions to Use

- Time to get dressed.
- Let's do it.
- Please lie still.
- Where's _____? (insert your little boy's name)
- I love you.
- Let's sing a song.
- Now you try it.
- What a good boy.
- What a clever boy.

Things Not to Say and Do

Don't expect your boy to sit still all the time you're dressing or undressing him. Don't say such things as:

- Why can't you keep still?
- Sit still, you bad boy.
- If you don't stop that I'm going to spank you.

Don't ever hit, shake, yell, or scream at your boy when he's fussing as you dress or undress him. Don't lose your temper if he gets his clean clothes dirty. That's what little boys do. Don't say such things as:

- I told you not to do that. Now you're all dirty.
- Can't you ever stay clean, even for a second?
- If you can't stay clean then you'll just have wear dirty clothes.

Words, Phrases, and Actions to Avoid

- You stupid boy.
- You're a dumb boy.
- I hate you.
- I don't love you anymore.
- Hitting.

- Shaking.
- Yelling.
- Punishing for not staying still.
- Punishing for not keeping clean.

EATING

◆

It's time to eat. If you're a nursing mother or a bottle-feeding mother or father, you look forward to this time with your boy when you and he are together, bonded in a wonderful ritual that shows how much you care for him. Of course you don't always love this at 3 A.M. and you can't wait for him to start sleeping through the night. But it's amazing how you have adjusted to a change in your sleep patterns for the sake of feeding your boy. And you marvel at his determination to feed himself at a very young age, even though at first more food ends up on the floor than in his mouth.

Things to Consider

Use mealtime to communicate your feelings of love and tenderness for your boy, whether you're nursing or bottle-feeding or your boy has decided it's time to feed himself. As he grows older and starts eating and drinking more than milk your boy will communicate his food preferences through facial expressions and physically accepting or rejecting things. He has acquired some of these preferences from you, while others are his own. Unless your boy shows extreme preferences in his diet, trust his judgment, because at this age he will, over time, choose a balanced diet as long as the choices are available to him.

Your boy's ability to feed himself will come early on. Encourage him in his efforts. Praise him for picking up each spaghetti strand and pushing it into his mouth with his fingers. Praise him for using his plastic spoon, at first upside down and backward, to shovel the bits of fruit into his mouth.

Your boy, say nutritionists, will become what he eats. In the first two years especially you must provide him with the food he needs for crucial development of his body and brain. His future as a normally functioning man depends on it. Experts acknowledge that mother's milk is best because it helps protect boys against certain infections. Infant boys are also more likely than girls to experience gastrointestinal and respiratory problems. A nutritious diet helps protect them against these.

Mealtime for your boy gives you the chance to communicate love, rules, praise, caring, encouragement, listening, and pleasure.

Three Things You Must Do

1. Communicate your love by giving your boy the food he needs.
2. Listen to your boy's food preferences.
3. Praise your boy's attempts to feed himself.

Things to Say and Do

Be attentive to your boy's demands to eat. Say such things as:

- Time to eat.
- I hear you. Let's have something to eat.
- Don't cry. I'm coming.

As your boy starts eating more than milk get your doctor's advice on letting him try a variety of fruits, vegetables, cereals, and other foods. Then respect his preferences. Say such things as:

- Do you like this?
- You don't seem to like this at all.
- I think this is your favorite.

Let your boy practice feeding himself from his mug and plate. Praise him for his efforts. Say such things as:

- What a clever boy you are.
- Here, let me help you hold this the right way.
- There, doesn't that work better?
- You're getting to be so good at that.

Always watch what your boy wants to put in his mouth. Tell him what things are not to be sucked on or eaten. Say such things as:

- Don't put that in your mouth. That's bad for boys.
- Ooh! You mustn't eat that. It will make you sick.
- That's a no-no!

Move anything dangerous to a height that your boy can't reach and secure your cupboards so he can't get at things that would make him ill. And never assume that anything is really safe from your baby boy. Always watch him and know what he's doing.

Words, Phrases, and Actions to Use

- You're a clever boy.
- It's time to eat.
- Here's your favorite.
- You do that really well.
- You're so clever, you can feed yourself.
- Do you like that?
- Let me help you.
- Not for boys.
- Show your boy how to hold his spoon and cup.
- Let your boy try to feed himself and help him when he needs it.

Things Not to Say and Do

Never ignore your boy's need to eat. This is not a choice at this age. Don't say such things as:

- You can't still be hungry.
- I'm not feeding you now.
- You just ate. I won't feed you again until later.

Once your boy has shown a desire to feed himself, never yell at him for trying and failing. Don't say such things as:

- You can't do it.
- I won't let you do it because you make such a mess.
- Don't be stupid. You can't feed yourself.
- You naughty little boy. Look at the mess you've made.

Words, Phrases, and Actions to Avoid

- You're a stupid kid.
- Shut up.
- Stop crying and eat.

- I'm not getting up again to feed you.
- Too much mess.
- Give up, you'll never get it right.
- Eat what I give you or you won't get anything.

GOOD BOY/BAD BOY

◆

You've just started feeding your little boy and he takes the spoon or fork out of your hands and insists on feeding himself, even though you know he's just going to make a terrible mess of it. Food goes all over his face, his hands, his hair, his clothes, the high chair, the floor, and maybe all over you too. Is he a good boy for trying to feed himself, or a bad boy for making such a mess? I hope you'll say to him, "What a good boy. What a clever boy for trying to feed yourself."

Things to Consider

Your boy is at the stage I call "What happens if I do this?" He is out to satisfy his male curiosity about this new world he's in. He will try to open, close, grab, hold, drop, pick up, move, hit, pull, and push almost anything and everything he can reach. You need to encourage him in this while at the same time protecting your home from total destruction. Child-proof what you can by moving it out of his reach. Put covers on electric sockets that are not in use. Secure the doors on cupboards that contain breakable or dangerous things. Model good behavior in the treatment of animals. Physically remove your toddler from temptation or from situations in which he is misbehaving.

Remember little boys are naturally more active and aggressive than little girls and you must allow for that in their behavior. Don't criticize your boy for doing what comes so naturally to him. But be firm and show him that there are strict rules about not hurting himself or others (including the cat), not being mean to others, and not being wantonly destructive. Your little boy needs to learn from your quiet teaching, your firm rules, and your consistency what's good behavior and what's bad behavior.

Use the phrase "Good boy" to communicate love, approval, right behavior, following the rules, permission, and admiration. Use terms like "Not for boys" or "That's not the right thing for boys to do" to communicate wrong behavior, disapproval, or danger.

Three Things You Must Do

1. Be consistent in your use of good and bad.
2. Use good and bad for your boy's sake, not yours.
3. Understand that little boys and girls have different needs and behavior patterns, and allow for those differences.

Things to Say and Do

When should you say "Good boy"? Use this phrase to reward your little boy for good behavior—behavior that will help him become a loving, respectful, and safe little boy. Use it also to reward curiosity, experimentation, trying new things, the successful opening and closing and manipulation of things, learning new skills, and practicing old skills.
Say such things as:

- Well done.
- Good boy.
- You did that just fine.
- What a clever little boy.
- What a nice boy you are.

Your boy is hardwired to be an aggressive male. Aggression is not bad in itself. Don't automatically try to discourage it. But you must consistently teach your boy to control it. Help him to channel it and to learn self-control. Encourage him to be gentle with people and animals. Reward him with words when he is. Say such things as:

- You are being nice and gentle with the cat.
- What a good little boy you are.
- I love you.
- You are really learning to behave like a nice little boy.

Let your boy win some battles with you. Don't think you have to win them all for him to be a good boy. Just be consistent in your insistence on good behavior and self-control. Say such things as:

- Okay, you win.
- You're a good boy so I'll let you have/do this.
- Yes, you can do that, good boy, but you must be very careful.

Don't use "Bad boy" with infants or toddlers. When your boy has broken something that he was told not to touch, or hurt himself or others in defiance of your repeated warnings, instead of saying "Bad boy," remove your boy from the situation. Talk to him about what he has done, why it has bad consequences, and why it shouldn't be done. If you have consistently rewarded your boy for good behavior and shown your love and care for him, he will much less often disobey you.

Words, Phrases, and Actions to Use

- You're a good boy.
- You're a nice boy.
- What a clever boy.
- What a gentle boy.
- What a clever thing to do.
- I'm proud of you.
- You are so good at that.

- Well done.
- Hug your boy for things well done or tried.
- Kiss your boy.
- Watch your boy and marvel at how much he has learned in so short a lifetime.

Things Not to Say and Do

Don't yell at your little boy unless he is in imminent danger. Don't say such things as:

- Watch out, you stupid little boy!
- Get out of there!
- STOP IT!

Don't threaten to withdraw your love from your boy just because he has done something bad. Don't say such things as:

- I don't love you anymore.
- If you ever do that again I won't love you.
- I don't love anyone who would do something like that.

Always remember that he is still very little and hasn't got the self-control or understanding or empathy that older children and adults have. Never do such things as:

- Strike or shake your little boy.
- Blame him for doing something that he doesn't understand.
- Blame him for breaking something that you ought to have removed from his level.

Don't think you have to win every battle. Don't say such things as:

- You must ask my permission for everything.
- When I say no, I mean no!
- Never do anything unless I say you can.

Remember to accept your boy's need to exercise some autonomy over himself, even when he's only a year old. Don't try to stifle his masculine instincts, just help him learn self-control and how to use his instincts to good ends.

Words, Phrases, and Actions to Avoid

- You're a bad boy.
- You're a little brat.
- You stupid little boy.
- You monster.
- I hate you.

- I don't love you anymore.
- You're not my boy.
- Never shake your little boy.
- Never hit your little boy.

MUSIC

◆

Your little boy loves music. He loves it when you sing to him. He loves listening to songs on television and music in the car. Now that he can stand up by himself you watch him dancing in rhythm whenever he hears music that he likes. Every night when you put him to bed you sing him a little lullaby. He lies still listening to your voice as you sing, even though you don't exactly sound like Jennifer Lopez or Luciano Pavarotti. He has even begun to sing little songs for himself. You tell your boy how much you like his singing and dancing.

Things to Consider

A few days ago my seventeen-month-old grandson was at a crafts fair when some musicians started playing a harp, recorder, and accordion. He immediately sat himself down in the middle of the floor and listened for ten minutes without moving, enthralled by the music. People around him got out their cameras to take a picture of this little music lover.

My grandson is the rule, not the exception. Young boys love music. They respond to melody and rhythm by singing and dancing, each in their own way. According to Sheila Moore and Roon Frost, authors of *The Little Boy Book*, music, especially soothing classical and country music, can be quite calming for a baby boy.

Little boys need to hear all kinds of sounds, including voices and music, to assist their normal development. Babies love the rhythm and sound in music. Some expectant parents play Mozart and other music for their babies while they are still in the womb. The effect this has on the baby after it's born can't be scientifically documented, but it seems likely that it can only help and not harm the fetus. And it certainly has a positive effect on the mom!

Play music for your little boy and enjoy both his enjoyment and the music itself. Use music, singing, and dancing to communicate love, happiness, beauty, serenity, and a sense of melody and rhythm.

Three Things You Must Do

1. Play music for your boy.
2. Sing to your boy.
3. Dance with your boy.

Things to Say and Do

- Play tapes and CDs for your boy.
- Play music in the car as you're driving him around.
- Buy your boy tapes and CDs of nursery songs.
- Sing along with him and the music.

Encourage your boy to sing. Say such things as:

- Sing, sing.
- What a good singer you are.
- Let's sing a song together.

Encourage your boy to dance. Say such things as:

- Let me see you dance.
- You're a good dancer.
- Let's dance together.

Expect your boy to want to hear the music he likes over and over again. Say such things as:

- Do you want to hear it again?
- Let's sing that song again.
- Let's dance to that music again.

Here's a song you can sing to say hello. You can also use it to say good-bye and goodnight by substituting one of those words for hello.

"Say hello to _____ *, (insert your boy's name),*
Say hello to _____ *, he's my little baby oh,*
Say hello to _____ *,*
How I love him so."

Words, Phrases, and Actions to Use

- Let's dance.
- Let's sing.
- Good singing.
- Good dancing.
- I love to hear you sing.
- I love to see you dance.
- Good music.

Things Not to Say and Do

Don't discourage your boy from singing and dancing. Don't say such things as:

- Stop singing.
- Stop dancing.
- Be quiet.
- Be still.

Don't play music that's too loud for your little boy. Don't discourage your boy from wanting to listen to his favorite music. Don't say such things as:

- Not again!
- You've listened to that too much today.
- I can't stand that music anymore.

Words, Phrases, and Actions to Avoid

- No singing.
- No dancing.
- Don't sing.
- Don't dance.

- I hate music.
- Music is a sin.
- Singing is a sin.
- Dancing is a sin.

PUNISHMENT

◆

You've just cooked a Thanksgiving turkey and the oven is still very hot. Your two-year-old son has been told again and again not to touch the oven door, keep away from the stove, and generally stay out of the kitchen. He's already quite good at conversing and he seems to understand your rules much of the time. But there he is again, toddling around the kitchen and going over to the stove. You wonder if you need to punish him because he keeps disobeying you?

Things to Consider

Babies and toddlers should not be punished. Think about it. What are you trying to teach them that punishing them would accomplish? You want your boy to learn some rules of behavior that will keep him safe and help him become a respectful, well-behaved young man. Will punishing a two-year-old do the job when he willfully disobeys you?

The answer is no. Don't even think of punishing your young boy as you might your twelve-year-old. You want to teach him discipline, but punishment is not the way at this age. You can best teach him discipline through love, kindness, and consistency in your rules for, and responses to, his actions. From the time he was old enough to smile at you and respond to your voice and your touch, you have been teaching him rules of behavior. You have encouraged him to learn about things in your home and you have watched how he gets better and better in his interaction with others in the family, including any family pets.

Your son, because he is a boy, is naturally very active and inquisitive, a risk-taker. At this age he wants to learn what will happen if he opens a drawer, drops his cup, turns that knob, pulls the cat's ear, or cries in frustration. Yet he wants to please you and you can see that he understands what you do and don't want him to do. He often does what you ask him to do, but not always. Sometimes he seems to simply ignore your rules.

Don't worry, and don't get too upset with him. Don't think of your role as the giver of punishment. It's much too negative. Think of yourself as a parent-teacher. Your job is to be consistent and firm in your discipline, yet be flexible enough to allow your son the chance to make mistakes and make his own decisions for some things. You are starting him off on the road to learning the most important kind of discipline of all, self-discipline.

Three Things You Must Do

1. Remember that newborns to two-year-old boys especially want to please.
2. Teach, don't punish.
3. Be loving, firm, and consistent when you teach him, and remind him of the rules.

Things to Say and Do

If you want your boy to behave, be a behaviorist. Reward him for good behavior. Say such things as:

- What a good boy you are.
- That's right. You did the right thing.
- Well done.

Help your boy please you. As he begins to understand language more and more remind him of the rules, and the right things to do. Say such things as:

- Remember that you must do this.
- You know what you're supposed to do.
- You know the rule.

When he does the wrong thing, gently tell him that it's the wrong thing to do. Say such things as:

- Remember, you mustn't do that.
- That's a no-no.
- That's not good for boys.
- No, you mustn't do that! It could hurt you.

Be kind and consistent in your teaching him the rules. Say such things as:

- That's right. You've learned that very well.
- What a smart boy to remember that.
- You know you're not allowed to do that.

Sometimes you must let him do his own thing (as long as it won't hurt). Say such things as:

- Okay, try it and see what happens.
- You go ahead, but I'm watching you.
- Be careful.

Don't punish him for disobeying. Do any or all of the following:

- Remove him from the situation.
- Explain what he did wrong.
- Show him the bad things that could have happened.
- Take him to a different part of the home where he can do other things.

Words, Phrases, and Actions to Use

- You're a good boy.
- Don't do that.
- What a clever boy.
- Be careful.
- You've learned that very well.

- What a smart boy.
- Go ahead.
- Thank you.
- You know the rule.
- You know what to do.

Things Not to Say and Do

Remember that he's still a baby even though he knows and does amazing things. Don't yell at him for disobeying. Don't say such things as:

- Stop it right now or I'll spank you.
- You silly little boy.
- How many times do I have to say don't do that?
- If you do that I'm going to punish you.

You must be consistent in teaching him how to behave. Don't say such things as:

- I know I said no, but it's okay this time.
- Do what you like.

Don't call your boy bad names or belittle him, his intelligence, or his abilities. Don't say such things as:

- You stupid little boy.
- You are so dumb.

- You're a little idiot.
- You just never learn, do you?

Don't let him hurt himself just to learn a lesson. Don't let him do any of the following without your being right there to help:

- Climb stairs.
- Descend stairs.
- Eat.
- Be outside.
- Be in the bath.

Never hit or shake your baby because he's disobeyed.

Words, Phrases, and Actions to Avoid

- You're stupid.
- You're dumb.
- You idiot.
- You bad little boy.
- I hate you.
- Why can't you ever learn?
- Do what you're told or you'll be punished.

- Hitting.
- Shaking.
- Pushing around.
- Knocking down.
- Scaring.
- Hurting in any way.

READING

◆

You read to your boy every day. You do it because he loves it and you love it. He has his favorites and he doesn't care how many times you read the same book to him. You have some special times for reading to him, but will read to him any time he asks you to. It's a time for bonding with him, and an especially good time for dads who don't have as many occasions to be close to their little boys as moms do. It's also a nice way to quiet your boy just before you put him to bed in the evening.

Things to Consider

Reading to your baby boy or toddler, just like talking to him, can only be a good thing for both of you. It helps your boy learn to identify houses, trees, chairs, tables, animals, bugs, birds, dinosaurs, and words as you read him the story and describe the pictures, often asking him to point to the appropriate word or picture himself. My sixteen-month-old grandson, Jonah, loves a book called *Animals*. He can point to elephants, donkeys, and ducks and make the appropriate sounds. The first choice of my seventeen-month-old grandson, Hunter, is *Snug as a Big Red Bug*, and he will listen to it endlessly, taking pleasure in pointing out the big red bug, and especially in turning the pages.

You love reading to your boy because he sits on your lap, or next to you in the chair or sofa, and you find it amazing that he will sit so quietly, looking and listening. It's a welcome relief from his endless activity during most of the day. It's a wonderful time of sharing.

I clearly remember sitting down to read to my first son, David, when he was two. We had just bought the first book of the Babar the elephant series. We sat on the couch. I opened the book and began to read it to him. I looked at the pictures and suddenly a flood of memories came flashing back. I realized this was the first book I could remember my mother reading to me when I was a toddler. What a feeling. Tears welled up in my eyes. Now I'm looking forward to reading Babar to my grandsons.

Besides the wonderful relationship reading to your boy produces, it's an important stimulant for the brain. Research has shown that talking to children is associated with increased brain activity in the child. Reading to your boy has the same result.

Read to your boy every day. Even after he can read to himself he will still enjoy a story from you. There are so many wonderful children's books being published these days that you and your boy are bound to find lots to share. This sharing will help him develop a love of reading that will hopefully stay with him for his whole life.

Three Things You Must Do

1. Read to your boy every day.
2. Buy him lots of books.
3. Let him choose his favorites.

Things to Say and Do

Start reading or telling stories to your boy when he's still a tiny baby. Girls have as much as a year-and-a-half advantage in reading skills over boys by the time they reach school, so it's important that your boy learn to love reading. Begin this love by reading to him early and often. Say such things as:

- Let's have a story before bed.
- Story time.
- I'm going to tell you a story about a mommy, a daddy, and their baby boy.

When your boy is old enough to understand you and to choose his own stories say such things as:

- Story time. What book would you like to read now?
- Go get your favorite book and I'll read it to you.
- Let's sit down and read your favorite story.

Encourage your boy to help you read. Have him point to things as you name them. Ask him to turn the pages. Say such things as:

- Show me the _____ (whatever you want him to point at).
- What's that?
- What does a cow say? What does a dog say? What does a duck say?
- Time to turn the page.

Words, Phrases, and Actions to Use

- . . . book . . .
- . . . book time . . .
- . . . story time . . .
- I'll read you a story.

- Pick your favorite.
- Show me.
- What does that say?

- I love reading to you.
- I love books.
- I love stories.

Things Not to Say and Do

Don't wait too long before you start reading to your boy. Don't say such things as:

- There's no point in reading to him. He's too young to understand.
- I'll wait until he can talk before I read to him.

Don't be sexist about reading to your boy. Don't say such things as:

- Books for young boys are a waste of time.
- Books are for girls.
- I don't have time to read to you.

Don't disparage the books your boy likes best. Don't say such things as:

- That's a silly book.
- I don't like that book. Choose another.
- Since I'm doing the reading, I'll choose the book.

Don't restrict your boy's books to ones that you think are uplifting and good for his character.

Words, Phrases, and Actions to Avoid

- You're stupid.
- You're bad.
- You're full of nonsense.
- You're a waste of time.
- That's not appropriate.

RULES

◆

You have realized from day one that you need to give your little boy rules to guide his behavior. You also know that your boy needs these rules, more than if he were a girl, to direct his energies and his naturally aggressive tendencies. On the other hand, you want your boy to be a real boy and realize that your rules have to fit his male biology. You are determined to have rules that channel his competitive and aggressive instincts in positive directions. Your rules will help him learn to be empathetic, thoughtful, and sensitive to others, but will not stifle his natural drive to take risks, be competitive, and to aggressively pursue his goals, without unduly endangering himself or others.

Things to Consider

Your little boy is not the same as every other little boy. He has his own individual temperament. He might be very daring in trying new things, or he might be cautious, always looking over his shoulder for your presence and reassurance. You have to know your little boy in order to know what rules are right for him.

On the other hand, there are some rules that apply to every little boy. For example, a good rule is that your boy is never allowed to hit his brothers or sisters. You need to provide a model for this rule by never hitting your children in anger or as punishment.

Experts agree that little boys have a natural desire to please their caregivers. Your rules should be such that they give your little boy lots of opportunities to do just that. At this age rules need to be simple and straightforward so that he can understand them. Rules need to be consistent with your boy's temperament. Make rules for his benefit, not just yours.

Here are some simple rules that baby boys and toddlers can begin to understand. Remember that these rules need to be adjusted to your and your boy's own personality, habits, family circumstances, and other, competing sets of rules. These are rules for your boy and for you.

SOME RULES FOR HIM
- He must treat others in the family with love and respect.
- He must never hit others in anger or as punishment.
- He must allow you to bathe him.

- He must allow you to dress and undress him and change his diaper.
- He must not climb stairs alone.
- He must not go into the kitchen alone.
- He must not go outside alone.
- He must go to bed when he is tired.

SOME RULES FOR YOU
- You will always treat your boy with love and respect.
- You will never hit your boy in anger or as punishment.
- You will provide food, shelter, and safety for your boy.
- You will encourage your boy to try out new things for himself.
- You will keep him from seriously hurting himself or others.
- You will explain your actions to him even though he may be too young to understand.

Three Things You Must Do

1. Have rules for your boy for his sake as well as yours.
2. Explain your application of those rules even when he is too young to understand.
3. Apply your rules consistently and with love.

Things to Say and Do

Whenever you apply or remind your boy of the rules be sure to explain the reasons for the rule even if he's too young to understand. Talking to him about what you're doing and letting him hear your intonation connected to your actions is a valuable form of communicating. You can generalize the rule or make it specific to your boy. Say such things as:

- I don't want you to do that. It's not safe for boys.
- Please don't touch that. You have to be five to do that.
- Boys don't do that. It can hurt them.

Consistently remind your boy of the rules as you do things. Say such things as:

- It's bath time for boys. It's important for you to be nice and clean.
- Be gentle with the pussycat. You can hurt her if you pull her ears too hard.
- You must lie still and let me change you. Dirty diapers are not good for little boys.

Tell your boy the rules you are following when you do something with him. Say such things as:

- I'm not letting you hit your friend because hitting people is wrong. It can hurt them.
- I'm changing your clothes because the day is over and it's time to have a bath and get nice and clean.
- I know you're hungry so here's something you really like. Eating will help you grow up to be big and strong.

Praise your boy for remembering the rules and trying to follow them. Say such things as:

- What a clever boy for doing that.
- Good boy for remembering the rules.
- You know the rules, don't you? What a bright boy.

If your boy doesn't respond to your rules just by your telling him, you can physically show him what to do or not to do. Do such things as:

- Remove him from places you don't want him to be and explain why you are doing it.
- Remove objects from his hands or reach and tell him what you're doing and why.
- Physically and gently restrain him if he won't listen, explaining what you are doing.

Words, Phrases, and Actions to Use

- ... rules ...
- That's not a good idea because ...
- No.
- Yes.
- Good boy.
- Remember.
- That's right.
- That's not good for boys.

Things Not to Say and Do

Don't punish your boy at this age for breaking or forgetting the rules. Don't say such things as:

- Stupid boy, can't you remember the rules? You'll remember after I punish you.
- I'm going to lock you in your room for breaking the rules.
- You broke the rules so you have to suffer the consequences.

Don't criticize your boy for breaking or forgetting rules. Don't say such things as:

- You haven't got a brain in your head.
- How come I have given birth to such a silly boy?
- Other little boys remember the rules, why can't you?

Never yell or shout at your boy, except in an emergency. Never hit, shake, or use violence of any kind against your boy for breaking the rules.

Words, Phrases, and Actions to Avoid

- You're stupid.
- You're dumb.
- You're retarded.
- You idiot.
- You're not my son.
- Hitting.
- Shaking.
- Punishing.
- Yelling.
- Criticizing.
- Belittling.

SAFETY

◆

Your first concern, always, is to keep your boy safe from harm. Nothing is more important to you than the well-being of your little boy. From the moment of his birth until this very moment you have done everything in your power to keep him from hurting himself and from getting sick. You have taken him for regular visits to your doctor to check on his development. You have gotten advice from family and friends on nutrition, health care, clothing, and behavior. You've read books on babies and made sure your baby gets enough to eat and sleeps enough. You take him to "mom and tots" playtime. He has his own toothbrush and he's gotten his shots. You have a proper child car seat for him. You wonder if there's anything more you can do.

Things to Consider

Boys, even when they are just babies and toddlers, move around more than girls, are more active, and are hardwired to take more risks. Because boys have better developed gross motor skills than girls and less developed fine motor skills, they do more dangerous things like creeping, climbing, sliding, and pulling themselves up on things. Boys enjoy doing more physically demanding things and need more space in which to do them.

As Sheila Moore and Roon Frost point out in *The Little Boy Book* "many little boys have activity levels that exceed their understanding." For example, one of my grandsons, at age ten months, was eager to crawl up and down steps, but had no sense of where a step was when he wanted to sit down and turn around. Without a parent there he would have plunged to the bottom. You have to constantly guard your boy from injury while at the same time allowing him the freedom to try to explore and test himself.

Once your boy can pull himself up and crawl you need to move all danger out of his reach, including putting plastic covers over unused electrical outlets, securing cupboards containing dangerous or valuable items, and moving small and heavy objects off low tables. Between five and eight months your boy wants to put everything into his mouth so you must be ever on your guard.

Your boy has his own danger threshold. You'll come to know how much risk he can tolerate. Even though babies and toddlers may not really understand danger, some little boys will look to their parents for reassurance in whatever they're doing, while others will bash on regardless of the risk. Get to know your boy's danger threshold.

Doing all this will help keep your boy safe, avoid confrontations, and avoid your constantly saying no to your boy or taking things away from him. Remember while you are doing all these things to talk to your boy about what you are doing. By doing this you teach him that you have his safety at heart. He will learn to recognize the tone of your voice when you want him to be safe, even if, sometimes, his reaction to this is cries of anger and frustration.

Three Things You Must Do

1. Boy-proof your house.
2. Know your boy's danger threshold.
3. Explain to your boy why you do things for his own safety.

Things to Say and Do

Encourage your boy to crawl, to pull himself up, and to walk when you're there to keep him safe. Praise him for his little successes. Say such things as:

- You can do it.
- You're crawling. What a clever boy.
- Crawl to me, darling.

Let him explore the outside. Take him to playgrounds and put him on swings and slides, but always be there to keep him safe. Praise him when he swings and slides. Say such things as:

- That's the way. I'm here to catch you.
- What a brave boy to go down that slide.
- You can do it. I'll help you.

When he goes off around the house exploring, climbing, and experimenting, follow behind him. If he's about to do something he shouldn't because it's dangerous, stop him and tell him why. Say such things as:

- You mustn't do that. That's too dangerous for boys.
- That will hurt you. You have to be five before you can do that.

When you go in the car put him safely in his seat and explain what you're doing. If you're out walking on busy sidewalks tell him why he must stay in his stroller or hold your hand. Say such things as:

- You have to sit here. This will keep you safe.
- I know you don't like this seat, but you must sit here until you're a big boy.
- You can't go off on your own. It's too dangerous for a boy.
- Hold my hand. I want you to be safe.

Words, Phrases, and Actions to Use

- Safe.
- Love.
- Be careful.
- That's too dangerous for boys.
- That's not for boys.
- You have to be five to do that.
- Remember what I said.
- I want to keep you safe because I love you.
- Always know where your boy is and what he's doing.

Things Not to Say and Do

Don't let your boy out of your sight either in the house or outside. Don't discourage him from taking all risks. Don't say such things as:

- You can't do that (for even the most innocuous things).
- I'm not letting you do that because it scares me.

Don't prevent him from developing his skills like climbing and running and roughhousing. Don't keep him out of play groups or playgrounds simply because it's possible for him to be hurt, unless the risk is too great. Don't say such things as:

- Don't play on the swing.
- Stay off the slide.
- Everything is too dangerous. Let's go home.

Don't punish him for trying new things. Don't criticize him for making mistakes and hurting himself. Don't say such things as:

- Stupid little boy.
- I'm going to punish you for doing such a dangerous thing.
- I told you not to do that. I knew you'd hurt yourself.
- It's your own fault.

Words, Phrases, and Actions to Avoid

- You're a bad boy.
- You're a stupid boy.
- You silly boy.
- Don't ever do that again.

- Stay off the swings.
- Stay off the slides.
- It's too dangerous.
- You're on your own.

TALKING, HUMMING, AND SINGING

◆

Your son is tired and rests in your arms as you slowly rock back and forth and sing him a lullaby. He responds to your voice contentedly and shuts his eyes. You feel his tiny body relax as your voice calms and reassures him. You continue to sing softly until you're sure he's asleep and then you gently lay him down in his crib, marveling that this little boy is really yours. You talk to him whenever you're with him. You use real words, telling him how wonderful he is. You make baby talk sounds also, which are nonsense, but to which he responds as though it were real talk. You hum melodies and you sing to him.

Things to Consider

In our culture boys get talked to less than girls, although experts say they enjoy being talked to just as much as girls.

The intonation and sound of your voice is more important to your boy at this age than the words you use. Baby talk works just as well as real words and you should use both. You can tell from your boy's response what works well and what doesn't. If you talk or sing too loud and frighten your baby, he'll quickly let you know.

Learn to sing nursery rhymes and other little songs from recordings and other moms and dads. If you remember the ones sung to you use those. You can have songs and chants for all occasions, including bedtime, wake-up time, eating time, playtime, and hello and good-bye. Your boy will quickly come to recognize them and may even start making familiar sounds himself as he gets older, around six or seven months.

Watch your baby's face as you talk, sing, or hum to him. As he matures you'll see how he grows in his reaction and recognition of your voice. Soon he will look around the room for you when he hears you.

Although your boy might not say any real words until he is one year or older, he will certainly start "talking" much earlier and will soon come to imitate your conversational intonation patterns. Before you know it he will be talking and singing back to you. Hearing you talk will teach him how to talk on his own. You can never talk, hum, and sing to him too much.

Three Things You Must Do

1. Talk to your boy.
2. Hum to your boy.
3. Sing to your boy.

Things to Say and Do

Talk to your boy from the moment he's born. Actually, you can begin as soon as he's conceived. Then never stop talking. Say such things as:

- I love you.
- You're such a beautiful boy.
- Hello, _____ (insert his name). How are you today?

Play hide-and-seek with him. Catch his attention so that he's looking at you. Then hide for a moment. He will wonder where you've gone. Suddenly reappear, smiling, and say "I see you!"

Sing "clap hands" to him. It's something my mother sang to me. It's silly but you can start this when he's one month old. Make up your own tune. Hold his hands in yours and clap them together to the rhythm of the song:

> *Clap hands, clap hands 'til daddy/mommy comes home.*
> *Daddy/mommy has money and baby has none.*

Use baby talk with him. I know it sounds silly and looks even sillier written down, but it works. He will love it just as much as real words. Say such things as:

- Boo, boo.
- Pooky, pooky, pooky.
- Diddle, diddle, diddle (while nuzzling your face in his tummy).

Hum your favorite melodies to him. Do it anytime you're with him.

Words, Phrases, and Actions to Use

- I love you.
- I see you.
- Peek-a-boo.
- There you are.

- Mama.
- Beautiful boy.
- Handsome boy.
- Brave boy.

Things Not to Say and Do

Loud sounds will frighten your boy and may make him feel insecure.

- Don't shout at your boy unless it's an absolute emergency.
- Don't argue with someone with your boy around.

Boys need extra talking to since they are spoken to less than girls.

- Don't assume others will talk to him if you don't.
- Don't ignore your boy.
- Don't discourage others from talking to him.

Encourage your boy to vocalize.

- Don't stop him from trying to talk.
- Don't criticize his efforts to communicate or create sound.
- Don't be too embarrassed to use baby talk.
- Don't discourage or embarrass others if they want to use baby talk.

Sing and hum to your boy even if you can't carry a tune.

Words, Phrases, and Actions to Avoid

- Don't.
- Don't talk.
- He can't understand.
- Be quiet.
- Shut up.
- Stop singing.
- You stupid little boy.

TOILET TRAINING

◆

Until your little baby was born you never thought that you could find joy in changing diapers and cleaning someone else's bottom. But you have, even though it's a chore that you would sometimes rather leave to someone else. However, your love affair with dirty diapers has reached the point where you wish your boy knew how to use the toilet. Your boy is eighteen months old and still hasn't shown any interest in using the toilet. What can you say to your boy to start him thinking about how nice it would be to go in the toilet, at least some of the time?

Things to Consider

It's an acknowledged fact that boys often take longer to toilet train than girls. Boys seem to develop bladder and sphincter control later than girls. Even by the time they start school boys have more bed-wetting problems than girls.

Although some boys start toilet training as young as eighteen months, Michael Gurian in *The Good Son* points out that it's normal for four- and even five-year-old boys to wear pull-up diapers at night. He suggests that boys of two and older can be successfully day trained. The secret is to help your boy learn at his own pace. After all, going to the bathroom is one of the few things within his control. You control almost everything else in his life.

Good communication, consistency, and pressure-free training seem to be the keys to helping your boy learn to use the toilet. It's hard, and counter-productive, to force toilet training before your boy is interested and physically ready. In England, where toilet training starts at an earlier age, the statistics report twice the number of bed-wetters than here.

First of all, you must know your boy's habits and interests. The best time to start is when he shows an interest. I read of pediatrician Dr. T. Berry Brazelton's system that encourages the child to use his own potty chair and let him control things from that point on. Here's the procedure:

- Introduce the potty chair.
- Explain how it's like the toilet you use.
- See if your boy shows any interest.
- Sit your boy on the chair with a shirt and diaper on.

- Read him a favorite story while he's sitting there.
- After doing this for a week or more start putting him on the potty without the diaper. Explain what it's for. He may not use the potty but he's getting the idea. Do this for at least a week.
- Each time he wets or soils his diaper bring him back to the potty and change him while he sits on the chair. Explain what you're doing.
- Once he seems to be interested in this routine encourage him to sit on the potty without diaper two or three times a day.
- Never pressure him to perform. Just explain the procedure.
- Praise him for any attempt or success.
- Don't move on to naptime or bedtime training until the daytime routine is firmly established and successful.
- Some parents prefer to put their boys in real underpants when they're training them because pull-ups absorb too well and provide little incentive to use the potty.

Remember that boys will respond differently to toilet training so don't upset yourself or your boy if things don't go smoothly. If you have any concerns talk to your doctor.

Three Things You Must Do

1. Start training when he seems interested.
2. Be low key. Don't pressure your boy.
3. Use explanations and praise, never punishment.

Things to Say and Do

Talk to your boy about using the toilet. Say such things as:

- Let me show you what big boys do.
- This is the toilet that Mommy and Daddy use.
- This is the way your brother/sister goes to the bathroom.
- Read your boy a story about using the toilet.

Introduce your boy to the potty chair. Say such things as:

- Let me show you what this is.
- This is what you'll use some day soon.
- This is a big boy's toilet.

Sit him on the potty with his diaper on. Say such things as:

- There, now you look like a big boy.
- I'm going to read you your favorite story.

Sit him on the potty with his diaper off. Say such things as:

- What a big boy you are.
- I'm going to read you your favorite story.

Get him into a routine each day. Say such things as:

- Potty time.
- Here we go again.
- Time to sit on the potty and have a story.

Praise him when he tries and when he succeeds. Say such things as:

- What a good boy.
- What a big boy.
- I'm so proud of you.

Words, Phrases, and Actions to Use

- . . . toilet . . .
- . . . potty chair . . .
- . . . bathroom . . .
- You're a big boy.
- Let's try.
- You're a good boy.
- It's story time.
- Good try.
- Well done.

Things Not to Say and Do

Don't pressure your boy to toilet train before he's ready. Don't say such things as:

- I want you to use the toilet.
- You're old enough to learn to go to the bathroom the proper way.

Don't criticize your boy if he's not interested. Don't say such things as:

- You're a bad boy for not using the toilet.
- Why can't you use the toilet like a big boy?
- You should be toilet trained by now.

Don't embarrass your boy if he's trained but still has accidents. Don't say such things as:

- Bad boy.
- You should know better.
- Why didn't you call me, you silly boy?

Don't compare him to other boys. Don't say such things as:

- All the other boys your age are trained.
- You're so slow compared to others.
- What's wrong with you? All the other little boys use the proper toilet.

Words, Phrases, and Actions to Avoid

- You're a bad boy.
- You silly boy.
- You're so slow.
- What's wrong with you?

Touching, Dancing, Holding, Kissing, Nursing, Rocking, and Stroking

You're looking at your new baby boy lying in his crib and he seems to be looking back at you. Of course, until he's about two months old he can't focus his eyes well enough to recognize you by sight. You reach down and gently stroke his cheek and he seems to respond to your touch. Your infant son wants and needs you to communicate with him through physical contact.

Things to Consider

Throughout their lives boys and men get held less than girls and women. Your baby boy needs physical contact with you as a way of making him feel secure as well as a way of bringing you and your son closer together as you bond physically as well as emotionally. Don't hold back because he is a boy, not a girl. Physical bonding can go far beyond simply holding him for feeding, changing, and dressing and undressing. Use your imagination to think of ways that the two of you can be in touch.

Fathers need to be particularly brave in their physical contact with their baby. Moms can help teach dads that their babies are very sturdy little creatures who don't break too easily. Some dads need to learn how to pick up and hold their son, although new dads are much better at this today than they were in my generation. One good piece of evidence that fathers are more than ever physically involved with their babies is the presence of changing tables in men's rooms at airports.

Physical contact is a major part of communicating with young children. You can use this contact to show your love and affection. Although ours is not as much a culture of touching as many others, especially among adults and boys and men, our culture is becoming noticeably more physically demonstrative. This is a good thing because touching and hugging can communicate feelings of love, support, affection, sympathy, and camaraderie better and more directly than words.

Touch your baby often. As the pediatrician and author Dr. Eli H. Newberger warns, don't come to associate touching your baby with the chores of feeding, cleaning up, and comforting. Don't get in the habit of thinking that a happy baby is one who doesn't need contact with you. Make physical contact a positive, pleasurable habit that expresses your love for your new son.

Three Things You Must Do

1. Hold your baby.
2. Stroke your baby.
3. Kiss your baby.

Things to Say and Do

With infants you can communicate really well by *doing*. Here are some ways to communicate with your baby son while he is still quite new.

Dance with your baby. It's a wonderful way to communicate love and happiness.

- Take him in your arms and move in time with music.
- Use real music from a radio, TV, computer, or stereo.
- Create your own music by humming or singing.

Holding your son contributes to his well-being and yours.

- Hold your baby in your arms just for the pleasure of having him near you.
- Carry your baby around with you as you work or walk. Use a carry pack that holds him securely in place on your chest.

Kiss your son often. Kissing expresses your love.

- Kiss him on his baby-soft cheeks.
- Kiss his tummy to tickle him and make him giggle.
- Kiss his hands and feet.

Rocking your baby in your arms has a soothing effect on him and you. Don't just do it when he's upset. Let the rhythm of rocking be a natural expression of your love for him.

- Sit in a rocking chair and let the chair do the work.
- Stand with him in your arms and swivel from one side to the other.

Most babies love to be stroked. It soothes and calms the body. Stroking teaches your son to be comfortable with physical touching that expresses love and affection.

- Stroke him in the quiet times.
- Stroke his arms and legs.
- Stroke his torso and head.

Touching can communicate many things to your infant son. Let it be a way to tell him that you love him, you cherish him, and that you are there to feed, clothe, and protect him.

Words, Phrases, and Actions to Use

- Carrying.
- Dancing.
- Holding.
- Hugging.
- Kissing.
- Nuzzling.
- Rocking.
- Stroking.
- Swaying.
- Tickling.
- Touching.

Things Not to Say and Do

Don't teach your son to associate physical contact with anger or unpleasantness.

- Don't hold him or touch him only when he needs changing or when you're putting him to bed or otherwise separating yourself from him.
- Never hit your baby boy.
- Never shake your baby boy.
- Never be afraid to touch your baby boy.
- Never discourage a father from holding his son.

Words, Phrases, and Actions to Avoid

- Abandoning.
- Dropping.
- Hitting.
- Ignoring.
- Neglecting.
- Shaking.
- Squeezing too hard.

PART 2

Preschool Boys

(3–5 years)

AGGRESSION

◆

You notice that your boy can be very aggressive toward the little boys and girls he plays with. Fights break out among the boys over toys, and sometimes your boy simply pulls toys out of girls' hands. You see your boy doing a lot of pushing and poking and in return other boys push and poke him. Boys seem to feed off each other, roughhousing and acting out violence they may have seen on TV. You are legitimately concerned about this aggressive behavior, but aren't sure what to say to your boy to change it.

Things to Consider

Both boys and girls are born with the estrogen, the female hormone, and testosterone, the male hormone. Experts on child development seem to agree that the male hormone, testosterone, which is present in much, much greater amounts in boys, shapes much of your boy's early behavior. Male behavior in virtually all species differs from the female insofar as males are much more aggressive, competitive, and combative.

Ask teachers of preschool or kindergarten classes to tell you about the differences between boys and girls and they'll describe boys' aggression and girls' organization and cooperation. Give them the choice and boys will wrestle and use toys to play many variations on war games, while girls will play with dolls and organize family games.

Of course this is our stereotype of boys and girls. Some people argue that we teach boys and girls this behavior, and therefore we have a choice. If we try we can teach boys to be more like girls and vice versa. But the evidence seems to be mounting that basic neurological and biochemical differences prevent us from making boys and girls behave similarly.

Your job, as the parent of a boy, is to help him make his aggressiveness productive and respectful of others while supporting his risk-taking and competitiveness. At this age your son needs space, he needs to move around and use his whole body in play. His energy level is higher than that of girls because his metabolism is much higher. You need to work with his high energy to help him develop confidence and mastery of basic physical activities at this age, while teaching him how best to get along with other children.

When he grabs a toy from another child, take it and return it, explaining to your son that he must respect the other child. Use your words, your facial expressions, and your body language to tell your boy that his aggressive behavior is appropriate or inappropriate.

Three Things You Must Do

1. Recognize your boy's aggression as a normal male trait.
2. Channel this aggression in appropriate directions by suggesting alternatives.
3. Teach your boy what's acceptable and what's unacceptable behavior by talking to him about it and explaining your views.

Things to Say and Do

When your boy gets angry and becomes aggressive toward other children, or starts throwing or breaking things, you need to first stop the behavior, and then explain why it's unacceptable. Say such things as:

- I think you know you must be nice to others.
- Tell me what's making you so angry.
- Let's take some time out and you can tell me why you're angry.
- Let's talk about why you mustn't do this.

When your boy pulls toys away from other children, return the toy and, if he resists, you might want to physically remove him from the situation while you talk to him. Say such things as:

- You mustn't take other children's toys. It isn't a nice thing to do and it hurts their feelings.
- Would you like it if someone took your toy? So you see, it's not a nice thing to make someone feel bad.

When your boy gets into a fight, say such things as:

- Fighting is not allowed. You may get hurt or you may hurt someone else. Now I want you and "Freddie" to apologize to each other and say you're sorry.

If your boy has a toy taken from him by another boy, say such things as:

- That was not a nice thing for him to do. I'm going to ask him to give it back to you.

If your boy lets others push him around, say such things as:

■ What "Johnnie" did is not acceptable. You must tell him that he is hurting your feelings when he does that and that's not a nice thing for boys to do to each other.

Words, Phrases, and Actions to Use

■ ... unacceptable ...
■ ... hurt feelings ...
■ You wouldn't like it if ...
■ No fighting
■ Don't take that.
■ Good boy.

■ Be nice.
■ Don't hit.
■ Be gentle.
■ I'm going to move you away from him.

Things Not to Say and Do

Don't encourage your boy to fight other boys. Don't say such things as:

■ If he hits you must hit him back.
■ Just hit him like he hit you.
■ Stand up for yourself.

Don't let him take others' toys. Don't say such things as:

■ He had it long enough.
■ If he really wanted it he'd come and get it.
■ You have as much right to it as he does.
■ He should share it with you.

Don't stop your boy from fun-fighting and roughhousing with other boys. Don't say such things as:

■ You mustn't do that. You'll get hurt.
■ No fighting, even in fun.
■ You don't need to play that way.

Don't let your boy be a bully. Don't say such things as:

- You're bigger and stronger so you win.
- Might makes right.
- If that sissy won't stand up for himself he gets what he deserves.

Words, Phrases, and Actions to Avoid

- You must learn to fight for what is yours.
- I'll teach you how to fight.
- Learn to take what you want.
- Hit him.
- If you want it take it.

BATH TIME

◆

Your boy has been playing outside this afternoon and he's in desperate need of a bath. When dinner is over you want to get him clean and ready for bed before he spends some quiet time with the family. You've set up a routine for him since he was a baby so he doesn't fuss about taking a bath. In fact he enjoys this time you and he spend together. You fill the tub with about six inches of water at just the right temperature for him. You let him turn the taps on and off if he wants to and show him how to test the water temperature. You make sure he has his favorite bath toys. You never leave him alone while he's bathing, even though he's been learning how to swim at the local pool. You point out how he's to wash himself, as you have done ever since you started bathing him as an infant. You ask him to tell you what he's doing as he tries, quite successfully, to wash himself. After he's clean and has had some playtime, the water has cooled off so that it's time to get out.

Things to Consider

Proper hygiene is so important for your boy, especially now that he's playing with other children, visiting their homes, and attending preschool. You want him to be clean and sweet-smelling, even though he's a rough-and-tumble little boy. The most important thing you've done in this regard is the routine you've established for baths ever since he was a baby.

Now he's old enough to take on some of the bathing responsibilities for himself. Under your close supervision you can let him run the bath. You can let him undress himself and put his dirty clothes in the hamper of the laundry room. You can teach him to get his pajamas ready to put on after the bath. You can let him use soap and a washcloth to clean himself. Of course you must still wash his hair for him, using a gentle baby shampoo that won't sting and still being careful not to get any soap in his eyes.

Bath time is a good time to communicate your love through talking about how much fun the bath is, how important it is to be clean, and how nice he smells after he's washed himself and you've done his hair. You can also use bath time to talk about safety in the bath, making sure the water is the right depth and temperature. You should always talk to him about what he's done during the day, how he's gotten so dirty, and what he's doing to clean himself up.

Three Things You Must Do

1. Keep him clean.
2. Teach him how to keep himself clean.
3. Talk about being clean.

Things to Say and Do

Remind him that he needs a bath because he's dirty and smelly. Say such things as:

- You've had a good time playing today. Now we need to get rid of all that dirt.
- Time to clean you up before bed.
- Now that you've finished playing what do we have to do?

Ask him to get the bath ready. Say such things as:

- Can you fill the bath?
- That's right. Turn on the water and let's make sure it's coming in at the right temperature.
- Are all your toys there?

Let him get undressed himself and get his pajamas ready. Say such things as:

- Take off all those dirty clothes and put them in the hamper.
- Can you bring your pajamas in from your bedroom?
- That's a clever boy for knowing what to do to get ready for your bath.

Let him play for a while, and play with him if he wants you to. Also let him wash himself when he's ready. Get him to talk to you by asking him questions. Say such things as:

- Can you rub some soap on the washcloth and clean yourself?
- Can you tell me where you need to wash yourself every day?
- Are you really clean? Did you wash all over?

Get his cooperation when you wash his hair. Say such things as:

- Now it's time for hair. Hold this cloth over your eyes and lean your head back.
- Hold still while I rinse the soap out.

Let him dry himself and then help him as he needs it, having a nice conversation with him all the time. Say such things as:

- Well, that was a nice bath and you smell so good.
- Was it a good bath tonight?
- Do you like washing yourself and being clean?

Finish off the bath routine by having him pull the plug. Also show him how you rinse out the tub, and help him get into his pajamas.

If your boy always refuses to take his bath you may want to talk to him to find out what's wrong, You also need to point out the consequences for him if he won't bathe. Say such things as:

- Why don't you want your bath?
- Is something wrong?
- Your friends won't want to be near you if you're not clean.
- If you don't take your bath I can't put clean pajamas on you.
- You must take your bath every day so you'll be nice and clean for your friends.
- Let me tell you a story about a boy who wouldn't take his bath.
- No bath, no television.

Words, Phrases, and Actions to Use

- . . . clean . . .
- It's bath time.
- You smell good.
- Let's play with your toys.
- Let me see you wash yourself.
- Fill the tub.
- Use lots of soap.
- What a clean boy.
- Good job washing yourself.
- Your bath is over.

Things Not to Say and Do

Don't fight with your boy if he doesn't want to take his bath. Be firm and remind him of the routine. Don't say such things as:

- I won't love you if you don't bathe.
- You're disgusting if you don't bathe.
- Everybody hates a dirty little boy.

Don't let your boy get away with not having his bath unless there is good reason to do so. Don't say such things as:

- I don't care if you bathe or not.
- If you want to be smelly and dirty it's all right with me.

Don't punish your boy, if he won't bathe, by taking away things that are good for him. Don't say such things as:

- No bath, no dinner.

Don't ever leave your boy alone in the bath.

Words, Phrases, and Actions to Avoid

- Hitting your boy.
- Shaking your boy.
- Depriving him of food.
- Cursing him.
- Forgetting he's still a very little boy.
- Assuming his actions are directed at you.

BEDTIME

◆

Your son is more physical in his play than he ever was. His days are full of activities, including his two hours in preschool every morning. However, he still fights you at bedtime. But you can use words to help him understand how important it is for him to get a good night's sleep. And he always enjoys it when you read to him or tell him a story, especially if you make him the main character.

Things to Consider

Your son's metabolism is higher at this age than it ever will be again in his whole life. To replace all the energy he uses up he needs lots of good food and lots of sleep. The experts agree that the most successful way to ensure this is through a consistent routine. A typical routine in our household for our boys was supper at six, followed by bath time and fifteen minutes to half an hour of quiet play or reading, then bedtime with a story at 7:30, and finally lights out with a lullaby and a goodnight kiss. This routine varied a little between summer and winter, but the basics remained constant.

Your son can take the initiative in this routine leading up to bedtime. For example, get him to tell you what happens next. At this age you can ask him to tell you which book he wants you to read to him. You can ask him questions about his day, and you can talk about tomorrow. He will love it if you make up a story about him and the family. You can base it on his experiences that day or on something you've done recently as a family, or something you're planning to do. You can ask him to tell you what happens next.

Three Things You Must Do

1. Have a bedtime routine and follow it.
2. Ensure your preschooler gets ten to twelve hours of sleep each night.
3. Make bedtime a special time for him.

Things to Say and Do

Your son needs his sleep to recharge his batteries. Start slowing him down and mentally preparing him for bed around dinnertime. Say such things as:

- Time to relax before supper.
- Let's talk about what you did today.
- Did you have fun playing with "Charlie"?

After dinner use his bath as a way to relax him and to talk in gentle tones about getting ready for bed. Say such things as:

- After we get you nice and clean and dry you can have a story and then it's bedtime.

After his bath let him do what he wants for about fifteen minutes to a half an hour, depending on how tired he is. Use this time to continue his winding down process. Say such things as:

- Now that you're nice and clean and in your pajamas you can play quietly or we can read a story. What would you like to do?

When it's bedtime be gentle, yet firm. Say such things as:

- Time for boys to go to bed.
- Time for bed and a story.
- It's 7:30. Time for boys your age to be in bed.

If he resists, as he very well might do, be firm and say such things as:

- You know the routine. It's time for bed and a story.
- Boys need to get a good night's sleep so they're ready to play tomorrow.
- It's bedtime. Here we go. (You can pick him up and carry him to bed.)

If he doesn't cooperate, sit next to him and start reading his favorite story, or tell him a story in which the main character is a boy like your son who refuses to go to bed.
    Remember to praise him for doing the right thing. Hug and kiss him goodnight.

Words, Phrases, and Actions to Use

- Relax.
- It's bedtime.
- It's story time.
- It's suppertime.
- It's bath time.
- What do you want to do?
- I love you.
- Sleep tight.

Things Not to Say and Do

Don't yell at your boy. Don't let disagreements escalate into battles of the will. Don't say such things as:

- You'll go to bed or else.
- You're a bad boy.
- I won't love you if you don't do what I say.

Don't play any violent games or let him watch anything on TV that might get him worked up. Don't deny him a story. Don't bargain with your boy if he refuses to go to bed. You are the boss. Don't say such things as:

- If you go to bed now, you can stay up later tomorrow night.
- If you go to bed I'll give you a special treat tomorrow.

Don't give up. Don't say such things as:

- I give up. Do what you like.
- If you don't want to go to bed I don't care.

Words, Phrases, and Actions to Avoid

- You're a bad boy.
- You're a rotten kid.
- I don't love you anymore.
- I'm going to punish you.
- Do you want a spanking?

COMPUTERS, VIDEO GAMES, MOVIES, AND TV

◆

Your preschool boy, as much as older boys, likes to use the computer, play video games, and watch movies and TV. You're not sure how to balance his fascination and enjoyment of these wonderful inventions with the potential dangers to your son's development. You can see that computers and video games emphasize spatial skills at the expense of verbal skills, just the opposite of what your boy needs. You know that watching movies and TV pose at lease two risks for him: that he will either be a passive watcher or that the violence he sees may make him act out aggressively in his play with other children. You have talked to your boy in very simple language about all of these things and you always monitor what he does, but you wonder if you're doing enough or doing too much.

Things to Consider

There are many different views on the beneficial versus the harmful effects that computers, video games, and movies and TV can have on young children, especially on boys, who seem hardwired to be endlessly attracted to such forms of entertainment.

Michael Gurian in his book *Boys and Girls Learn Differently* points out some of the dangers computer use presents to preschool boys. It may restrict development of those parts of your boy's brain (temporal lobe and left hemisphere) that control his communication abilities, an area in which boys already lag behind girls. Computer use in young children may also adversely affect the imagination function located in the right hemisphere. Finally, reading and writing ability, which depend on both right and left brain, may be inhibited because whole brain function develops less well in the presence of spatial stimulants like the images on a computer, TV, or movie screen.

None of this suggests that your boy should never use a computer, play a video game, watch a movie, or watch TV. But it does tell you that *too much* of this kind of visual stimulation can be bad for your boy because it affects the normal development of the brain. The compounding factor is that boys are more attracted to these computers and games than girls, yet they hurt boys precisely in those areas of communication development in which they already lag behind. For video games and computer use you may want to restrict access for your boy to an hour a day. You may also want to restrict movie and TV watching to an hour a day.

Video games, movies, and TV also pose an additional concern: appropriate content. Content includes language, subject matter, and violence. Many child psychologists and psychiatrists believe that violence in movies or video games is bad for children, and especially for young boys. These doctors argue that this violence causes boys to become violent and, more important, provides very bad behavior role models for boys.

You cannot depend on TV stations, cable operators, satellite services, program advertisers, or video game creators and video stores to police the content for your boy. That's your responsibility. You make the rules, you program your TV to restrict access to certain channels, you decide what he can watch, you determine which video games are okay and which are not, and you decide when and where he can watch or play, whether it be at home, at a friend's, or at the movies.

Dr. Eli H. Newberger, author of *The Men They Will Become*, has some very sensible suggestions regarding television watching, which I've expanded to include movie watching, electronic game playing, and computer use. I summarize them here:

1. Use movies and games that you've previewed, rather than "live" movies or games you don't know.
2. Watch movies and play games with your boy, talking to him about what he sees and understands.
3. Use things other than television watching, playing games, or time on the computer as a reward for good behavior or as a baby-sitter when you have other things you'd rather do than look after your boy.
4. Balance TV watching, game playing, and computer use with other worthwhile activities, like playing with other children, reading, running, jumping, skating, and riding bicycles.

One last thought. It's important for your little boy, especially as he gets older and starts school, to be able to talk to his friends about the things they all know about, like movies, TV shows, video games, and computer things. He needs to have some of the same experiences they do, so don't totally restrict him from these things.

Three Things You Must Do

1. Limit your boy's use of computers, video games, movies, and TV.
2. Monitor your boy's use of computers, video games, movies, and TV.
3. Talk to your boy about his use of computers, video games, movies, and TV.

Things to Say and Do

Talk to your boy about computer use at home, at a friend's home, and at preschool. Say such things as:

- I'll teach you how to use the computer, and we'll use it together.
- Does "Bobby" have a computer at home? Do his mom and dad let him use it? Are you allowed to use it when you're at his house?
- I know you use a computer at preschool. What kinds of things do you do on it?

Talk to your boy about the video games he and his friends like. Say such things as:

- What's the best video game?
- Will you tell me about it? Why is it great? What happens in it?
- Do your friends have it?

Talk to your boy about movies and TV. Say such things as:

- What's your favorite movie/TV show?
- How come?
- What do your friends like?
- Do you want to watch it together?

Don't be afraid to make rules about using, playing, and watching. Say such things as:

- Let's decide when you can use the computer/play that game/watch that movie/ watch TV.
- That's not a good game/movie/program for boys.
- You have to be six to play/watch that.
- You can only use/play/watch that with me.
- That's enough for today. Let's read a book together.

Words, Phrases, and Actions to Use

- Too much . . .
- Good boy.
- Bad.

- That's not for boys.
- That's okay.
- Let me see it.
- Tell me about it.
- You know the rules.

Things Not to Say and Do

Don't let your boy have free choice to do or watch whatever he wants. Don't say such things as:

- Watch what you want. It can't hurt you.
- You need to learn to use the computer as early as you can because they make you smart.
- I'd rather have you playing on the computer than playing outside.

Don't use these things as baby-sitters too much. Don't say such things as:

- I'm busy. Go watch TV.
- Here, turn on the computer and play around while I do other things.

Don't let your boy do these things at the expense of playing games with playmates. Don't say such things as:

- I'd rather have you in here where I can watch you.
- You play too rough with those kids. Stay in and watch TV.

Don't ignore your boy if he wants to talk about any of these things with you. Don't say such things as:

- I'm too busy to talk about it.
- Figure it out for yourself.

Words, Phrases, and Actions to Avoid

- Do whatever you want.
- Shut up.
- Don't bother me.
- Watch what you like.
- You can do whatever your friends do.

EATING

◆

Your little boy has decided that Fruit Loops, macaroni and cheese, and pizza give him all the nourishment he will ever need at breakfast, lunch, and dinner. No peas, carrots, salads, fresh fruit, eggs, or meat for him. He drinks milk, thank goodness, but only on his Fruit Loops. You prepare good meals for the family but your four-year-old pushes them away. Your doctor wants to see him if he persists in this behavior at mealtimes. You recognize that little boys have preferences for toys, clothes, playmates, books, and many other things, and you want to respect his wishes as much as possible. But when it comes to eating you know he needs a balanced diet to grow and flourish. You pray that he'll come to his senses as you continue to offer him nutritious alternatives to his current tastes.

Things to Consider

Because your boy's general physical and neurological development is galloping along during these years and because his metabolic rate is higher than it will ever be again, you recognize that his need for healthy food is more important than ever. What's a good diet for him? That's for you and your physician to work out. Your little boy, when given the options, will likely choose a balanced diet. If he doesn't, then you must seek professional advice. In the meantime you can keep giving him good choices at mealtimes and talking to him about good nutrition, good food, and regular eating habits.

Don't prepare a special menu for your boy. You can give him healthy choices, but don't cater to his extremes for any extended time. Let him eat as much or as little as he likes. But if he refuses to eat what you offer at dinnertime, don't give him unhealthy or inconvenient alternatives. If he refuses to eat dinner offer him something at bedtime so that he doesn't go to bed hungry.

Above all, choose your battles wisely. As much as you can, tell your boy that you will respect his preferences as long as they are healthy. If you can plan your week's menu with these preferences in mind you will make your life, and his, much more enjoyable, without sacrificing a healthy diet. If you do this you can even occasionally indulge him in his not-so-healthy choices.

Finally, be sure that your boy's teeth are in good shape. Your boy may prefer foods that are easy to chew because he has a problem. Don't wait until his adult teeth begin to come in to take him to your dentist for a checkup.

Three Things You Must Do

1. Offer your boy a healthy diet.
2. Respect his healthy preferences.
3. Check with your doctor on any persistent eating problems.

Things to Say and Do

Talk to your boy about food and the importance of eating a healthy balanced diet. Refer to his role models and heroes as people who eat well and grow big and strong. Say such things as:

- If you want to be big and strong like him, you have to eat good food.
- Boys have to eat well if they want to become men like your daddy.
- Good food makes you grow up. Then you can be big and strong like your hero.

Talk to your boy about his preferences in food, even though you probably know them already. Praise him for his healthy choices. Say such things as:

- What are your favorite things to eat at breakfast/lunch/dinner/snacktime?
- What good choices you make! Those are really good for you.
- Eating that will help you be big and strong.

If you can, tell him what different foods are good for. Make it very personal to him. Say such things as:

- Drinking milk will make your bones really strong.
- Eating your carrots will make your eyes see like an eagle.
- This meat will give you strong muscles like your favorite action hero.

Be a good role model for your boy. Talk about what you like to eat and why you like to eat it. You can even tell him your preferences for junk food. If you can tell him about your childhood food preferences that would be even better. Say such things as:

- Your daddy/mommy and I try to eat what's good for us and we want you to do the same.
- When I was your age I wouldn't eat carrots, but now I love them.

- I love sour cream and onion potato chips, but if I eat too many I don't like them anymore.
- When I was your age I ate a whole chocolate turkey at Thanksgiving and got really sick to my stomach. It was a long time before I ate chocolate again.
- You can eat whatever you like as long as most of it's healthy and good for you.

Words, Phrases, and Actions to Use

- . . . balance . . .
- This is good food.
- Those are healthy choices.
- What are your choices?
- That's nutritious.

- That's good for you.
- That's bad for you.
- Let's compromise.
- That's too much.

Things Not to Say and Do

Don't tell your boy he can eat whatever he likes even if it's not nutritious. Don't say such things as:

- I don't care what you eat.
- Have more pizza.
- You can always eat as much ice cream as you want.

Don't discourage him from eating vegetables. Don't say such things as:

- I hate vegetables.
- You don't have to eat salads at your age.
- Anything green is so boring.

Don't be too indulgent of his unhealthy preferences. Don't say such things as:

- You can eat as much junk food as you want. It won't hurt you.
- Have some more Twinkies.
- Here are your favorite potato chips.

Don't prepare special meals for him unless your doctor recommends it.

Don't force your boy to eat everything you put in front of him. Don't say such things as:

- If you don't clean your plate you get no dessert.
- Eat it all up or you'll be punished.
- I don't care if you don't like it. You're going to eat it.

Words, Phrases, and Actions to Avoid

- Eat what you like.
- Junk food is okay.
- You don't have to eat that. I'll make you something special.
- Pizza, ice cream, and cookies have all the food groups.
- You'll be sorry if you don't eat it.
- You'll eat it or else.
- You're a very bad boy.

FEELINGS

◆

**You love your little boy and would never want to do anything that might hurt
his feelings. But he's moved a little beyond the beautiful innocence of being a
baby and toddler. Now he has a strong will of his own, he seems less totally
dependent on you, even though he still needs you for almost everything in his
life, and he is asserting his independence more and more. You know what he
wants and how he feels both by what he does and what he says. He has minor
confrontations with you and with his playmates. Teaching him how to appropriately express his feelings in words rather than actions is high on your list of
priorities.**

Things to Consider

Boys express their feelings at this age in ways that are often different from girls. Part
of the reason is that boys seem hardwired to act out their feelings while girls talk about
them. Because of this you need to encourage your boy to verbalize his feelings. You
don't want him to feel inhibited or guilty about them; you just want him to express them
in ways that will strengthen his self-esteem and relationships with others.

This is an especially important thing to learn *before he starts school*. Acting aggressively or angrily in school will hurt his relationships with his teacher and schoolmates, and can affect his learning. Appropriate expression of feelings is an acutely
important social skill that you must teach him.

What are the right ways for him to express feelings? You need to teach him to put
into words how he feels about people and things. You do this by modeling the talk. Tell
him how you feel about things and ask him to tell you how he feels. Show him that it's
good to say nice things about people, but also important to say when someone bothers
or hurts him, or makes him feel sad.

Use words to show him what to say to get along with his siblings and playmates,
and with adults. Encourage him to ask for what he wants rather than to cry or take.
Reward him whenever he uses words rather than actions to express his feelings. Of course
actions like hugging, singing, dancing, skipping, running, and jumping are positive ways
to express feelings. And you should also reward him for that. Because boys will almost
always want to express their feelings physically rather than verbally, you need to encourage talking about them much more than acting them out.

Three Things You Must Do

1. Encourage your boy to express his feelings.
2. Teach him to use words rather than actions.
3. Model appropriate talk about feelings.

Things to Say and Do

Encourage your boy to talk about how he feels. Say such things as:

- I think you're feeling sad. Can you tell me why?
- I want you to tell me how you're feeling.
- Do you feel angry? Let's talk about it.
- How do you feel now?

Teach your boy how to talk about feeling unhappy and angry. Say such things as:

- You look unhappy. Can you tell me what makes you feel unhappy? Was it something that I did?
- How do you feel? You're feeling sad. What makes you feel sad? Say the words that make you sad.
- I think you're feeling angry. Did I make you angry? What did I do?

Encourage your boy to talk rather than act out his feelings. Say such things as:

- It's not nice for a boy to hit anyone, even when he's angry.
- Taking that boy's toy makes him feel sad. Would you like someone to make you feel sad?
- I know you really want that toy. How do you feel about it?

Model good talk about feelings in language your young boy can understand. Make it simple and direct. Say such things as:

- The sunshine outside makes me feel very happy. How does it make you feel?
- I'm feeling very sad today. I wanted to take you to the playground but it's too wet outside.
- I get angry when another little boy takes away your toy.
- I don't like it when boys hit other children.

Words, Phrases, and Actions to Use

- I feel good.
- I feel bad.
- I feel angry.
- I feel happy.
- I love you.
- How do you feel?

- What do you feel like when you're happy?
- No hitting.
- No kicking.
- No crying in anger.

Things Not to Say and Do

Don't encourage your boy to act out his aggression or anger. Don't say such things as:

- If he takes your toy just take it back.
- Don't let him do that to you. Hit him.
- When I'm angry I cry and throw things.

Don't be a bad role model for your boy. Don't say or do such things as:

- Shout.
- Hit.
- Use very aggressive language.

Don't discourage your boy from expressing his feelings. Don't say such things as:

- Be quiet.
- Don't be such a baby.
- Big boys don't cry.

Words, Phrases, and Actions to Avoid

- You're a bad boy.
- You're a sissy.
- You're a baby.
- Shut up.

- Hitting your boy when he cries.
- Punishing him when he tells you he feels angry.
- Shaking him.

GENDER IDENTITY

◈

Your little boy is clearly aware that he has a penis. If he has a sister he is aware that she doesn't. You are interested and maybe a bit embarrassed by your son's budding curiosity in his own body and that of others, even though you know it's totally innocent and immature. Gender identity and sexuality become an ever more important topic for you to talk about with your boy. You certainly want him to grow up with a healthy and respectful attitude toward his own body and that of others. One of the most important things you want to teach him is that his body belongs to him—others must respect his privacy as much as he must respect others. The last thing you want to do is make him feel guilty about his male identity.

Things to Consider

Your boy is going through the first stages of learning what it means to be a boy. He will begin to realize that some of his body parts are the same as everybody else's, while others are what makes him a boy and not a girl. However, at this age he will not realize the permanency of gender identity, even though you try to explain it to him. He might simply assume that someday his sister will also grow a penis. Not until he's in school does he begin to understand the idea that gender identity doesn't change (usually)—boys and girls remain boys and girls.

Your preschooler will notice that males and females have different sex organs and that boys and men pee standing up. Of course you have explained this to him and in his toilet training you have shown him how to do this. Other body parts will also begin to take on significance for him. He'll notice that his dad's face gets rough when he hasn't shaved. He will see that his mom shaves her legs. He'll see that his mom's hair may be longer than his dad's. He might even notice it feels different because it has a different texture. He'll notice many other gender differences as well—in clothes, makeup, and behavior. It's up to you whether or not you let your boy see you naked. Whatever makes you comfortable. But your boy will certainly be curious and you may find him and a little girl comparing bodies.

You'll talk to your boy about these gender differences whenever he asks. You won't stop him from trying out makeup or dressing in female clothing because you know he still doesn't understand that gender is a permanent thing. You'll talk to him about boy things and girl things without trying to shut him off from his feminine side. But as time goes on your boy will notice things about his gender identity. As a result he will likely become quite rigid in his ideas of what's right for boys and what's right for girls. He may avoid playing with girls and try to be a macho man by imitating his male heroes. Your concern then is that he may play so much at being male that he tells you he wants to be treated like a boy, not a girl, and rejects your hugs and kisses.

You want your boy to become comfortable with his male identity, but you don't want to ignore his need for your love and nurturing. At his age you must make it clear to him that you are always there to comfort and console and protect him.

Three Things You Must Do

1. Accept his growing interest in gender and sexual identity.
2. Remember that his interest is innocent, immature, and very limited.
3. Answer all his questions about gender honestly in language he can understand.

Things to Say and Do

Use the proper names for body parts when he asks you about them. This will save you and him embarrassment later on. Say such things as:

- This is your penis. Boys and daddies have a penis.
- Girls and mommies have a vagina.
- Everyone has breasts. Big girls and mommies have bigger breasts than boys and daddies.

Explain some of the fundamental differences between males and females. You don't have to be too detailed unless he asks. But if he has the chance to see you pregnant explain what's happening. Say such things as:

- Boys grow up to be daddies.
- Girls grow up to be mommies.
- Mommies carry the new baby in their tummies until it is born.

Because your boy doesn't understand gender permanence at his age you may see him go out of his way to do what he thinks is really male. Don't criticize him for this but make sure he doesn't get out of control. Say such things as:

- Boys do this. But girls can do it too.
- Boys are allowed to do this.
- Real boys don't hit girls or other boys.
- Daddies never hit mommies.

Your boy will look to his dad for a male role model. Be a good one. Do such things as:

- Show that your masculinity can be good for everyone.
- Don't be ashamed to cry.
- Show your boy your warm, nurturing, loving side.
- Show your boy your strength and courage.
- Be present in your boy's life so that he knows what his dad does through experience.

Words, Phrases, and Actions to Use

- You're a real boy.
- Someday you'll be a man.
- Girls are different.
- Girls become women.
- Someday you'll be a daddy.
- Girls become mommies.
- It's all right to do this.
- Boys don't do this.
- Boys and girls do this.

Things Not to Say and Do

Don't make your boy feel guilty about his interest in gender. If he plays with himself in the bath don't criticize him or stop him. Don't say such things as:

- That's disgusting.
- Leave yourself alone.
- Boys mustn't play with themselves.

If your boy asks about his sister's or mom's genitalia, don't ignore or criticize him. Don't say such things as:

- That's none of you business.
- You're too young to know.
- That's a dirty thing to ask.

If your boy sees you naked don't overreact. Don't say such things as:

- EEEEEEEE YAH!!!!!!!!!
- Get out of here.
- Go away, you naughty boy.

Don't deny your boy the right to be afraid, to be upset, to cry. Don't say such things as:

- Big boys don't cry.
- There's nothing to be afraid of.
- Be a man.
- Don't be a sissy.

Don't condone your boy's behavior if he hurts someone else. Don't say such things as

- Boys will be boys.
- He's just learning to be a man.

Words, Phrases, and Actions to Avoid

- You're a bad boy.
- You dirty boy.
- You nasty little boy.
- That's a bad thing to do.
- Go away.
- Don't ever say things like that.
- If you do that everyone will call you a sissy.
- You're no better than a little girl.

GIRLS

◆

Your little boy used to have little sense of gender when he was younger. He seemed to be quite happy playing with girls. But suddenly he won't have anything to do with them. You want to encourage him to play with girls but he doesn't want to. Girls are not acceptable as playmates now. He's only interested in playing with boys and doing boy things. And he's drawn a line in the sand that separates girl things from boy things. It's as though gender differences were suddenly the most important thing in the world to him and he exaggerates them as though he was afraid that his male identity was at risk. All of this is quite normal and has important practical developmental explanations.

Things to Consider

Male and female brain differences and body chemistry show themselves in boys and girls very early. Even in their preschool years boys and girls differ in their preferences for games, toys, and playmates. At this age girls are more verbal and can use their talk in play much better than boys. For girls, dolls are babies, mommies, and daddies; for boys, they are action figures. You must be careful not to blame or discourage your boy from seeking out those who play like him, which is probably mainly boys.

Girls at three to five years are already socially aware in their games, while boys are much more task-oriented. Girls' play already includes talk about relationships, other kids' clothes, and friendships, while boys get together to build things, take them apart, roughhouse, and play action hero. Researchers have found that young girls seem quite focused on their play, carrying one game or activity to its end, while in the same time period boys switched their attention to new games, new people, new toys three times more often than girls.

Girls are more likely to cry when they are hurt, while boys often cry out of anger or frustration. The fact is that girls can verbalize anger and frustration, while boys of the same age express themselves by crying or lashing out. Girls seem to welcome new children into their play group more readily than boys.

In summary, although you are anxious to raise your son to recognize girls as equal to boys, the tide of your boy's mental and physical development at this age works against you. Preschool boys have developed quite rigid gender stereotypes. So don't be too upset when he seems to reject everything you've told him about girls being able to do anything boys can do. Don't give up. Simply continue to talk to him about this, pointing out examples from real life. Also help him come to understand that he will always be a boy, just as his sister will always be a girl. Give him the right names for anatomical differences. Let him choose whom he wants to play with. Just keep talking to him about girls and how they are the same as and different from boys.

Three Things You Must Do

1. Understand the neurobiological differences between girls and boys.
2. Realize that your son's preference for boy playmates reflects a stage in his development.
3. Keep talking to your son about similarities and differences between girls and boys.

Things to Say and Do

Let your son make his own choices of playmates even if they are, all of a sudden, only boys. Say such things as:

- You choose who you want to play with.
- Who do you want to play with?
- Who's your best friend?

Keep talking about girls as potential playmates. Say such things as:

- "Amanda's" a nice girl. Why not play with her?
- You like "Sarah." You've played with her before.
- Girls make good playmates.

Be prepared for rejection. But get your boy to talk about his reasons. It's important to encourage him to put his feelings into words. Say such things as:

- Why don't you want to play with "Amanda"?
- Can you tell me what you don't like about "Sarah"?
- What don't you like about playing with girls?

When your boy stereotypes girls make sure to correct him with real examples. But don't criticize him or make him feel stupid. He's just going through a specific stage in his development. Say such things as:

- Of course girls can fly planes.
- Girls drive big trucks.
- Girls are strong and can carry heavy things.

If you are the mom, show him what you can do and point out other female activities that your boy may consider to be purely male. Boys need to learn early about the wide range of gender roles and activities that transcend stereotypes.

Help your son realize that girls and boys don't normally change their gender. You can help him by telling him. Experts also suggest you tell boys the correct names for vagina, breasts, and penis. Point out similarities and differences in other areas of gender relations, such as occupations, sports, musculature, hair, voice, clothes, makeup, and jewelry. Say such things as:

- You are a boy and you're always going to be a boy.
- Your sister is a girl and she will always be a girl.
- Mommy was always a girl.
- Daddy was always a boy.
- Girls can do most things boys can do, and boys can do most things girls can do.
- Girls are also different from boys in very nice ways.
- You are a boy but you can play with girls' toys and girls can play with boys' toys, if you want to.

Words, Phrases, and Actions to Use

- . . . different . . .
- . . . same . . .
- You're a boy.
- She's a girl.
- You're a male.
- She's a female.
- Those are boys' toys.
- Those are girls' toys.
- There is no difference.
- Everyone can play with dolls in their own way.

Things Not to Say and Do

Don't force your boy to play with girls if he doesn't want to. Don't say such things as:

- You have to play with "Amanda" whether you want to or not.
- If you won't play with "Sarah" you can't play with anyone.

Don't discourage your boy from playing with girls if he wants to. Don't say such things as:

- Real boys don't play with girls.
- I won't let my son play with girls.

Don't make your boy feel guilty if he wants to play with dolls. Don't say such things as:

- You can't play with dolls.
- There must be something wrong with you.

Don't let your boy be aggressive toward girls. Don't say such things as:

- You can hit a girl if she deserves it.
- You're only doing what boys do.
- Boys always hit girls. It's human nature.

Don't frighten your boy by telling him he's going to turn into a girl. Don't say such things as:

- If you play with girls you'll turn into one.
- Playing with dolls will make you a girl.
- You're going to become a little girl if you keep playing that way.

Words, Phrases, and Actions to Avoid

- You're a sissy.
- You're acting like a girl.
- What's wrong with you?
- Real boys don't play with girls.
- You're a bad boy.

MORAL DEVELOPMENT

◆

You have been teaching your boy to be a good boy ever since he was born. Every time you said, "Good boy," or "Bad boy," or "That's not a nice thing to do," you've been giving him feedback on his behavior, telling him what's right and what's wrong. Now that he's a preschooler with a growing command of language, you can talk about reasons for things being good and bad, right and wrong. He's still too young to really put himself in other's shoes so he can't really understand the meaning and the consequences of his actions for others, but he certainly knows what he likes and what he doesn't like when it happens to him. You want him to have fun and be happy, but you also know that you must say "No" to some things, even if it makes him sad, because that's how you teach him the difference between right and wrong.

Things to Consider

You teach your boy moral lessons by showing and telling him the difference between right and wrong. You talk to your boy about the good and bad actions that you, he, and others take and you try to model moral behavior. Your boy develops moral reasoning as he slowly learns to put himself in another's place and recognizes that his actions have consequences for himself and others.

Eventually you want your boy to be honest, trustworthy, gentle, kind, considerate, and compassionate. This can't happen overnight. And it doesn't happen automatically. It requires years of training, talking, experience, reflection, and self-discipline. Your boy will learn it in stages as he changes mentally and physically from being a completely self-centered baby consumer of love, food, and shelter, to being an adult provider of love, food, and shelter for his children. Moral development requires practicing The Golden Rule: do unto others as you would have others do unto you.

Completely permissive parenting won't help your boy become a good, moral person, nor will strict authoritarianism. As with most things in life it's the middle road that works best. Teaching moral development to your preschool boy means teaching in words that he can understand. It means gradually giving him some control over his life so that he can make good choices. You can teach him right and wrong by your reaction to what he says and does, using your smile, your body language, your words, and your tone of voice. If you are too strict your boy cannot develop an independent moral sense because he will be too dependent on you. If you are too permissive your boy may never learn to control his male aggression or his male impulsive behavior. He may never fully develop that self-discipline and respect that allows him to treat others like himself.

Your boy wants to be like you. Give him a good model to imitate. Love him and be firm, fair, and consistent in your discipline. Also apologize when you are wrong, discuss his behavior, and yours, and encourage him to verbalize his thoughts and feelings.

Three Things You Must Do

1. Model love, respect, and fairness in your relationship with him and others.
2. Talk about his behavior and yours.
3. Be firm and consistent in teaching him the differences between right and wrong.

Things to Say and Do

You teach moral thinking and behavior by talking about the actions of your son and others. Be specific in speaking of things in concrete terms rather than abstract ones. Say such things as:

- That was nice when you shared your toy with "Mary."
- Hitting "Felipe" was the wrong thing to do. It hurt him and made him cry. You must apologize to him and never do that again.
- I'm going to take you home now because you have behaved very badly toward me. When I told you to let your friend on the swing you ignored me. Why did you do that?
- You're such a good boy for letting your sister play with you and your friends.

Help your boy learn to empathize with others. Ask him to tell you how his actions affect his friends, or you, or how their actions, or yours, affect him. Say such things as:

- How would you feel if "Logan" hit you?
- Do you think "Latrelle" likes it when you take his toy away?
- When I tell you that you did something naughty how does it make you feel?
- What makes you happy?
- What makes you unhappy?

Be firm in your teaching. Say such things as:

- You must never hit anyone because you're angry.
- You must never try to hurt your sister.
- Whenever you take a friend's toy you have to think about how you would feel if they took yours.

Talk about your boy's behavior and your reaction to it. Say such things as:

- You and I have talked about the rules. Are you allowed to do what you just did? Can you tell me the rule?
- What do you think I should do with you?
- I think that was a nice thing to do. Can you tell me why?
- I love you and think you're a good boy. Do you think you're a good boy? Why?

Model good behavior for your boy. Do such things as:

- Be loving.
- Be fair.
- Be forgiving.
- Be kind.
- Be gentle.
- Be compassionate.

Words, Phrases, and Actions to Use

- You're a good boy.
- You're a bad boy.
- You're naughty.
- That was a nice thing to do.
- That was the right thing to do.
- That was the wrong thing to do.
- Why did you do that?
- Love others and yourself.

Things Not to Say and Do

Don't think that your boy will automatically become a good boy. Don't ignore his behavior. Don't say such things as:

- I don't care what you do.
- You can do whatever you want.
- Hitting him was the right thing to do.

Don't be too strict and authoritarian. You need to give your boy some control over his own behavior. Don't say such things as:

- Don't do anything without my permission.
- You will only do what I tell you to do.

Don't be a poor role model for your boy. Don't do such things as:

- Hit your boy.
- Hit others.
- Fight.
- Curse.

- Be cruel.
- Be unloving.
- Be unforgiving.
- Be unfeeling.

Words, Phrases, and Actions to Avoid

- You're a terrible boy.
- I'm going to hit you.
- Go on and hit him.
- You should fight him.
- Other people don't matter.
- Do it to others before they have a chance to do it to you.

PRESCHOOL

◆

You're trying to decide whether or not to enroll your boy in a preschool program. You know that your boy will benefit from being in a formal setting with other boys and girls. You've read about the advantages of giving your son experience in structured situations where he will learn to follow instructions, play with others, and engage in many different kinds of creative activities. You also know how much you look forward to having some time for yourself, even if it's only half a day. Yet you feel slightly guilty about the whole thing. You love your boy very much and want to spend as much time with him as you can before he actually starts school, yet you look forward to having someone else look after him for a while. You wonder what the best way is to tell him that you're going to be sending him to preschool. What will you say when he says he doesn't want to go?

Things to Consider

There are many things to consider, including your boy's personality and physical and social maturity, when deciding to enroll him in preschool or not. Is your boy an easy mixer or does he prefer to be on his own? Is he physically able to stand up for himself in a group of other boys? Is he toilet trained? Does he make friends easily? Does he hit? Can he make himself understood or does he need to physically act out his needs and emotions?

The kinds and reputations of preschools in your area are an important factor. Research suggests that young boys do better in well-structured preschool environments than in more permissive ones. Structured schools teach them appropriate behavior and other social skills more effectively. Boys, more than girls, have trouble adjusting to the demands of kindergarten and grade one, so learning these skills in preschool can be a distinct advantage. Less important to learning these skills is the actual academic skills that some preschools may introduce. If your boy is physically and socially ready for school when he's six years old, he will have no trouble doing the academic work expected of him. The boys who are behaviorally and socially immature are the ones who most often have problems when they start regular school.

Choose a preschool that emphasizes developing good social relationships, learning to listen carefully to instructions and to follow rules, learning good time management skills, learning to ask for things rather than taking them, and learning to verbalize one's feelings rather than acting them out in some aggressive way. Look for a preschool that recognizes and balances your boy's needs for physical activity and rough-and-tumble play, as well as his need to develop and practice his verbal and fine motor skills.

You need to explain preschool to your boy. Boys typically find it harder than girls to be separated from their mothers and are more likely to cry when first left at preschool. This may not be true for your boy, but you know him best and can decide how much preparation he might need. If you think being left at preschool will upset him be sure to tell him how much he will enjoy it and why. If he has any older siblings at preschool be sure to take him along to theirs before he has to go himself. Once he's there talk to him and his teachers about how well he has settled in. If he has problems it's much better to nip them in the bud in preschool than wait until regular school.

Your boy's preschool experiences will give you lots of things to talk about and lots of new activities you can share.

Three Things You Must Do

1. Decide if preschool is right for your boy.
2. Choose the right school and the right time to send him based on his needs and strengths.
3. Prepare him for the first time with lots of talk and a preview if possible.

Things to Say and Do

Before you come to any decision talk to your boy about preschool and get his reaction. See if he seems to like the idea or not. If he has older siblings or friends already at preschool he should feel more comfortable about going. Say such things as:

- Would you like to go to school?
- Do you know what children do at school?
- Do you think that would be fun?
- Your friend "Johnny" goes to school. Does he like it?
- Would you like to go to his school?

Talk to your boy about all the fun things he would do at school. Let him tell you before you tell him. Say such things as:

- Do you know what children do at school?
- Do you think that would be fun?
- There are lots of other boys and girls to play with at school.

- You learn lots of things you need to know when you go to the big children's school.

Visit the preschools in your area. Ask the directors and teachers what their philosophy of preschool is. Ask if you can observe. Talk to friends who have preschool experience. Once you've placed your boy in preschool carefully monitor his experience there. Go and observe the school. Talk regularly to the director and teachers about your son's behavior and work there. Talk to your boy about his experiences. Say such things as:

- Can you show me what you did today?
- Who are your friends at school?
- Is your teacher nice to you?
- Are the other children nice to you?
- Do you like it there?

Words, Phrases, and Actions to Use

- Preschool is exciting.
- You can have fun there.
- You can play there.
- You will make new friends there.
- Boys and girls go to school.
- You can play games there.
- Learning is fun.
- Talk to me about school.
- Does the thought of school make you happy?
- Does it make you sad?
- Does it make you angry?
- Schools have rules.

Things Not to Say and Do

Don't send your boy to preschool solely to give him an academic head start on other children before he starts kindergarten or grade one. Preschool for boys should encourage fun, socializing, creativity, verbalizing, and learning how to follow rules and gain self-discipline. Let your boy follow his own pace in reading, writing, and arithmetic. If he's not ready to learn these things until he begins formal schooling, that's okay. Don't say such things as:

- You've got to go to preschool to learn how to read and write and add and subtract, or you'll be behind everyone when you start regular school.
- Preschool isn't just for fun and playing around. It's for hard work and learning.

Don't think you have to send your boy to preschool. If he's a normal, well-adjusted young boy, he will do very well even without preschool. Just putting him in a regular play group, or having him go to the playground where he can meet and play with other children, is enough, as long as you work with him at home on giving him little tasks to do like helping you clear the table after dinner, picking up his clothes, and providing him with stimulating things to do. Don't say such things as:

- You're going to preschool whether you want to or not.
- If you don't go to preschool you'll be way behind the other kids.
- Go play by yourself. I'm too busy.
- There will be plenty of kids to play with when you start kindergarten.

Words, Phrases, and Actions to Avoid

- You must know how to read and write before you start school.
- Preschool is about work, not fun.
- You're going to preschool no matter what you say.
- You'll do what I say.
- You stupid boy.

PUNISHMENT

◆

You and your spouse disagree when it comes to punishing your boy for doing something he was told not to do. You were raised in a household where words were used to punish and hands and belts were not. You can't remember ever being spanked or physically punished. Your spouse grew up being spanked for disobedient behavior and claims that it was a good method of punishment. So far you have prevailed. Your son has never been spanked. But as he grows older your spouse has started to argue that the only way to really teach a boy a lesson is to spank him when he seriously misbehaves.

Things to Consider

Some parents take the old saying "Spare the rod and spoil the child" quite literally and feel that corporal punishment is a good and necessary part of raising children, especially boys. Many more boys than girls are physically disciplined at home and in school. Other parents recognize the need to discipline their children, but opt for other methods of punishment and would never spank or hit them, not even their boys.

You need to ask yourself what do you want to accomplish when you punish your boy? Child development expert Dr. Eli H. Newberger asks the following question: "Is spanking, even for the sake of loving deterrence, the only or best method of nurturing a boy's character and capacity for making wise choices?" The research findings on the effects of corporal punishment on boys are ambiguous, but common sense tells us that it's not the best way to solve behavior problems. What we do know is that there is a clear relationship between boys who have been spanked or hit and their own violent behavior as they grow up. These boys are more violent and aggressive. They get into more fights at school and hit their wives and children more than boys who were not spanked or hit. Even if there is no way of knowing which came first, the spanking and hitting or the aggressive and violent tendencies, why take the chance?

If there's a good possibility that hitting a child causes aggressive behavior, then common sense would tell us to use other ways to teach good behavior. I would urge you to change your notion of punishment altogether from the principle of retribution, making your boy suffer the consequences of disobedience, to the principle of communication, teaching your boy to understand and accept your values. This may not seem as immediately effective, nor may it feel as satisfying as a good wallop on his bottom, but in the long run it is a better way to teach your boy the kind of self-control, discipline, and deep, long-lasting values that you have as your goal for him.

How does this work? Your goal is that your boy learn self-discipline and that the source and foundation of this self-discipline comes out of his relationship with you. The sooner you begin to talk to him about each behavior that is morally wrong, socially wrong, or just dangerous, explaining why it is wrong or dangerous, the sooner your son will start building his own set of standards for right and wrong behavior. Each time he misbehaves you will take the time to explain your standards of judgment. You will use your love for him as your foundation. You will praise him for his good behavior and accomplishments. You will point out, explain, and, whenever possible, prevent bad behavior.

Above all you will be consistent and reasonable, helping your boy discover good behavior and the reasons for it through constant talk with you about what's good and what's bad and why. He will learn the limits and rules of good behavior by example and experience, not as an abstract set of rules you lay down. You will be firm and just, and your son will learn that he must live with the consequences of his actions. You will not cover for him if he breaks the rules. But he will understand what he's done wrong because he has internalized the meaning of good and bad moral and social behavior.

Three Things You Must Do

1. Love your little boy.
2. Be consistent and reasonable and don't expect or demand perfection.
3. Empathize when you talk to him about good and bad behavior, remembering that he is a living, feeling little boy.

Things to Say and Do

Aggressive behavior in little boys changes around age four from grabbing other's toys to fighting with the intent to hurt. You need to have started to teach your boy either kind of aggression is wrong because it hurts others. You must physically prevent it and you must talk about the reasons with your boy. Say such things as:

- You mustn't take "Bobby's" toy. It makes him feel bad.
- Even though you share your toys, some boys don't like to. It's very good to share, but you must never take any toys from children who don't like to share.
- Hitting "Johnny" was wrong because it can really hurt him. You wouldn't want someone to do it to you because it would hurt you and make you cry.

Rather than talk about punishment for breaking the rules help your boy develop his own set of rules by pointing out the good and bad things he and others do. Say such things as:

- How would you feel if someone made you cry? Would you ever want to make someone else cry? Do you think what you did to "Mary" was a good thing to do?
- Why shouldn't we hurt someone?
- Do you know why you mustn't throw rocks at anyone? I'm going to take you home now because you did that and I want to talk to you about why you must never do it again.

Emphasize the importance of trying to make up for what you've done wrong. Making restitution is a very important principle in this kind of disciplining. It helps develop a sense of responsibility toward oneself and others. Talk about restoring damage to things and relationships. Say such things as:

- You hurt "Sarah's" feelings. You need to make her feel better by apologizing to her. It will make you feel better too.
- You broke "John's" toy because you were being too rough with it. I know you didn't mean to do it, but now "John" doesn't have his toy to play with anymore. You must tell "John" how sorry you are that you broke it and then you and I will have to talk about what we can do to get him a new one. What do you think we should do?
- You know what you did was not very nice, don't you? Why was it not nice? What do you think you can do to make it better?

Talk about what the limits to your boy's behavior are and ought to be. Say such things as:

- Who do you think is the nicest friend you have? Why?
- What does it mean to be nice to someone?
- Why shouldn't you take someone's toy?
- Why shouldn't you hit someone?

Remember that your goal is to teach your boy self-discipline.

Words, Phrases, and Actions to Use

- Nice work.
- Well done.
- You're such a thoughtful boy.
- Thank you.
- I'm sorry.
- Please.

- That was a wrong thing to do.
- You hurt her feelings.
- You hurt him.
- Why did you do that?
- What should you do?

Things Not to Say and Do

Don't think of behavior in terms of a rigid set of rules that your boy must automatically obey. He is not in the army. He's your little boy and you want him to learn good moral and social behavior. Don't say such things as:

- Do it because I say so.
- You're in big trouble, kid.

Don't forget that your boy is a human being with feelings and motives like anyone else. Don't say such things as:

- I'm not interested in reasons. You're a bad boy.
- I don't care why you did it.
- I won't talk about it. You know the rules and you broke them.

Don't ever do either of the following things:

- Don't hit or spank your boy.
- Don't shake your boy.

Words, Phrases, and Actions to Avoid

- You're a bad boy.
- You're going to get a spanking.
- Hold still while I hit you.
- I'm going to give you the strap.

RULES

◈

You want to be loving, kind parents and you don't want to be too hard on your boy. You realize that sometimes "boys will be boys." But you also understand that your boy needs to learn self-discipline. You know that your boy needs rules more than his sister does because he is more adventurous, aggressive, and risk-taking. Most of all, your boy needs to learn the rules that will make him a good person. Good behavior toward others is one of those. You started teaching him rules when he was a toddler and now that he's a preschooler you're ready to go beyond those simple rules to more complicated ones—rules that will help him develop good moral character as well as rules for safety and consideration for others.

Things to Consider

You have given your child unconditional love and respect from the time he was born. In doing so you have modeled one of the most important rules he will ever learn in life: do unto others what you would have others do unto you. This is the Golden Rule and one of the best guideposts for your boy's life.

When your boy was just an infant or toddler his focus was on himself rather than others. He trusted you to provide for his essential needs: food and shelter, safety and love. Because you consistently gave him these things your boy's trust in you and his immediate world blossomed into a healthy trust of others and the world in general.

Now that your boy is a preschooler he has reached the age at which you want him to start thinking about himself in relationship to others and the world around him. Because he can now think of himself apart from you, he can also begin to understand that his actions have consequences. Your job is to help him understand that the rules you are teaching him will help to do things that have good consequences and avoid doing things that have bad consequences. Believe it or not he wants to please you.

The most important rule you can teach him at this age is respect for himself and others. Be respectful of things as well. Show him how to respect the world around him by modeling respectful behavior yourself, and by talking about it. Always say "please" and "thank you." Never take others for granted. Be kind to people and pets. Be considerate of others' feelings. Don't hit or fight. Don't yell or scream. Don't lose control of yourself or your temper. Use nice words, saving bad words for very special occasions.

Compliment your boy when he tries to do the right thing, and gently and respectfully correct him when he doesn't.

Above all, be consistent with your rules. Don't make too many rules and don't make them too difficult to understand and follow. At this age allow for lots of mistakes and forgetfulness. Remember he is just a little boy and the rules are for his benefit, not yours. Even if he breaks your rules, they are giving your boy the foundation for good moral character and good behavior throughout his life.

Three Things You Must Do

1. Make rules appropriate to your boy's age and understanding.
2. Make the first rule respect of himself and others.
3. Remember that he is still a little boy and be gentle with him.

Things to Say and Do

Talk to your boy about the rules that are most important for him to learn. Don't get too philosophical. Keep the rule and the explanation practical and tie it to a specific occasion. Say such things as:

- Always say "thank you." People like boys who say "thank you."
- Always say "please." People like boys who say "please."
- Never hit your brother or sister. You don't like being hit and they don't like it either. It makes them feel very sad.

Talk to your boy about respect for himself and others. Model respectful behavior in your relationship with him. Say such things as:

- That was a very nice thing to do. You are a good boy.
- When I do nice things it makes me feel good. Does it make you feel good when you do nice things?
- You must never do something to other people that you wouldn't want them to do to you.

Instead of yelling at your boy when he forgets a rule, simply remind him of the rule. Say such things as:

- Remember that you must pick up your toys.
- Don't forget to say "thank you."

- Don't forget to say "please."
- Remember not to hit.
- Remember to be gentle with the kitty.

Remember to keep calm when your boy does something wrong. He's just a little boy and he's no more perfect than you are. Simply be consistent in reminding him of the rule. If his forgetting creates a bad situation for others, like fighting or hitting other children, remove him from the situation and then talk about the rule. Say such things as:

- That is not a nice thing to do. It makes other children sad and it hurts them. You wouldn't want them to do that to you.
- If you're going to do that then you cannot play here anymore. That's not a nice thing to do. You are making the other children and parents angry with you. We have to leave now.

Words, Phrases, and Actions to Use

- Show respect . . .
- Rules show I love you.
- Rules help you get along with other children.
- Treat others like yourself.
- Be gentle.
- Be nice.
- Be good.
- Don't be bad.
- Don't hurt . . .
- "Please" is a good word.
- Thank you.
- I'm sorry.

Things Not to Say and Do

Don't expect your boy to remember all the rules all the time. Don't say such things as:

- I told you never to do that. Why can't you remember?
- You stupid little boy. Can't you remember the rules?
- You have a rule for everything and I expect you to remember and obey.

Don't punish your boy when he makes a mistake. Don't say such things as:

- You're going to get it now.
- I'm going to punish you.

- Every time you break a rule I'm going to hit you on the bottom. That will help you remember.

Don't make the rules for your benefit rather than his. Don't say such things as:

- You'll do what I say because I tell you to.

Don't be inconsistent. Don't say such things as:

- I know I said don't do that, but now I want you to do it.
- Don't question me. Just do what I tell you right now.
- Go ahead and hit him. He deserves it.

Words, Phrases, and Actions to Avoid

- You're stupid.
- You bad little boy.
- I'm going to smack you for that.
- You need to be severely punished.
- Hit him.
- Kick the dog if he bothers you.
- Watch what happens when I pull the cat's tail.
- Whatever you do is right.
- I don't care what you do.

SHARING

$\diamond$

Your preschooler loves playing with other children. You want him to be as generous with his toys as the other children seem with theirs. Sometimes your boy won't share. Sometimes he will, but he gets angry when other children won't. Above all you want to avoid fights over toys. You're afraid if your boy doesn't share like the other children their mothers and fathers won't be happy with your boy playing with their children, and that would be a disaster. You want your boy to learn to be willing to share his toys, his cookies, and his friendship because sharing is one of the most beautiful things we can do in our lives.

Things to Consider

Sharing, in its most important aspect, involves giving up something you value and letting someone else have it or use it. Boys at this age don't understand abstract concepts like generosity, but they do know what it means to share, whether or not they like sharing. Boys, perhaps because of their aggressive, male nature, get very attached to their possessions and often don't always like to share them, especially once they get past the toddler stage.

You have to model sharing for your boy. Much of his attitude toward giving and receiving will come from what he sees you do and say about possessions. Of course it goes beyond material possessions. Sharing extends to sharing your time, your love, and your enthusiasm. Ask yourself what kind of a model you are for your boy when it comes to giving of yourself and your possessions. If your boy wants your attention and you often say, "Not now, dear, I'm too busy," he learns that you don't willingly give of yourself.

On the other hand if your boy sees you welcome your friends and his into your home, treat all people with equal care and attention, and you willingly give to good causes, volunteer your time to work for others, and lend your valued possessions to friends, you will be giving him a wonderful model of sharing.

Most boys respond well to social pressures and explicit rules that teach him to share with others. Preschool or organized play groups do this as well, or better, than any other way because they put your boy in supervised situations where adults and other children encourage him to share and model sharing for him.

Have rules for sharing that you and your boy talk about and decide on. You may even decide to have a box of toys that are specifically for sharing, thus preserving the new, most highly prized toys for your boy, while putting all the other toys in the sharing box. Labeling your son's toys so that he can always identify them may ease his anxiety about sharing them.

Boys tend to be less welcoming to outsiders and less likely to foster relationships with new children than girls, so you must give boys as much practice in doing this as you can. You want your boy to learn to share himself, to welcome others into his home, his play, his trust, and his confidence, as well as to share his material possessions. In this area of sharing preschool experience is a great teacher. Any social situation in which your boy must play with other children can teach him how to share himself, but you must be there, at least in the beginning, to help the process along. You need to be there to ensure that all children are welcome to play and none is rejected, because rejection is children's unwillingness to share themselves, their toys, their games, and their friendship. It is possessiveness, the opposite of sharing.

Three Things You Must Do

1. Give your boy the opportunity to play with other children where he can be on the giving and receiving end of sharing.
2. Praise your boy when he is generous and shares his possessions or himself.
3. Model generosity and sharing.

Things to Say and Do

Encourage your boy to share his toys with other children. Say such things as:

- "Bobby" would like to play with that for a little while. I think you would make him feel very happy if you would let him.
- When you let him play with your toys he will learn to let you play with his.
- Everyone likes a boy who shares his toys.

Encourage your boy to include all children in his games. Say such things as:

- Everyone can play. You would be very sad if someone said you can't play.
- Sharing your games is like sharing your toys. It's a nice thing for a boy to do.
- Let's talk about a really important rule of sharing: you can't say you can't play.

Make your boy feel comfortable about sharing his possessions. Do such things as:

- Have a sharing box in which your boy puts all toys that he's willing to share.
- Put your boy's name on his toys so he won't be afraid of someone else claiming they are his own.

Talk to your boy about how he would feel if others didn't share their toys and games with him. Say such things as:

- How would you feel if "Johnny" didn't let you play with his toys?
- Would you like it if "Ramon" said you can't play in his game?
- Do you ever not want to share? How do you think it makes your friend feel?
- How do you feel when someone says you can't play?

Praise your boy when he shares, especially when he shares without prompting. Say such things as:

- You're a very good boy to share your toys.
- I like it when you let everyone play in your game.
- That was a very nice thing you did, letting "Bobby" play with your new toy.

Model generosity and sharing for your boy. Do such things as:

- Volunteer for a charity or hospital.
- Buy food for a food bank.
- Always have time for your boy and his friends.

Words, Phrases, and Actions to Use

- . . . give . . .
- . . . lend . . .
- You're a good boy.
- Nice sharing.
- Say "you're welcome."
- Here's mine.
- You can play with it.

Things Not to Say and Do

Don't encourage stinginess. Don't say such things as:

- You don't have to share anything if you don't want to.
- Don't let them play with your toys unless they let you play with theirs.
- I don't like sharing my things with others. They never take proper care of them.

Don't blame your boy for sharing. Don't say such things as:

- You shouldn't have to let anyone touch your new toy.
- Don't come crying when someone breaks your new toy.
- If you let others play with your toys you have to expect them to get lost or broken.

Don't be a bad model of sharing yourself. Don't say such things as:

- I don't have time for you just now.
- I'm too busy to talk to you.
- Don't come to me complaining.

Words, Phrases, and Actions to Avoid

- Don't.
- You're a bad boy.
- Sharing is a bad idea.
- That's only for you to use.
- Go away.
- Don't bother me.
- It's your own fault for sharing.

TOILET TRAINING

◆

Your boy is already three years old and he's still not completely trained. You've heard that all your friends' preschoolers and even two-year-olds seem to be trained and yet you're afraid to let your boy go without diapers, especially at night. It seems that all the other children in his play group are trained. You're beginning to be concerned and you're getting pressured from your parents and your spouse's parents, not directly, but in little remarks like, "You mean he isn't trained yet?" You think your son may have a medical problem so you've decided to ask your doctor for her opinion.

Things to Consider

As long as you've been following the advice in the earlier infants and toddlers chapter on toilet training you probably have nothing to worry about. You simply need to relax, be patient, and persist in your training efforts. Above all, don't transfer your anxiety to your boy. As I said in the previous chapter, the rate of bed-wetting among older boys is much higher in societies that insist on children being toilet trained by age two.

Most experts agree that the age at which a boy becomes toilet trained can vary by as much as two years. It is not uncommon for boys to be trained by age two, but some boys are four years old before they are daytime trained. The important issue here is that training success depends on a combination of factors, some of which you can't control. Boys with older brothers will probably train easier and earlier than boys who are the oldest child. It's also well known that toddlers and preschoolers who are trained often regress when a new baby comes into the family.

A second factor is muscle control. Boys vary in the development of sphincter and bladder control. Remember to keep this in mind when you hear of your boy's friends already doing what you wish your boy was doing.

The best advice for you is to carry on gently and consistently training and encouraging your boy to use the potty or the toilet. Make it a pleasant occasion. Use yourself and his older siblings as models. Above all, don't make it an issue! Never punish your boy for not being trained or for having "accidents." Pressuring him will not help and will probably only delay success. And it may do harm that will come back to haunt you and your boy.

Finally, be aware that it's not unusual for four- and five-year-old boys to wear trainers at night, so even after you boy is daytrained, don't expect perfection at night. (As I said in the previous section, some parents prefer to use real underpants that provide a greater incentive for a boy to use the potty since they don't absorb as much as trainers.) For your own peace of mind and for the sake of your boy, if you think he does have a physical or emotional problem with toilet training, then discuss it with your physician. The chances are good that it is nothing more than a maturational situation, but expert opinion is always reassuring.

Three Things You Must Do

1. Make toilet training a nonissue by being supportive, gentle, and consistent. (Follow the suggestions in the toilet training section in part one.)
2. Allow your boy to learn at his pace, not yours.
3. Don't compare your boy to others.

Things to Say and Do

Remember that it doesn't help your boy to learn potty training through pressure. The best approach is gentle, consistent encouragement through talk, stories, and example. Say such things as:

- It's potty time.
- You sit there and we'll read that story you like so much about the little boy learning to use the grown-up potty.
- Soon you'll be using the potty just like your older brother and sister.

Allow for individual differences among boys. Don't expect him to do things at the same time as his friends. Say such things as:

- The important thing is that you're trying to use the potty.
- You're a good boy for trying.

If your boy is trained but still has accidents during the day and night, make it seem perfectly normal that he wears trainers. Say such things as:

- Even older boys wear trainers.
- These trainers will help you learn to use the potty.
- If you wear these then you don't have to worry about accidents.

Be positive. When your boy has success praise him warmly. Say such things as:

- What a big boy you are.
- Well done.
- You're really learning.

Words, Phrases, and Actions to Use

- You're a good boy.
- Don't worry.
- You'll learn in your own good time.
- You'll do it when the time is right.
- Let's go to the potty.
- It's time to go use the potty.
- Let's read a book on the potty.
- That's all right.
- All boys have accidents sometimes.
- Well done.

Things Not to Say and Do

Don't make toilet training a life-and-death issue. Don't say such things as:

- You're old enough to know how to use the potty.
- Won't you ever grow up?
- I'm sick and tired of changing diapers. When will you learn?

Don't compare your boy to others. Don't say such things as:

- Why can't you use the potty like your friends?
- Your brother and sister were both trained by your age. What's wrong with you?

Don't assume your boy has something wrong with him if he's not trained by age three. Don't say such things as:

- You must be sick.
- There's something wrong with you if you still have to wear a diaper.
- I'm taking you to the doctor because I think you should be trained by now and you're not.

Don't punish your boy for not being trained, or for accidents. Don't say or do such things as:

- You go to your room and stay there. That's punishment for wetting your pants.
- I'm going to spank you until you learn to use the potty.
- Why can't you get up at night and use the potty? I'm keeping you home from play group until you can.

Words, Phrases, and Actions to Avoid

- You're a bad boy.
- Why can't you use the potty like your friends?
- You dirty little boy.
- I don't want to have to clean up any more messes.
- There's something wrong with you.
- You're going to learn to use the potty or else.
- If you're not trained you can't go to preschool.

TOYS

◆

**You take your boy to Toys "Я" Us with some anxiety because you know he'll
want every toy in sight. You've had confrontations with him in the past when he
wants a toy and you won't buy it for him. You've had confrontations when he
takes a toy from another child and you have to tell him that's not what boys
should do. The other issue that you worry about with your boy is violence and
the distinction between boy toys and girl toys. He wants guns and action figures.
This year the hot seller is called Rescue Heroes. In my day it was G.I. Joe, and
more recently, Teenage Mutant Ninja Turtles. Should you give in to gender-
specific toys so that boys get cars and trucks, building blocks, toy guns, and action
figures, and girls get playhouses, clothes, and dolls? What, you wonder, should
you do about getting him to understand that he can't have every toy in sight,
that the toys he does have he must share with his friends, and that you don't
really want him to play with guns and aggressive, violent, action heroes?**

Things to Consider

You are perfectly right not to give your boy every toy he wants. It's important that he
learn self-discipline right from the start. A first step in that direction is teaching him that
he can't have everything he wants. Help him in this by talking to him about the toys he
likes best, those he has, and those he would like. Get him to tell you which ones he
likes. Then put this to the test in two ways. First, watch him while he plays with his
toys and see which ones he likes most. Second, when he wants a new toy, tell him he
must give one up that he already has, and see which one he chooses.

Another good idea is toy swapping among friends. Meet with the parents of your
boy's friends and arrange to have seldomly used toys put in a box and taken to the play
group where the children can choose toys from this box. Any toys not chosen, but still
in good condition, can then be given away to thrift shops.

You can allow your boy to spend any gift money he receives on new toys. He will
have to make some hard choices. But make any new purchase of a toy contingent on
your boy's willingness to share it with his friends, after a week or so of it being exclu-
sively his.

The gender-specific, violent toy issue is a more difficult one. Boys are hardwired to be aggressive and they play fighting and war games without being taught. Boys don't feel pain as quickly and acutely as girls. Studies have shown that boys will use toys in an aggressive way, even when the toys are not so designed. They will often use dolls as action figures for fighting. But this doesn't mean you have to buy your boy toy guns and violent video games. Probably the most important issue for your boy is having toys that his friends approve of. Most preschool and older boys will say they do not approve of boys playing with girls' toys. So you must decide if you want your boy open to ridicule from his friends.

The violent toy issue can't be taken in isolation. You have to ask yourself if your boy seems inclined to violence and aggression beyond the norm for boys. Has your boy been exposed to real violence in his everyday life and do you risk overstimulating him if you allow him to have toys that embody violence? Most boys can play with violent toys and never be adversely affected. They will become well-adjusted, kind, peace-loving, and compassionate men. So the issue is more likely whether or not you approve of violence in your boy's play, regardless of its likely affect on him.

Three Things You Must Do

1. Teach your boy that he can't have every toy he wants.
2. Make sharing a condition of having toys.
3. You must decide whether or not violent toys are for your boy.

Things to Say and Do

Be consistent in teaching your boy that he can't have every toy he wants. Say such things as:

- You know the rule. You must choose which toy you want most.
- You can't have every toy you want. That's not good for boys.
- Toys come on special occasions like birthdays and Christmas or Hanukah.

Make sharing a condition of having toys. Say such things as:

- If you get this toy you have to share it with your friends, not right away, but later.
- Toys are for sharing. You get to play with others' toys and you must let them play with yours.
- Are you ready to share your toys with your friends?

Explain how you will make your boy's toys safe. Say such things as:

- I'm going to write your name on your toys, so even if you share them everyone will know they're yours.
- Let's make a box of toys to share with friends.

Use toys to teach sharing and generosity. Say such things as:

- Did you know that some boys don't have lots of toys? Let's go to the store and buy a toy for children whose mommies and daddies can't buy them some.
- Let's pick out toys you don't play with and give them to boys who don't have many toys. Is that okay with you?

Explain how you feel about your boy not playing with violent toys. Ask your boy's opinion. Say such things as:

- I know you want to play with guns like your friends, but we don't think guns, even toy guns, are nice to play with.
- We don't think "killing" other people, even bad people and monsters, is a nice way to play.
- Do you like playing with guns? Do you like shooting people? Why?
- Are you angry with us because we won't let you have toy guns?

Words, Phrases, and Actions to Use

- You have lots of toys already.
- Play make believe.
- Don't be greedy.
- Choose what you like best.
- Share your toys.
- Be gentle.
- Don't hit.

Things Not to Say and Do

Don't let your boy have everything he wants. Don't say such things as:

- Of course, my little darling, you can have any toy you want.
- Whatever you want you can have.
- We can afford it so why shouldn't you have all the toys you want?

Don't discourage your boy from sharing. Don't say such things as:

- Don't let your friends play with that new toy. They'll only break it and then you won't have it anymore to play with.
- I don't think sharing favorite toys is a good thing.
- Don't share your toys unless your friends share theirs.

Don't ignore your boy's need to play aggressive games with toys. Don't say such things as:

- You cannot play war games.
- You cannot play "kill the monster" games.
- Use that doll as it was supposed to be used, not for fighting.

Don't keep your boy from playing with boys' toys. Don't say such things as:

- Boys' toys are too violent. I don't want you playing with toy guns or violent games.
- I want you to play nice games like your sister and her friends.

Don't encourage your boy to play violent, macho games. Don't say such things as:

- Shoot him before he shoots you.
- Stab him with your sword.
- Shoot the ray gun at him.
- War games are great fun. You can kill all the bad guys.

Words, Phrases, and Actions to Avoid

- You're a sissy.
- Don't play with those sissy toys.
- Boys don't play with dolls.
- Boys don't play with girls.
- Guns are great.
- Blow them up.

PART 3

Young Schoolboys

(6–8 years)

ANGER

◆

You allow yourself to get angry, and you show it. You have tried to model anger management for your boy, showing him how anger can be made productive rather than destructive. You've used your anger as a source of energy to get out and do what it takes to fix the situation that made you angry in the first place. When a situation was beyond your control, you said so and tried to make the best of it rather than steaming around all day, cursing and shouting and taking your anger out on your spouse and children. You recognize that your son, at his age, has very little control over his own life at home or at school, so his frustrations can often lead to angry confrontations if you don't help him channel his anger productively. If you teach your son good anger management you will be giving him a priceless gift that will last him the rest of his life.

Things to Consider

Your boy has endless amounts of energy and curiosity. He needs plenty of space for his activities, many of which involve fairly aggressive behavior like play fighting, playing rough-and-tumble games, and testing out toys to see how hard it is to break them or take them apart. Your boy's energy and curiosity combined with numerous adults telling him where he can and cannot go and what he can and cannot do, can and cannot say, and can and cannot have will make even the most patient boy angry on occasion.

However, your boy, like most boys his age, is impatient. He wants to get on with things. He is still soaking up everything around him, learning much about himself—what he likes and doesn't like—and testing the limits that surround him at home and in school. There are many times during his day that he comes up against the rules that you and others have made. You know they are for his own good, but he doesn't always see it that way because his energy and curiosity need more outlets than he has available. Because of this he gets angry with you, his teacher, his siblings, and his friends.

You can help him cope with this anger in three important ways. First, you can model good anger management yourself, never yelling and screaming at him and never hitting him or punishing him in a fit of rage. Second, you can help him use his energy in constructive ways. Taking part in sports could be described as a constructive use of anger. Encourage your boy to play sports, both organized and unorganized. Give him the support he needs to do this. It's a great way to help him burn off all that energy and aggression. Third, when your boy gets angry move him to neutral ground, away from the source of his anger, whether it's a person, thing, or situation. Then walk and talk about it. Don't tell him he shouldn't be angry. Just listen, nod your head, and make sounds of agreement.

After he is talked out, you can say a few things to help him see other sides to the issue that made him angry. From the age of six, boys can begin to see other points of view and you can use this situation to give him practice putting himself in someone else's shoes. But listen carefully to your boy's reasons for being angry. React to his anger in proportion to its seriousness. If his anger is based on something done to him that is wrong and unacceptable, be ready to say so and to take some action yourself. It may mean talking to your boy's teacher or school principal, or to your boy's friends or his friends' parents. In other words, don't automatically assume that your boy's anger is unwarranted. It may have a cause that you need to remove.

Three Things You Must Do

1. Teach your boy to control his anger and make it productive.
2. Recognize that his anger often comes from lack of control over his own life.
3. Listen sympathetically when your boy tells you why he is angry and react appropriately.

Things to Say and Do

Expect your boy to get angry sometimes. If you can, remove him from the situation that's making him angry. Say such things as:

- I know you're angry. Let's get away from here so we can talk.
- I think you need to calm down. Let's go for a walk.
- Let's go to your room so we can get you calmed down.

Once you have him in a quiet place, ask him to tell you about why he's angry. Don't judge him. Just listen and prompt him to say more. Say such things as:

- Okay, now tell me what happened.
- Why are you so angry?
- Who did it? What exactly did they do?
- What else happened?
- I understand. Go on.

When your boy's anger has quieted down, ask him if he wants you to do anything, even if you already have a plan of action. Say such things as:

- Okay, is there anything I can do?
- What would you like me to do?
- Do you want me to talk to your teacher?
- Do you want me to talk to "Johnny's" mother?

Encourage your boy to play games and sports. If he's already doing that go and watch him and see how he handles himself. Emphasize the fun and sportsmanship aspects of games. *Never get angry, yell, or scream at the other kids, coaches, parents, or officials during the game or after.* This presents a terrible role model for your boy. Be a good anger management role model for your boy. Say such things as:

- I know how you feel. I get angry too. But I try to let it help me do things so that I won't get angry again.
- When I get angry I go for a walk.
- When I get angry I go to my favorite place and read.
- When I get angry I play my favorite music.
- When I get angry I write down on a piece of paper why I'm angry and put it in a drawer. That makes me feel better. Often when I look at it the next day I wonder why I got so angry.

Words, Phrases, and Actions to Use

- Calm down.
- Tell me about it.
- Let's talk.
- I believe you.
- Go on.
- I understand.

- I'm listening.
- I can help.
- Let's go somewhere quiet.
- Anger isn't fun.
- Write it down.
- Take some deep breaths.

Things Not to Say and Do

Don't dismiss your boy's anger as insignificant or foolish. It's very real and significant to him. Don't say such things as:

- Don't be so silly. There's no need to get so angry.
- You're getting angry over nothing.
- What a dumb thing to get angry about.

Don't avoid talking about it with your boy. Don't say such things as:

- It's your problem, not mine.
- I don't have time to talk about it. I'm too busy.
- I'm not interested in talking about it just now.

Don't leave your son to deal with a serious problem on his own. He can't. Don't say such things as:

- I know it makes you angry but there's nothing I can do.
- Don't expect me to help you. You caused the problem so you have to solve it.
- No, I won't talk to your teacher. She's probably right.

Words, Phrases, and Actions to Avoid

- You're stupid.
- It's your own fault.
- You deal with it.
- I'm too busy.
- Go away.
- I can't help.
- Work it out for yourself.
- It's not important even though you think so.

BULLYING

◈

Your boy is in grade one. He was terribly excited about going to school in September but he doesn't seem excited anymore. In fact, he seems reluctant to go off in the morning. He says there's nothing wrong, but you think he's hiding something. He's not eating as much breakfast as he should and there's no excitement in his voice when he talks about school. His body language tells you that he doesn't really want to go. It's such a difference from earlier this year that you wonder what's wrong. He seems unwilling to say what's wrong, although you know him well enough to know that something is really bothering him. You think you will go to the school and talk to his teacher to see if she can tell you what the problem is.

Things to Consider

Boys are much more likely than girls to be either bullies or bullied. It seems to be the way boys work out the "pecking order" among themselves. Bullying in some form can be found in every school. If your boy is young for his grade, less developed physically or socially, or visibly different from the other children in his school, he is more likely to be bullied.

It doesn't matter whether your son is the victim of bullying, a bully himself, or one of the crowd who joins in the activity or simply tolerates it. Bullying is wrong, hateful, destructive, and, sadly, a very real fact of life for many students. I am sure that virtually every one of you reading this book experienced bullying, or the somewhat less offensive teasing, in some way when you were a child. I know I did, and I'm ashamed when I think back to that time that I did nothing to stop it.

The root cause of bullying among young boys is lack of empathy. Among six- to eight-year-old schoolboys empathy is an emotion that is just developing. So you can expect your son to be involved in bullying in some way or another. On the one hand, he may be little more than an onlooker while others are teasing children who are new or different. On the other hand, if your son is quiet, well-behaved, and passive, he may be the victim of bullying. If he is socially and physically advanced for his age he may be the bully.

The reasons for, and the consequences of, bullying for young boys can be simple or complex. However, your reaction to evidence of bullying should be simple and immediate. Bullying is unacceptable. As an adult you must take the lead in stopping it.

First of all you must know your son's role in the bullying. For example, if he is the victim in school you must find out all the circumstances and talk to the teacher and administrators concerned who must talk to the offending children, usually boys, and their parents. You must make sure that their message is clear: bullying will not be tolerated. And anyone who witnesses bullying and does not speak up or do something to stop it is as guilty as those who do the bullying.

Boys need to hear this message at home and in school starting in kindergarten or grade one. Your obligation is to teach your boy that you expect him to do the right thing, even if it means that his friends will stop being his friends. You can point out that any boys who don't want to be friends because you're doing the right thing are not very good friends anyway. You also need to be sure that your boy's school has a clear and well-publicized policy against bullying. If it doesn't you need to work to have one put in place.

Finally, you can help promote good relationships between children by teaching them to empathize with all other children and by showing them that differences among people should be celebrated and embraced, not held up to ridicule. Help him to understand how stressful it is to be someone who is bullied or constantly teased. You need to model this kind of behavior for your boy, as well as talk to him about it.

Three Things You Must Do

1. Know about your boy's role in bullying of any kind.
2. Make it clear to your boy that you will not tolerate his bullying or being bullied.
3. Make sure your boy's school has a clear and workable policy against any kind of bullying.

Things to Say and Do

Be aware of any marked change in your son's behavior that's abnormal or out of character. Any loss of appetite, loss of enthusiasm for school, persistent attacks of upset stomach, or other malady, especially at schooltime, should be carefully investigated. Say such things as:

- How are you feeling? What's actually wrong? Does something hurt?
- If you're not well I think we should go to the doctor and have you checked out.
- You're acting strangely. It there something wrong?

Always know what's going on in your boy's life, especially in school. Talk about his time in school on a regular basis. Say such things as:

- Did you have fun in school today? What did you do?
- Who are your best friends in school? (Your boy should be able to name best friends without hesitation. If he can't check with his teacher.)

Ask your boy about bullying and teasing in his school. Say such things as:

- Have you ever been bullied?
- Do other kids at your school get pushed around and teased?
- Who are the bullies in your school?

If you have any concerns talk to his teacher regularly. Don't wait for parent/teacher interviews. Say such things as:

- Is bullying a problem at school?
- Does my son get bullied, or does he bully others?
- What does the school do to prevent bullying?
- How do you deal with bullying when it happens?
- I'd like to volunteer in your class this week.

Make your son understand that bullying is unacceptable whether he is a victim, a bully, or merely a bystander. Make it clear that you expect him to tell you about any bullying he sees. Say such things as:

- We need to talk about bullying. I want you to understand what the right thing to do is when you see someone being bullied.
- If you ever see any bullying you must tell your teacher and me.
- If you see someone being bullied you must tell the bullies to stop.

Model tolerant behavior for your son. Show that you accept differences and promote acceptance of everyone for whom they are.

Words, Phrases, and Actions to Use

- . . . love . . .
- . . . tolerance . . .
- Bullying is unacceptable.
- Teasing is hateful.
- What's the school policy against bullying?

- That behavior is destructive for everyone concerned.
- This is the right thing to do.
- Embrace differences.

Things Not to Say and Do

Never condone bullying or malicious teasing. Don't say such things as:

- He got what he deserved.
- I don't like people who look that way either.
- Some kids just ask for it.

Don't model bullying. Don't say such things as:

- Pick up your toys or I'm going to beat you.
- I had to hit your mom. She deserved it.
- I'm not a bully. I'm just showing these people why they better do what I say.

Don't blame your son for being bullied. Don't say such things as:

- If kids bully you it's because you're probably asking for it.
- Don't come crying to me. You have to stick up for yourself.
- I'm not going to talk to anybody about this. You have to work it out for yourself.

Don't encourage your boy to go along with bullying. Don't say such things as:

- Don't you tell on anyone. Then you'll get in trouble.
- Just go along with the crowd. Be thankful you're not the one being bullied.
- If you tell on your friends they won't be your friends anymore.

Words, Phrases, and Actions to Avoid

- Fight them.
- Beat them up.
- You're a wuss.
- You're a whimp.
- You're a coward.
- You better go along with it.
- Don't be a snitch/tattle-tale/informer/traitor.
- There is no right or wrong, only what's best for you.
- Bullying is a fact of life.

CHILDREN WHO ARE DIFFERENT

❖

You want your son to be tolerant of children who are different, whether that difference is religious, ethnic, or a mental or physical disability. Your son's school has children from many different backgrounds. Some of your son's classmates, you have heard from his teacher, other parents, and your son, bully and tease some of the children who are different. You don't want your son to grow up thinking that that's acceptable behavior. How, you ask yourself, can you teach him tolerance, respect, and compassion for children of all backgrounds and circumstances? You have been wondering yourself how sincerely you can teach your son the tolerance and acceptance of all children of goodwill, regardless of who or what they are.

Things to Consider

Your first responsibility as a parent is to give your boy food, security, and love. This is what all parents want for their children, regardless of their circumstances. Beyond that your most important work is to teach your boy to be a good, moral human being. Tolerance and respect for children who are different from your son is one of the most critical aspects of this teaching because when you teach him to accept children who are different from him simply because they are fellow human beings, you are teaching him the universal message of human relationships: to love his neighbor as himself.

Intolerance is a fact of life among schoolboys. Boys of school age often single out children whose appearance is different from theirs. Even within their own group they jockey for positions of dominance and submission. Both within and outside their group they are quick to find children with weaknesses and pick on them. Girls engage in such things too, but among boys these dominance activities often include threats of aggression and actual aggression, both verbal and physical. And they stigmatize the outsider.

You can teach your boy tolerance and understanding of other children in many different ways. One of the best ways is to model this behavior in your own words and deeds. Show your boy that you tolerate and try to understand people who are different, whatever that difference might be. Show him that the only thing you won't tolerate in others is hatred and intolerance. Make it a point to say things that show respect for people who are visibly different. Don't make fun of people with disabilities. Don't criticize or dehumanize people with different religious beliefs. Don't be suspicious of people who are different. Practice good human values of love, tolerance, and understanding.

Teach your boy these values by asking him how he would like it if other children picked on him, or teased or bullied him, simply because he was different. Talk to him about differences in children that are important and differences that don't matter. Intervene when you see your boy being mean to others. Talk about the need for tolerance and acceptance of differences.

Differences that are important are things like children not being able to speak English well, children who need special help because of mental or physical disabilities, children who need friendship because others tease or bully them, and children who need friendship because they have no friends. These are the differences that make a difference.

Encourage your boy to go out of his way to help those who need help, to welcome differences among his classmates, to understand the source and meaning of differences, and, above all, to intervene when he sees others being intolerant. Also talk to him about differences that *don't* make a difference. Emphasize that most people have many more things in common than are different. It is more important to focus on things we share than on things we don't.

Three Things You Must Do

1. Talk to your boy about differences in children.
2. Make it clear that you won't tolerate intolerance of people of goodwill.
3. Be a model of tolerance of people who are different.

Things to Say and Do

Begin by talking to your boy about the differences he sees in his class and his school. Ask him to tell you about the different kinds of children he sees there. Say such things as:

- Tell me about the kids in your school. Are there many different kinds of kids?
- What are the important differences that you see?
- Do your friends say anything about these kids?

Talk to your boy about what he sees happening to these children. Say such things as:

- Do these kids get bullied or teased? Do you ever think about how they must feel when that happens?

- How do the teachers treat these kids?
- Do you have any problems with these kids?

If your boy is visibly different from most of the other kids in his class or school keep him talking about his relationships and be alert for any problems. Say such things as:

- Do you have lots of friends at school?
- Do kids pick on you?
- Do you ever get into fights with other kids? Why?

Talk to your boy about differences that make a difference. Say such things as:

- Do you think kids who can't speak English well need help?
- Do you have kids in wheelchairs in your class?
- Do some kids in your class need special help?
- Are there kids in your school who get picked on because they look different or sound different?

Talk to your boy about differences that don't make a difference. Say such things as:

- Does it matter what kids look like?
- Do all your friends look the same?
- Why do you like "Pablo" so much?

Make it clear that you will not tolerate intolerance of people of goodwill. Say such things as:

- I try to be nice to everyone even though I don't always succeed.
- People may be different from us but they are still good people.
- I try to like people as long as they are nice people. Nothing else about them really matters.
- You must be nice to people just like you want them to be nice to you.

Words, Phrases, and Actions to Use

- . . . tolerance . . .
- . . . respect . . .
- Be nice.
- If you like others they will like you.

- Friends are the most important thing.
- Be a nice boy.
- There are differences that make a difference.
- There are differences that don't make a difference.
- Good people come in all colors, shapes, and sizes.

Things Not to Say and Do

Don't encourage or condone intolerance in your boy or his friends. Don't say such things as:

- It's okay. Boys will be boys.
- You're just doing what comes naturally.
- You don't have to like everyone.

Don't model intolerant behavior. Don't say such things as:

- If people are different they have to suffer the consequences.
- I think they should keep to themselves.
- If they were like us they wouldn't have these problems.

Don't use racial or religious epithets. Don't use stereotypes in talking about people. Don't say such things as:

- We know what _____ are like.
- They're dirty.
- I don't think they believe in God.
- They're all violent and gang members.

Words, Phrases, and Actions to Avoid

- They're bad.
- They're sneaky.
- They're rotten.
- They're untrustworthy.
- They're stupid.
- They're retarded.
- They're worthless.
- I don't like them.
- I don't trust them.
- I don't want you to be friends with those kinds of kids.

CLOTHES

◆

Clothing becomes an issue as soon as your boy is born. If he's a firstborn boy and has no older cousins, and if you don't have friends with older boys, you have to start buying baby clothes from scratch. Of course he grows so fast you've barely bought him a sleeper before he needs a new one. This problem continues throughout toddlerhood and becomes even more extreme now that he has begun school. You have a number of concerns about his clothes. First, he already pressures you for clothes like those of his friends. Shirts and pants have to be the right color and the right style. At his age you can still avoid disputes over labels, but not for much longer. Second, you want him to dress for the weather, not for style. He needs to wear rain jackets and winter jackets when appropriate, regardless of what he says his friends are wearing. Third, you want him to learn to care for his clothes. You're concentrating on getting him to keep his clothes in drawers and hangers, not on the floor.

Things to Consider

Pick your battles wisely. At this age fights over clothes are really not necessary. As your boy gets older he demands, and deserves, more and more control over his own life. Clothing becomes an issue when the dress code of your boy's peer group in school starts to be a bigger and more important factor in his life. All parents have struggles with their children over the color, style, cost, appropriateness, and care of clothes.

You should still make sure that your boy wears clothes appropriate for school, your place of worship, and other special occasions. But as long as his clothes are reasonably priced, clean, and modest, don't fight about style or color. With coats, sweaters, pants, shirts, and shoes, let him have his way. You just want him to be warm enough and comfortable in what he wears, and you want him to take care of his clothes. If you let him choose his own clothes, as long as you're there to monitor fit, quality, and cost, you can make control contingent on care. If he gets to choose his clothes, then he has to take good care of them. Don't let style and color bother you. He needs to dress for his friends, not for you.

You can help him when he asks for it, but don't make an issue out of clothing. You can help him care for his clothes by making it easy for him to hang them up. Make sure wall, door, and closet hooks and rails are at his height. Have dresser drawers that he can reach and open and close easily. Help him remember what goes where by labeling drawers and hooks with words and pictures.

Make sure your boy gets up early enough on school mornings so he has time to dress himself. Don't insist on dressing him just because you're impatient. He needs to learn to do it all himself. Guide and help him, but let him feel a sense of accomplishment in doing this for himself.

Finally, model good clothes care for him. Make sure you keep your own things neat and tidy.

Three Things You Must Do

1. Recognize your boy's need to dress like his friends.
2. Concern yourself with price, fit, and protection, not with style, color, and fashion.
3. Responsible care of clothes should go along with your boy's right to choose.

Things to Say and Do

Give your boy increasing control over the style and color of clothes he wears. Avoid fighting with him about the superficial aspects of clothing. Say such things as:

- What kind of pants, shirts, shoes, coats do your friends wear?
- What would you like to buy?
- Let's look at the choices.

Your concern should be about price, fit, and protection. You have to stay within your budget. His clothes, especially his shoes, have to fit properly. Say such things as:

- You can get the clothes you want as long as they're not too expensive.
- Your shoes have to be the right size.
- Your coat has to be warm enough for winter.

Link your boy's right to pick out most of his own clothes with the responsibility for their care, with your help, of course. Say such things as:

- Let's make a deal. You can pick out the clothes you want, but you have to promise to hang them up and, not leave them on the floor. I'll help you.
- You like to drop your clothes on the floor and expect me to pick them up and put them away for you. But that's going to stop. If you're old enough to choose your own clothes then you're old enough to take good care of them.

Keep control of what your boy wears for special occasions. Make sure he dresses properly when you go to your house of worship, the theater, nice restaurants, and holiday celebrations. But don't go overboard. Make sure your standards don't embarrass him because you're out of touch with what six- to eight-year-old boys wear to these events. Say such things as:

- I'm letting you choose your own clothes that you wear to school or to play in, but you have to wear nice, clean clothes to church/mosque/synagogue/temple. And I'm going to be the judge of what's nice and clean.
- Special occasions require special clothes. I want you to look good when you go out with us.
- I've been watching what boys your age wear to church, and I think what I am asking you to wear is pretty much in line with what they wear.

Give your boy the help he needs in dressing himself, but don't be overbearing and impatient and insist on doing it for him. Say such things as:

- Well done. You can really dress yourself very well.
- I bet most of the boys in your class can't dress themselves as well as you can.
- Take your time and do it right. You have enough time to do it if you concentrate.

Model nice dressing for your boy. You can't model style for him, but you can model cleanliness, proper fit, and appropriateness for the occasion.

Words, Phrases, and Actions to Use

- Wear nice clothes.
- What's the style?
- What do your friends wear?
- You can choose.
- Your clothes must be clean.
- Pick them up.
- Hang them up.
- Wear special clothes for special occasions.

Things Not to Say and Do

Don't fight with your boy over clothes. Let him dress like his friends. Don't say such things as:

- You can't go out wearing something like that.
- You'll wear what I want you to.
- I have the say 'cause I have to pay.

Don't let your boy buy shoes that don't fit. Don't say such things as:

■ If you want them you can have them, even if they don't fit.
■ I don't care anymore. Buy what you like.

Don't insist that he has no say in what you buy him to wear. Don't say such things as:

■ I'm buying you this and you'll wear it because I say so.
■ As long as I pay the bills you will wear what I tell you, or you'll go to school naked.
■ Boys your age aren't competent to choose their own clothes. I'm going to do it for you.

Words, Phrases, and Actions to Avoid

■ No, you can't.
■ I do the choosing.
■ That looks awful.

■ I don't care what your friends have.
■ I don't care how you look.
■ You can do whatever you want.

Computers, Video Games, Movies, and TV

◆

Your boy is a child of the electronic revolution. He already knows as much as, or more than, you do about websites, the Internet, play stations, and handheld electronic games. He and his friends talk about action heroes, war games, destroying the enemy, killing the robots, and saving the world from the space invaders. He likes movies and TV shows that includes animals, action, violence, robots, spaceships, and stories about young boys being the heroes and routing the bad guys. Your boy has a much more intense interest in everything electronic than does his sister or most other girls. Your biggest concern is to protect him from the many obnoxious, violent, hateful games, Internet sites, and movie and TV shows. They are not suitable for a young boy, you tell him, and you make sure he doesn't have access to them at your house. But you worry about him when he's at a friend's house where you have no control over his play or watching.

Things to Consider

What differentiates today's young boys from young boys when you were your son's age is not a taste for action and violence in games, movies, and TV; it is the endless new machines and inventions that give your boy easy access to these things. In one sense your job is no different from the one your parents had. They were concerned with inappropriate movies and TV shows. You are concerned with violent, obscene, or pornographic games, Websites, movies, and TV shows.

However, your boy has many more opportunities than you ever did for finding these things. They pop up everywhere, and there is very little control over them, apart from the control that you, as a parent, must exercise. There are many ways to control these things. The best way is to be involved in your boy's life and know what he likes and doesn't like. Keep your computer in a public area so you can easily see what he's doing on it. Put a filter on it to keep out objectionable websites. Know what his friends like. Know the games they have. Know what their parents allow. Program your TV to keep out the objectionable programs.

Above all, exercise your parental responsibility to shield your boy from games and content that teach the wrong values. Take every opportunity to talk to your boy about the games he plays and what he sees on TV, in movies, and on the computer. It's never too early to teach him to think critically about everything he hears, sees, and reads.

There is a debate over the educational value of computers. I, in my work, have been using e-mail since it first began in the 1980s and I think computers are a wonderful tool. They may help you think, but they don't make you more intelligent. I see no need for schools to spend thousands of dollars for computer hardware and software and high-speed Internet access. This money would be more wisely spent on hiring more teachers and lowering class size so that more good, personal, human interaction can take place.

Another issue comes from research on young children's brain development. Experts suggest that too much early dependency on electronic devices adversely affects a boy's attention span and imagination, and his proficiency in reading and writing, because it understimulates the whole brain and overstimulates the right brain, which is already highly developed in young boys. Boys lag behind girls in school precisely because girls have better whole brain and left brain development, areas that are crucial for school success.

Having said that, I think you ought to have a computer in your home. They are a useful tool and, wisely used, will help your boy's work at school. Some research suggests that boys learn math better through computer games than through ordinary lessons in which girls do well. If computers help boys learn, or if they make learning easier or more attractive to boys, then they are worth having at home. At their worst they will make your boy more informed, even if not always better informed.

Three Things You Must Do

1. Accept that your boy will want to be totally involved with computers.
2. Exercise your parental responsibility to make sure that your boy is shielded from objectionable electronic games, TV programs, and computer sites.
3. Show your boy your values, and the values you hope he will develop, by talking to him in simple terms about the content of the games, shows, and sites he's exposed to.

Things to Say and Do

Electronics are an important and inescapable part of modern life for your boy. Encourage him to use these inventions wisely and with reflection. Say such things as:

- I know you love electronic games. Let's talk about what kinds there are and what you think about them.

- What games do your friends have? What do they like playing?
- I like getting you these games, but I don't like all of them. Let me tell you why.

Talk to your boy about the Internet sites you like and encourage him to go to. Don't talk about the objectionable ones because it might simply serve to whet his curiosity. Say such things as:

- The Internet has some great things on it. What are your favorites?
- I think there are some sites that would help you in school.
- Let's play some games on the Internet.

Talk about what your boy does on the computer at school or at friends' homes. Say such things as:

- You use the computer in school. What do you use it for?
- Who supervises you on the computer at school?
- Can you go to any Internet site you want to at "Johnny's" house?

Talk about TV shows. Know the ones your boy likes best and make sure you talk about them with him. Say such things as:

- I know you like watching _____. Why do you like it so much?
- Do you like the same shows your friends like?
- Do you think there's too much fighting in that show?
- What do you think those people fight for?

Talk about movies that your boy wants to see. Make sure you know the content of these movies. Don't simply rely on the rating system. If you're going to let your boy see them on home video it's a good idea to preview them. Say such things as:

- What movies do you want to see? What are they about?
- Have your friends seen them?
- What movies do you and your friends talk about at school?

Make your own values and wishes regarding games, movies, TV, and Websites known to your boy. Say such things as:

- I don't like violent games or movies. I know you do. I think we need to watch any of these together and then talk about them.

- I like movies in which people are nice to each other and in which people do good things.
- I don't want you to watch movies or TV in which people keep killing each other. Do you like them? How do they make you feel?

Talk about computers as a learning tool. Say such things as:

- Does your teacher teach you things using the computer? What sorts of things?
- Do you like learning things from the computer? What do you like best?

Words, Phrases, and Actions to Use

- Computers are good in moderation.
- Games can be fun but mustn't be too violent.
- We must talk about which movies are right for you.
- Some TV shows are not good for boys your age.
- You can't play that game.
- That's too violent.
- I don't want you to watch things in which people are killing each other.
- That's too old for you.
- Let's talk.

Things Not to Say or Do

Don't allow your boy free access to any of these electronic games. Don't say such things as:

- You want that, you can have it.
- I don't care what games you play. They can't hurt you.
- You can have whatever your friends have.

Don't ignore what movies your boy sees. Don't say such things as:

- You can watch whatever you want.
- You know movies are just make-believe.
- You're old enough to know the difference between reality and fiction.

Don't give your boy unlimited and unsupervised TV use. Don't say such things as:

- Watch whatever you want.
- I don't care how much TV you watch. I love to watch TV too.

Don't let your boy spend all his free time at the computer. Don't say such things as:

- You don't have to go out and play.
- The computer is there for you to use as much as you want.

Don't avoid talking to your boy about what he does and what he watches. Don't say such things as:

- I don't have time to talk about that with you.
- What good will talking do?
- I'm busy. Ask me later.

Words, Phrases, and Actions to Avoid

- Do whatever you want.
- I don't care.
- I'm too busy.
- The world is violent.
- Everything about computers is wonderful.
- Computers will make you smart.

DISCIPLINE

◆

Your boy is in school now and you know that he needs good self-discipline. You don't want him getting into trouble at school or anywhere else. As he was growing up you tried to be fair and consistent in your discipline so that he knew what he could and couldn't do, and knew what the penalty was when he did something against the rules. You have never disciplined your boy by hitting or spanking him. You have tried to teach your boy the self-discipline that comes from a well-developed moral sense of what's right and wrong and an ability to empathize.

Things to Consider

Boys are punished more often and more severely than girls. Some parents are especially punitive in their disciplining. Hopefully you are not one of them since your boy isn't a fool and he will judge you by the difference between what he thinks is an appropriate punishment and the punishment you give him. Harsh discipline will create a boy who fears and resents you. Your discipline should be firm, fair, and consistent, and filled with love and understanding

You and your boy haven't always agreed on what is appropriate behavior. Sometimes it is a battle of wills. Your boy wants his own way and you want yours. As a parent you sometimes need to put your wishes ahead of your boy's. He will resist this, and this is a perfectly natural thing for him to do.

As your boy gets older he will show ever more resistance to being told or forced to do things he'd rather not do. By the time he's a teenager you won't be able to physically force him to do anything because he will probably be bigger and stronger than you are. You will have to depend on his self-control, and on the relationship of trust you have developed with him over the years of his growing up.

In school, at home, and in the community, cooperation with others is a key component in discipline. If you have taught your boy to cooperate with others as he was growing up, you have done him a great service. Self-discipline means that your boy will cooperate because he knows it's the right thing to do. But the real question you have is what if your boy isn't like that? What do you do with your boy if he refuses to cooperate, if he consistently disobeys you or his teachers, and if he's always getting into trouble? Here are some suggestions.

The first and most important thing is to know your boy. Know his temperament and his ability for self-control. Know his habits, trouble spots, and things that set off misbehavior. Then work with him on these things. Talk to him about what he does that gets him into trouble. See if you can understand what motivates him. Look back on his early childhood to see if there were any experiences, or any actions on your part, that initiated this behavior. Some little boys are naturally impulsive. If your boy is like this you need to help him build a space between an impulse and action, a time for quick reflection on what he wants to do and why he ought not to do it.

Second, you need to have taught your boy good standards of behavior. By talking and modeling good behavior you have helped your boy understand what's expected of him. He knows, for example, to respect people's privacy and property, to follow the rules you and his teachers set, and to always try to put himself in the other person's place before he acts.

Third, you need to understand that your boy misbehaves for a reason, even if you don't agree with or understand that reason. Therefore, it's your job to try to understand that reason. Ask your boy why he's done something. Then *listen* to his answer. His reason may not excuse the action, but it will help you understand your boy and prevent future bad behavior.

Specific disciplines that are good for your boy include the following. As you impose them be sure to explain to your boy exactly why you're giving him this punishment so that he understands your motivation and what you think he did wrong.

- Time-out. Have your boy stay by himself for a while to think about what he's done wrong.
- Take away his privileges.
- Remove your boy from the situation in which he has misbehaved.
- Explain what your boy did wrong or, better still, have your boy explain what he thinks he did wrong.
- Have your boy apologize to anyone he may have hurt by his actions.
- Have your boy compensate any victims of his misbehavior.

The experts I have read all seem to agree on one thing. Violent punishment such as hitting your boy with your hand, a strap, a stick, or anything else is not discipline or punishment; it is child abuse. Not only is it abuse, but research shows it can do long-term physical and mental damage. It may seem to work in the short run, but in the long term it doesn't solve the problems that cause bad behavior.

The alternative to violent discipline is disciplining with words. If you've begun doing this with your infant and have consistently used verbal discipline (as well as physically removing your boy from a bad situation) you should be successful in using it throughout your boy's childhood. Experts point out that the benefits of nonviolent discipline include lower rates of adult violence, masochistic sex, depression, and alcohol abuse, and better chances of completing high school and achieving a higher income. This should be a good incentive for you, and all parents, to discipline your boy with words, love, and caring, rather than through anger and violence.

Three Things You Must Do

1. Know your boy's temperament and the kind of misbehavior he's likely to engage in.
2. Be fair, firm, consistent, kind, and loving in your discipline.
3. Never use violent forms of punishment.

Things to Say and Do

Talk to your boy about the rules for behavior. Let him know your standards. Be positive. Say such things as:

- You know that doing that will hurt someone. That's why you shouldn't do it. You don't ever want to hurt someone, do you?
- If you get in trouble at school you will be hurting yourself and us. Is that what you want to do?
- When we ask you not to do that do you understand why? What do you think about doing that?

Listen to your boy's reasons for any misbehavior. Let him tell you his side of the story. Say such things as:

- What you did was wrong as far as we can see. Why did you do it? Would you do it again?
- Tell me why you wanted to hit "Jimmy"? Let's talk about it to see what you were thinking.
- Your teacher said you did this. Did you? Why?

Explain to your boy why you're punishing him. Discuss it with him so that you're sure he understands. Say such things as:

- We're asking you to take some time alone to think about what you did. Then we'd like to talk about it with you so we can hear your side of the story and you can hear our side.

■ We're doing this because we love you and want you to learn how to avoid getting into trouble by doing the wrong thing.

In words that your boy can understand talk to him about the reasons he must learn self-discipline. Say such things as:

■ Do you like people who take toys from you or hit you? That's why you mustn't do it to anyone else.

■ You have to learn to do the right thing even when we're not there to tell you what the right thing is.

■ Big boys and men learn to control themselves and never hit others. You need to learn other ways to express anger to people.

Praise your boy for doing the right thing. Say such things as:

■ I know you were angry but you didn't hit "Bobby." You were very good. You did the right thing.

■ You're getting to be such a big boy. You didn't let your temper make you do the wrong thing. Well done!

■ You showed me that you know the right thing to do. You're such a good boy.

Words, Phrases, and Actions to Use

■ How would you feel . . . ?
■ You're a good boy.
■ Never hurt others.
■ Put yourself in their place.
■ Well done.

■ Who gets hurt?
■ Practice self-control.
■ Practice self-discipline.
■ Doing this will make you happier.

Things Not to Say and Do

Don't encourage your boy to misbehave. Don't say such things as:

■ If someone hits you hit them back.
■ Don't ever let someone take something from you.
■ Be a man. Hit the boy.

Don't use violent punishments. Don't do such things as:

- Hitting your boy.
- Kicking your boy.
- Using an object to hurt your boy.

Don't yell or scream at your boy. Don't say such things as:

- You dumb kid. I'm going to get you for that.
- You're not my boy anymore. Get out of my sight.
- I don't love you anymore. Go away.

Don't discipline your boy with threats. Don't say such things as:

- If you do that you'll be sorry. I'm going to really punish you.
- If I ever hear that you were bad in school you'll get a whipping.
- Spare the rod, spoil the child, that's my motto. So watch what you do.

Words, Phrases, and Actions to Avoid

- You stupid kid.
- You're not my kid.
- I don't care what you did, or why you did it.
- You're getting a whipping.
- Get me the belt.
- You'll never learn.

EATING

◆

Your boy is now in school, and proper nutrition and eating is a more important issue than ever for three reasons: (1) you're not always there to supervise what he eats, (2) he can't eat on demand because he's in class, and (3) young boys respond to fashions in food and he will want to eat what his friends eat. You want him to eat the right foods, not just the junk food he sees advertised on TV, his heroes eating, and his friends eating. Experts agree that the food your boy eats can profoundly affect his behavior and learning. A healthy diet means giving him the right foods at the right time.

Things to Consider

Research into children's brain development and functioning shows that foods that are high in protein and fiber and milk products, such as yogurt, are excellent breakfast foods. They help cell growth and neural connections. Carbohydrates and sugars are not as good at breakfast time because the energy from high blood sugar concentrations doesn't last and can make your boy jittery and impulsive.

Certain fatty acids, such as those found in fish, are a very important part of a balanced diet for your boy because they make his brain grow properly. Lack of such fatty acids in a child's diet have been linked to Attention Deficit Hyperactivity Disorder (ADHD), a problem found mainly in boys, as well as other behavioral and learning problems. Some of these problems don't appear immediately but take years to develop.

If you find that your boy is impulsive and aggressive, has problems in his gross or fine motor skills, doesn't seem able to pay attention in school or when you are talking to him, or seems to have an attention span so limited that he's constantly moving around without settling down, you need to ask your physician if your boy's diet needs to be changed. A good way of observing your boy's behavior is to volunteer at his school. You can see if he shows any of the above behaviors. Also discuss this with his teacher if you have reason for concern.

We are lucky to live in a society where there is abundant food for most of our children, although, shamefully, not all. Your boy has the benefit of a well-stocked pantry and refrigerator. You always encourage him to eat well and to try everything you put before him. However, you need to be careful about his eating habits, not that he will not eat enough, but that he will eat too much. In our society obesity in children is probably a bigger problem than malnutrition. And it can lead to long-term health problems as he grows older.

Don't let your boy overeat. Children can be cruel to each other and children who are fat will often suffer the cruelest treatment. They will be teased, taunted, excluded from games, and generally made fun of. You certainly don't want your boy to endure this kind of treatment. He will have enough problems to cope with as just a normal child.

In this matter of nutrition and eating it is you and your boy's older siblings who must provide good role models. Buy good, nutritious food, avoid junk food, serve moderate portions, and don't make food a source of comfort. Watch your own weight and show your boy that there is great wisdom in the Latin saying, *mens sana in corpore sano*, a sound mind in a sound body.

Three Things You Must Do

1. Know what makes for good nutrition for boys.
2. Feed your boy the most nutritious food you can afford.
3. Be on the lookout for food-related behavioral disorders, and for overeating.

Things to Say and Do

Talk to your boy about good eating habits. Combine that talk with giving him good, nutritious food. Say such things as:

- Breakfast is a very important meal for a young boy.
- Here's some good breakfast food. This will help you learn and pay attention in school.
- I'm giving you some good snacks for later. These will help you grow big and strong.
- Here's a good sandwich for lunch. It has lots of vitamins and other good things for a growing boy.

See if your boy has learned anything about nutrition in school. In some schools he will be taught in grade one or two about the good food groups. Say such things as:

- Does your teacher ever tell you about the good things to eat?
- Do you know what the food groups are?
- Do you know what nutrition means?

If you notice your boy being jittery or impulsive, ask him if anything he eats makes him feel funny. Say such things as:

■ Do you feel strange when you eat some things?

You can also try eliminating certain things from his diet if you think they are making him behave strangely. But it is best to do this only after talking to your physician. Encourage your boy to eat healthy foods. You can go to fast-food places occasionally, as a special treat, but make sure your boy knows that only some of the food served there is really nutritious. Say such things as:

■ This is the kind of food that tastes really good but it's not for everyday eating.
■ Burgers and fries are fun sometimes, but you can't grow big and strong eating just those foods.
■ I don't mind bringing you here because when you eat at home you eat food that will make you grow big and strong.

Be careful that your boy doesn't develop a weight problem. Don't let him have an unlimited supply of cookies, ice cream, potato chips, and candy. Say such things as:

■ You can have sweets for treats, but not too much.
■ I want you to eat things that taste good, but that are also good for you.
■ If you eat too much of that stuff you won't be healthy.

Be a model of good nutrition and weight control. Eat a healthy, balanced diet. Eat a good breakfast. Don't binge eat, don't "pig out" on sweets, and don't get fat.

Words, Phrases, and Actions to Use

■ That's healthy.
■ That's nutritious.
■ That's delicious.
■ That's good for you.
■ That's bad for you.

■ You should eat all the food groups.
■ This is a good food for snacks between meals.
■ You want to eat well to grow big and strong.

Things Not to Say and Do

Don't let your boy eat too much junk food or fast food. Don't say such things as:

■ I could eat at this place every day. I love burgers and fries and I don't care whether they're good for me or not.

- I eat what I want.
- I only eat what I like.

Don't let your boy always choose his own food. He will often make bad choices because of the influence of his friends and advertising. Don't say such things as:

- I don't care what you eat. You choose.
- You can eat whatever your friends eat.
- I know you'll choose what's best for you.

Don't let your boy become overweight. Don't say such things as:

- Eat whatever you want.
- If you eat everything on your plate I'll give you a double serving of cake and ice cream.
- You need to put more flesh on those skinny bones. At your age a chubby boy is a healthy boy.

Don't ignore the evidence that good brain development depends on good nutrition. Don't say such things as:

- I don't believe all that research on food. We didn't think about that kind of thing when I was a kid and I grew up healthy.
- Your brain will grow, no matter what you eat.
- You need lots of carbohydrates and sugar in the morning to get you going.

Don't be a bad nutrition role model. Don't eat poorly, don't overeat, and don't develop or ignore a weight problem.

Words, Phrases, and Actions to Avoid

- Eat whatever you want.
- Have more ice cream and chips.
- Let's finish this box of cookies.
- You're fat.
- You can never be too skinny.
- You don't have to eat it if you don't like it.
- Potato chips and ice cream have all the food groups.
- Let's go to the burger place again tonight.

EMPATHY

◆

You realize from your own experience that being able to put yourself into others' shoes is one of the most important abilities your boy needs to develop. You ask your boy to try to put himself in another child's place when he has acted aggressively toward that child, as boys will often do. You ask him to think about how you feel when you ask him to pick up his clothes in his room, or to help clear the dishes from the dinner table, and he says no. You ask him to think about what his schoolmate might be feeling when he is teased or bullied by the other kids. You want him to imagine himself as a child who is somehow different and who suffers because of it. You are putting major emphasis on empathy as a way to channel your boy's naturally aggressive feelings into understanding how he can use these impulses to help rather than hurt others.

Things to Consider

Empathy is an emotion that can be seen in very young children. A baby will respond to another baby's crying. By the age of six months you can see them trying to comfort other unhappy babies. By the time your boy reaches school age you will have spent four or five years urging him to think about the effects of his actions on others. Dr. Eli H. Newberger in *The Men They Will Become* reports that one year olds will cry, or seek comfort themselves, upon hearing another child crying. However, he observed young children who have been abused in a day care center and pointed out that they showed little empathy for other children in distress. In fact, they often showed fear, anger, and aggression toward those children.

Although your boy has his own temperament, you can encourage him to develop empathy from an early age by giving him opportunities to socialize with other children. Socializing with him yourself will also help him to learn good social behavior from your own example. By the age of six your boy should have no trouble seeing things from another's perspective. See how he shows this in his comments on situations in which he observes someone else's frustration, pain, fear, anxiety, or anger. You are looking for words or actions that show he understands someone else's needs. He will do this better if you have shown him how to do it in your own words and actions as he's been growing up.

You need to put your feelings for others into words that show you empathize with them. If you have been warm and positive in your talk and actions in your relationship with your boy, he is more likely to be warm and positive in understanding other's feelings. If you have abused your boy emotionally or physically by being too punishment oriented and too unforgiving—basically, by showing a lack of empathy for your little boy as he has been growing up—you are more likely to have a boy who will show a similar lack of empathy for others as he grows up.

Now that your boy is in school look for signs of growing empathy toward children who are different, as well as people who are sick or in need of any kind of assistance. Give your boy a chance to empathize by letting him do simple forms of charity work through your place of worship or your community groups such as scouts or school clubs. Tell him how much you value this kind of empathy, and give him lots of hugs and kisses for it.

Finally, encourage your boy to put his feelings into words, especially his aggressive feelings. Boys are naturally more physically aggressive than girls, and therefore less likely to feel empathy for the objects of their aggression unless they're forced to stop and think about the other person and to put their aggressive feelings into words. Show your boy how to listen to his own words and ask him to imagine how he would feel if he were on the receiving end of them. Emphasize to him that physical violence is always unacceptable.

Three Things You Must Do

1. Model empathy for your boy as he's growing up.
2. Encourage him to socialize with other children, and socialize with your boy yourself.
3. Reward him with praise, hugs, and kisses for showing that he understands others' feelings.

Things to Say and Do

The most important thing you can do is model good empathetic behavior for your boy. For example, show him the feelings you have for him when he hurts himself, or is feeling sad. Say such things as:

- Oh honey, I'm sorry you hurt yourself. That must feel very sore.
- Do you feel sad? I know what it's like to feel sad.
- It makes me sad when you're sad. What can I do to make you feel better?

Talk to your boy about your feelings for others who are sick, disabled, poor, or in trouble. Say such things as:

- Grandma isn't feeling well. I wish there was something we could do to make her better.

- See that man skiing. He only has one leg. I think it's wonderful that he hasn't let that stop him from doing something he loves.
- It's our responsibility to give to others who aren't as lucky as we are. Imagine how you would feel if you didn't have nice clothes, good food, a safe, comfortable place to live, and a little money?
- Soon you can come with us when we volunteer at the food bank each week.
- The bottle drives your school organizes for the homeless shelter are a good way of learning how to do things for others who need help. Imagine what it must be like to have no home.

Talk explicitly about the importance of empathy. Say such things as:

- We've talked a lot about how important it is to try to put yourself in someone else's place.
- I think you're pretty good at imagining what it would be like to be someone else, especially when they're in trouble or hurting. Can you tell me what you say to yourself?
- I always try to put myself in your place when I ask you to do something. Do you do that too? I never want to ask you to do something that I wouldn't want to do myself.

Encourage your boy to volunteer his time and effort for others at your place of worship, at school, or with some community group. Say such things as:

- I'm glad you go on bottle drives to raise money for charity.
- When I was your age I used to volunteer with my scout group to take disabled veterans in hospitals to church services. We'd push their wheelchairs to the chapel. Does your scout group ever talk about doing anything like that?

Words, Phrases, and Actions to Use

- . . . kindness . . .
- . . . gentleness . . .
- How would you feel if . . .
- Do unto others what you would have others do unto you.
- Imagine what it's like to . . .

- Try to understand.
- Let's talk.
- Tell me what you're feeling.
- Put yourself in his shoes.
- Would you like to feel that way?
- What if you were in his place?

Things Not to Say and Do

Don't be a poor role model. Don't make rude or nasty comments about others. Don't say such things as:

- I don't care about poor people. They're only poor because they're too lazy to work.
- Those people deserve whatever bad things happen to them.
- I don't like them because they're not like us.

Don't condone teasing or bullying of any children. Don't say such things as:

- I'm not surprised that kid gets picked on. He was asking for it.
- If other kids tease you or bully you, you probably deserve it.

Don't belittle your boy's desire to help others. Don't say things like:

- You have to help yourself. You can't be worrying about other people.
- Why should you help them? They wouldn't lift a finger to help you.
- There are plenty of people doing charity work. You don't have time to do it.

Don't discourage your boy from talking about his feelings for others. Don't say such things as:

- Don't be a Goodie Two-shoes. You don't have to like everyone.
- I don't have time to listen to how you feel about those people.
- Keep your feelings to yourself.

Words, Phrases, and Actions to Avoid

- Do it to others before they have a chance to do it to you.
- Hate is good.
- You're a loser.
- It's a dog-eat-dog world.
- I don't care.
- They don't deserve your sympathy.
- You come first.

FEARS

◆

Your young schoolboy likes to pretend that nothing frightens him. He sees himself as a macho man like the heroes in his books, movies, and games. But you know better. You know he's afraid of the dark when he thinks he's alone. He invites you to join him when he's watching a scary movie. You tell him that you're there to protect him and care for him. You say that while he doesn't have much to fear, we all need to be careful in our lives because there are always possible dangers at home, at school, or elsewhere.

Things to Consider

At a very early age a combination of culture and body chemistry tells your boy that if he is a real man he must be fearless, a protector of girls and women, a fighter against evil, and a mentally and physically strong and self-reliant individual. There are many good things for boys to emulate in this stereotype. But this image of masculinity can also be destructive if it forces your boy to hide normal and realistic fears that he experiences in his life.

You, as his parent, have the responsibility to provide your boy with the love and security he needs to grow up into a confident, loving, caring man who can cope with his own fears and those of others. As a result of the recent attacks in New York and Washington, many parents and teachers have been wondering about the best way to calm their children's fears and convince them that they are safe. There are a number of things you can do to prevent your boy from being needlessly afraid, and to help him feel secure when he is afraid.

First, you must recognize that your boy is probably afraid of something, whether it is staying home alone, being separated from you, being abandoned (as in a marriage breakup), being in the dark, being bullied or teased, encountering ghosts or demons, experiencing an enemy attack on his home or school, or simply being afraid. Look for signs of abnormal behavior of any kind, such as a loss of appetite, unwillingness to leave the house or your company, reluctance to go to school, or reluctance to answer questions about why he is acting strangely.

Second, you must get your boy to talk and you must listen, *without judging him*. Hopefully you have a good communicative relationship with your boy so he will readily talk to you about almost anything. Just listen to his fears and comfort him. No matter how real the fear, tell him he has nothing to be afraid of, that you are there to protect him. It's vital, at this age, that you assure him that he's safe with you. Tell him that it's all right to be afraid. Don't perpetuate the myth that real men must never show fear. Help your boy to be a well-adjusted man by showing him that sometimes being afraid and showing it is the most sensible and heroic response.

Third, regardless of the cause of the fear, you and your boy must share your feelings and thoughts. Even if you don't have all the answers, you must talk about effective strategies for overcoming the fear, either by removing its cause or changing your behavior in light of it. For example, if your boy is afraid of being home alone after school because you work, arrange for him to stay at a day care or a neighbor's until you can get home. If your boy is afraid of going to school, visit his teacher and principal to discover any good reasons why he might be afraid.

Realistically, you need to assess the cause of your boy's fear in order to know what to do next. You need to know how closely your child has been affected by whatever is frightening him.

If your boy's fears persist, seem irrational, or you feel helpless to eliminate them, don't hesitate to seek professional help.

Three Things You Must Do

1. Recognize that your boy may be afraid.
2. Listen to his fears.
3. Give him lots of love and hugs and make him feel safe with you.

Things to Say and Do

Encourage your boy to talk about anything that's really worrying him. If you've always had time to listen to him talk about his life and encouraged him to do so, if you've also regularly had conversations with him and talked to him about yourself, and if you've listened to him without judging him or getting angry with what he's told you, then you'll find it more likely that he'll tell you about his fears. Say such things as:

- Is something bothering you?
- I think you're afraid of something. Can you tell me about it?
- I know what has happened has frightened you. Let's talk about it.

Talk about the specific things your boy is afraid of. Say such things as:

- Is there something at school that's bothering you?
- Let's talk about things that make you afraid. I'll tell you what makes me afraid and then you can tell me what makes you afraid.
- We all have some things that frighten us. What frightens you?

Reassure your boy that you are there to love him and keep him safe. Say such things as:

- Nothing can hurt you as long as we're here to protect you.
- We love you and will never let anyone harm you.
- There's nothing to fear when you're with us.

Tell your boy that it's all right to be afraid. Say such things as:

- All boys and men are afraid of something. Don't think that because you're a boy you shouldn't be afraid of some things.
- It's good to be afraid of some things. Then you can avoid them.
- It's silly not to be afraid of people or things that can really hurt you. Let's talk about them.

Words, Phrases, and Actions to Use

- Fears are normal.
- Tell me about your fears.
- Don't worry.
- I love you.
- Give me a hug.
- Let's talk.
- You're safe with us.
- We'll protect you.

Things Not to Say and Do

Never dismiss your boy's fears as silly or groundless, no matter what you may really think about them. Don't say such things as:

- That's silly.
- What nonsense. There's nothing to be afraid of.
- You're worrying over nothing.

Don't make this a gender issue. Don't say things like:

- Real men don't feel fear.
- You're acting like a girl.
- Don't be a sissy.

Don't abandon your boy and expect him to work it out for himself. Don't say such things as:

- You're getting to be a big boy now so you work it out for yourself.
- I'm not going to help you. You deal with it.

Don't reject your boy's need for love and protection from you. Don't say such things as:

- Don't be a baby.
- I'm just as much afraid as you are.

Don't refuse to talk about your boy's fears with him. Don't say such things as:

- I don't want to discuss it.
- It's so silly it's not worth talking about.

Words, Phrases, and Actions to Avoid

- It's nothing.
- That's stupid.
- That's silly.
- That's groundless.
- Don't be a sissy.
- Be a man.
- You deal with it.
- I'm busy.
- Later.

FIGHTING

◆

Your boy likes to play. He likes climbing and wrestling and running around with packs of other boys. Sometimes his play gets very rough and your boy gets into a fight with another boy, or he and his pack of little boys start to taunt and call another pack of little boys insulting names. You don't want to squelch your boy's natural male instincts for aggression, but you want it channeled into productive activities. You don't want him fighting with other boys and especially not with girls, even girls who are older, bigger, and stronger than he is. You want to know how to teach your boy not to fight, without limiting his need for activities in which he competes and tests himself.

Things to Consider

William Pollack in *Real Boys* acknowledges that boys and men are incomparably more violent than girls and women. But he also points out that boys do not have a "violence chromosome." Part of the reason boys tend to fight, he suggests, is that they have been taught that anger is one of the few acceptable emotions for them to show. They learn that other, gentler emotions such as sorrow, pity, empathy, compassion, and a willingness to "kiss and make up" are for girls and women.

You can do something about this by showing your boy from an early age that these gentler emotions are there for him to use without them threatening his masculinity. As a father, you can show him that you settle problems through talk and conciliation, not through fighting. As a mother, you can show him that you love and respect the courage men show when they settle their differences peacefully, rather than through violence.

Accept the fact that boys are programmed for aggression, although not necessarily violence. Try some practices experts say can help you channel your boy's natural instincts in a positive direction.

Because young schoolboys are going through a period in their lives when their tendency to fight increases and therefore can be unduly influenced by violence in movies, TV shows, and electronic games, try to monitor and limit your boy's watching and play. Always talk about the meaning and purposes of these movies, shows, and games with him and make sure that you emphasize peaceful, rather than violent, ways of solving his problems.

Young boys, much more than girls, find it hard to distinguish between the make-believe and real aspects of violence in entertainment. You can help them develop a critical sense of this by talking to them about how and why these movies, shows, and games are made so that they understand what is real and what is not.

Imaginative play is very important to the development of your boy's ability to deal with problems, real or imagined. Encourage your boy to play fantasy games and to use his imagination in building things, painting, playing music, or doing physical activities, rather than having him sit and watch television. Encourage him to read books, write stories, write poems, or write plays and act them out alone or with family and/or friends. Work with him to read and write his own fairy tales in which tensions, frustrations, and problems get resolved.

Show your boy through your own behavior and relationships that peaceful solutions are worth working for. Never resort to fighting or physical violence with him, or with any other family member.

If your boy does get into a fight, intervene if you can. Remove him from the site. Talk to him about the cause and alternative solutions. Insist on his doing the right thing, apologizing, if he was at fault, but most certainly reconciling with the other child. Don't let him believe that fighting was the best solution to the problem.

Listen carefully to your boy talk, and watch the way he behaves toward others, including pets and other living things. See if he seems to be unusually angry or fearful or cruel. Talk about these things if they seem evident.

Finally, work with your boy to create a physical or mental space where he is free to express his emotions nonviolently. This space allows him to be angry, afraid, sorry, tearful, sad, frustrated, and so on. This space can be bedtime, a short walk around the neighborhood, a quiet time after dinner, or a weekend morning.

Three Things You Must Do

1. Recognize that your boy is programmed for aggression, but not necessarily violence.
2. Teach your boy that gentle emotions are good for a boy and that fighting isn't a good solution for problems.
3. Be a model of good conflict resolution.

Things to Say and Do

Help your boy understand that the fighting that he sees on television, in movies, and in electronic games isn't a reality to be imitated. Talk to him about the creation and purposes of such games. Say such things as:

■ Let's talk about this program you're watching. What do you think about all the fighting that goes on here?

- Tell me what you think is real and what's make-believe in this movie.
- The games you're playing are just made-up things, not real. Do you realize that?
- Let's you and I make up a story about you and your friend having a fight at the playground. Is that real? Tell me about why you'd fight him. Can you think of a better way to do things than fighting?

Encourage your boy to use his imagination to come up with better solutions to problems than fighting. Say such things as:

- Do you ever think about fighting someone? Tell me about it. Why do you want to fight? Is fighting the best thing to do?
- Here's a nice story about two boys who were friends but had an argument. Tell me how you think they settled their argument.
- Let's draw a picture of two friends. Do you think they would ever want to fight each other? Why? Is that the best way?

Model peaceful solutions to problems. Don't ever fight with anyone. Talk to your boy about your way of solving problems. Say such things as:

- Have you ever seen me fighting with anyone?
- Why do you think I never get into a fight with my friends?
- Have you ever seen grown-ups fighting? How does that make you feel?

Don't let your boy have a serious fight. If he does get into a fight remove him from the scene. Say such things as:

- Why were you fighting?
- How do you feel about fighting? Do you think it's the right thing to do?
- I want you to think about what happened and tell me if there is a better way than fighting.
- You have to say you're sorry to your friend. It doesn't matter whose fault it was. You must both apologize.

Create a peaceful space with your boy, a physical or mental space that has no violence. Say such things as:

- When you go to bed and we have talked and I tuck you in and you're all nice and cozy and comfortable, how do you feel?
- When do you feel really good? It's nice to have that feeling, isn't it? Would you ever want to fight when you feel that way?

- Can you think of some place that's really nice and safe, where nobody would ever be fighting?

Words, Phrases, and Actions to Use

- ... peace ...
- ... safety ...
- ... security ...
- Solve your disagreements.
- No fighting.

- Imagine.
- Find a better way.
- Be friends.
- Stay calm.

Things Not to Say and Do

Don't let your boy watch or play any shows or games he wants to. Don't say such things as:

- I don't care what TV shows you watch. They can't hurt you.
- I love that game in which everybody kills everybody else.
- That's a good show. It teaches you how to be a good fighter.

Don't condone fighting as a solution to problems and disagreements. Don't say such things as:

- You were right to hit him.
- Sometimes you have to fight for what you want.
- Don't ever let anyone push you around. Just punch him out.

Don't be a bad role model for your boy. Don't do and say such things as:

- Fighting with your spouse.
- Fighting with your boy or other children.
- Getting into a rage and threatening to fight another person.
- Sometimes we fight, but it's good for us.
- I only hit your mom when she deserves it.

Words, Phrases, and Actions to Avoid

- Hit him.
- Fight him.

- Don't take that from anybody.
- Punch him out.
- I'll teach you to fight.
- Sometimes you need to hit someone who's bugging you.

FRIENDS

◆

Your boy has started first grade. One of the things you notice is that your son has a new friend. This is a boy from his class at school. He's a nice boy and you're glad he's found a good friend. You're a little jealous also, because your son clearly wants to spend all his free time after school, on weekends, and during school holidays with this boy. But you recognize that one of the most important aspects of your son growing up is his developing strong and lasting friendships. This shows good personal and social skills in your boy and you would be much more concerned if he had trouble making and keeping friends. You also recognize that as your boy gets older, and especially by the time he is a teenager, his friends will seem much more important to him than you are. You're prepared for this and you see his first real friendship at school as a good beginning.

Things to Consider

Boys and girls seem to differ in their reasons for friendships. At this age both choose friends of the same sex—boys choose boys and girls choose girls—although successful cross-sex friendships do exist. Experts have noticed that boys and girls will describe their friendships differently. Boys talk about the things they do with their friends, while girls speak of the trust and closeness of the relationship. This is no reflection on the quality or intensity of the friendship. Boys express their friendship in shared activities—running, climbing, playing games. They also, like girls, have intimate, quiet moments of talk. But boys are less likely to see this as the essence of their friendship.

Your boy's friends are most likely to be other boys from his school and neighborhood that share his need for active, physical play. Boys this age like to form packs, even though they will have special friends within these packs. These friendships will help your boy develop important life skills such as negotiating, compromising, reconciling, defusing, empathizing, and sympathizing. Boys negotiate the games they'll play and whom they'll play with and against, they'll compromise if no decision can be reached, they'll reconcile themselves to doing what the majority of their friends want to do, they'll defuse potential fights among friends or between different packs of boys, they'll learn to see things from their friend's point of view, and they'll sympathize with friends whose parents won't let them play that afternoon.

Your boy's friendships will help him learn how to handle aggression in himself and in others. The situations that all friendships create, in which there are conflicting motives, methods, and goals, will force your boy to confront alternative actions. He must decide to resist, run, or compromise. It is in situations like this that your boy will develop important verbal skills because he will find that talking is a better way than fighting to settle differences with friends, and others.

Your boy's friendships are also important for teaching him about himself. He will learn to measure himself against his friends in terms of self-esteem, self-assertiveness, aggression, physical and mental ability, and emotional needs and resources. Your boy will also learn about his need for friends, his preferences for certain kinds of friends, and his friends' families, how they are similar to or different from his own.

During these early years of school and friendship your boy will begin to explore a wonderful world of variety. His friends may be different from him in many ways— religion, race, family structure, economic resources, and cultural traditions. His friends will teach him about new ways of thinking about himself and others, new foods to eat, new holidays to celebrate, new expressions to use, new values to choose from, and new places to be from. They will teach him these things explicitly and implicitly.

Your boy will look to you for your reaction to his friends—what you say about them and their family background, what you value and what you reject. He will see from what you say and do how open you are to his new friends and their similarities and differences. This is a chance for you to show your boy your true values regarding others.

Three Things You Must Do

1. Encourage your boy to have friends.
2. Welcome your boy's friends into your home.
3. Know your boy's friends, and his friend's parents if possible.

Things to Say and Do

Always encourage your boy in his friendships at this age. You will know the boys he likes to play with because they will be from his school or neighborhood. Say such things as:

- I like to see you playing with your friends.
- Your friends are always welcome at our house.
- Tell me about your friends. Who is your best friend? Who is your worst friend? Why?

Talk about the backgrounds of your boy's friends. See how much he knows about them. Say such things as:

- Some of your friends seem very interesting. Do you know if they come from other places?
- Are all your friends from around here?
- Do you like your friends' moms and dads?

Talk about the differences your boy's friends may have. Encourage your boy to learn all he can about them. Say such things as:

- What church/synagogue/mosque/temple do your friends go to?
- What country does your friend come from?
- Your friend's family seems to have a different background from ours. I think that's great. You can learn so much from a friend like that.

Your boy will learn useful things about himself and about life from his friendships. Talk to him about these things. Say such things as:

- What do you like best about your friend?
- How is he different from you?
- Do you ever get angry or fight each other?
- Do you like all the same things as your friend?
- How well does your friend do in school?
- Is he as good at running as you are?
- When you disagree on something how do you decide who's right?

Words, Phrases, and Actions to Use

- Friendships are wonderful.
- Who's your best friend?
- Playing together is good.
- Do you talk about things?
- Does he like the same things?
- Never fight with your friends.
- Look after each other.
- Understand each other.
- Forgive each other.
- How is your friend the same and different?

Things Not to Say and Do

Don't try to pick your boy's friends. It generally doesn't work. Even at this age he will choose his own friends. Don't say such things as:

- I forbid you to play with that boy.
- He is not a suitable friend for you.
- I don't like him and I don't want him to be your friend.

Don't show any prejudice or discrimination (in the pejorative sense) toward your boy's friends because they are from a different background than your boy. Don't say such things as:

- I don't want you playing with that kind of boy.
- He's not our kind and I don't want you being friends with him.
- He's the wrong sort of boy for you.

Don't always compare your boy to his friends. Don't say such things as:

- Your friend is much better than you in school. What's wrong with you?
- Why can't you be as good at sports as your friend?
- Why aren't you the leader of your friends?

Words, Phrases, and Actions to Avoid

- He's not suitable.
- He's not our kind.
- Don't be his friend.
- He's better than you.
- Why can't you be more like your friend?
- I don't like people who are different.
- We're far superior to them.
- You can't play with him.
- You don't need friends.

REPRODUCTION

◆

Your boy has been interested in his penis since he was a toddler, and has caused you some embarrassment by playing with himself in the bath and in public. You haven't known what to do about his innocent sexual interests and now that he's in school you want to know how best to teach him about sex in a way that he will understand. You don't want him to feel guilt because of his interest in male and female genitalia and the reproductive process, but you do want him to learn to treat himself and other children with respect. You recognize that he may have engaged in sexual play with other boys or girls when he was a preschooler, but now that he's a young schoolboy you want him to exercise self-control that shows he recognizes other children's right to privacy.

Things to Consider

It's clear that boys, from a very young age, are more sexually active and curious than girls. Boys want to know about bodies, body functions, and especially gender differences. Normally your boy won't have a reproductive sex drive until he reaches puberty and adolescence. But, as Sheila Moore and Roon Frost point out in *The Little Boy Book*, because a young boy's genitals are external his curiosity about them is more obvious than a little girl's.

You can start now introducing your boy to the facts and language of reproduction, but in a simple way to match his level of understanding. If you have had any children after you had your boy, you will already have told him that babies grow in the mommy's tummy. Now he might want to know how the baby got there in the first place. It might be easier for you to talk to your boy about the facts of reproduction at this age when he is still too young to fully understand the fairly abstract ideas of sexuality than to wait until your boy is older.

If your boy asks questions about the process in his own naïve way, there is no reason not to tell him the truth in straightforward language, using the proper names for body parts and functions. At his age you can talk to him about gender differences and reproduction as a natural part of life. He won't be embarrassed, and neither should you. In talking about reproduction you have the chance to give your boy a positive lesson in morality by making this wonderful human process and experience seem as natural and miraculous as you can.

At the same time you can begin to teach your boy simple ideas about the sanctity of the human body, of human relationships, and reproduction. You want to satisfy your boy's curiosity without making him feel ashamed or threatened or guilty. You also want him to learn that his own and others' bodies are private. While satisfying his natural curiosity about girls and his interest in how babies are made you can point out that understanding these things will come as he grows older.

This approach means that you need to know what and how much your boy understands about sex and reproduction. Hopefully, you have developed an open and easy communicative relationship with your boy by never being judgmental or negative in your response to what he says. Just listen, ask him questions, and give him straightforward, simple answers to his questions. Your boy, at this age, will probably have a good idea of the physical differences between boys and girls, but he will still have a very simple, childlike understanding of what these differences mean.

As you talk to your boy about reproduction, as you decide what's appropriate for him to see and explore in his sexually innocent way, always base your decisions on what you know about his level of understanding. You don't want him to experience things that are impossible for him to properly understand. This includes sexual exploration with playmates, whether or not he should be allowed to see you naked, or to see in movies and TV shows sexuality that is far beyond his understanding. Rather than trying to say too much, let your boy's questions be your guide as to what you tell him.

Three Things You Must Do

1. Give your boy a positive attitude toward sexual differences and the reproductive process.
2. Never criticize him for the questions he asks.
3. Always keep your explanations honest and at his level of understanding.

Things to Say and Do

Accept your boy's natural curiosity about genitalia and reproduction. Never make him feel ashamed or guilty for asking about them. Say such things as:

- Do you know the proper names for what boys have and what girls have?
- Do you know why boys and girls are different?
- Let's look at this book that shows pictures of the differences between boys and girls.

Match the facts and language about reproduction to your boy's age and understanding. Try to find out how much he knows about where babies come from. Say such things as:

- Babies grow in their mommy's tummy. Isn't that interesting?
- Boys and girls are different so that when they become men and women and get married they can have babies, just like we had you.

Explain how babies are conceived. Use the correct terms. It helps to connect the process with love and marriage. Remember your boy's age and be ready for unexpected reactions to your explanation, such as "Disgusting," "No, it can't be," or "I'm never going to make a baby." Say such things as:

- It takes a man and woman together to make a baby. Usually they love one another, get married, and then decide to make a baby.
- Babies begin as tiny little seeds that the daddy plants inside the egg of the mommy. He does this by putting his penis inside the mommy's vagina and squirting the seeds into the mommy's egg that lives in the mommy's stomach in a place called the uterus, which is the warm place where the egg will grow into a baby. When the baby is ready to be born it comes out through the mommy's vagina.
- I know this sounds funny to you, but it's really the way daddies and mommies make babies.

Assure your boy that this is a very natural and beautiful process when the mommy and daddy love one another. Say such things as:

- This is one way that mommies and daddies show their love for each other.
- All people make babies the same way.
- Boys and girls can't make babies until they are older and shouldn't make babies until they are grown up, like we are.

Emphasize the sanctity of the love relationship that produces babies and the privacy of boys' and girls' bodies. Say such things as:

- Your body is your own and nobody can touch it without your permission.
- You should never touch anybody else's body without their permission.
- If anyone touches you without your permission you must tell us.

Make sure your boy knows he can talk to you about anything he wants to and you will try to explain things to him. Say such things as:

- If you ever have any questions we'll always try to answer them for you.
- Don't ever be ashamed to ask us about something.
- You'll understand a lot of what I've told you when you're older.

If you find that your eight-year-old boy violates the privacy of others' bodies or has an abnormal interest in sex, you may want to seek professional advice.

Words, Phrases, and Actions to Use

- . . . penis . . .
- . . . vagina . . .
- . . . reproduction . . .
- . . . babies . . .
- . . . seed . . .
- . . . sperm . . .
- . . . egg . . .

- . . . uterus . . .
- . . . fertilize . . .
- . . . love . . .
- . . . marriage . . .
- Life is sacred.
- Our bodies are private.
- Sex is beautiful.

Things Not to Say and Do

Don't ever make your boy afraid to ask you about sex and reproduction. Don't be critical of his comments and questions. Don't say such things as:

- That's not something boys should talk about.
- You don't need to know about that now.
- Don't ever let me hear you say those words again.

Don't assume that because your boy knows about reproduction that he will want to have sex with the little girl next door. His sex drive won't begin until puberty. Don't say such things as:

- I can't tell you about that because it will only cause trouble.
- The less you know about sex, the better.

Don't lose your temper because you find out your boy and the girl next door have been comparing body parts. Don't say such things as:

- You dirty little boy.
- Good boys never look at little girls.

Words, Phrases, and Actions to Avoid

- That's dirty.
- That's filthy.
- You pervert.
- Don't ever talk about that.
- If I ever catch you peeping at a girl I'll punish you.
- You're a bad boy for saying that.
- You're abnormal.
- Don't ask.
- You'll have to find out for yourself.
- Ask your friends.

RESPONSIBILITIES

◆

You want your boy to take responsibility for some of the things in his life. It's your way of starting him on the road to adulthood. Now that he's in school you realize that he has to be in control of some things because you can't always be watching him and helping him, even though you are always there for him. You want him to take responsibility for the things he's old enough to do and do competently. He already has to help clear the dishes from the table after meals. You also insist that he clean up the toys when he's finished playing, that he turn off the machines when he's finished using them, and that he keep his clothes off the floor of his room so that it can be easily cleaned. You know that your boy may complain a little about some of these responsibilities, but that he really is pleased and proud that you trust him to do so much for himself. It makes him feel grown-up.

Things to Consider

Continue teaching your boy to be helpful around the house by giving him new responsibilities as he gets older. Now that he is in school he needs to practice at home the kinds of responsibilities he must take on at school. This includes keeping his room neat and clean, picking up his clothes off the floor, keeping his school things in order so that they are ready every morning, and bringing home school announcements and giving them to you.

Remember that your boy is young and still working on developing fine motor skills so you need to be very tolerant with him. You want to reward and praise *effort* and *willingness* rather than success and perfection. If your boy willingly takes on responsibilities for looking after his own things as well as helping with chores in the house you should be very pleased with him.

Giving your boy increased responsibility as he shows himself capable of accepting it gradually moves him closer to being the grown-up, autonomous, self-reliant young man you want him to become. While you are there to help him with all parts of his life at this age, you are beginning to learn to stand back a bit, relinquish a little of your control and authority, and let him be responsible for some small, yet important parts of his life.

In addition to wanting to give your boy more responsibility, you may have to give him a share of responsibility because of your family circumstances. If you are a single parent, or married with both of you working, and if you have other children, everyone in your home needs to be responsible for some aspects of their own lives, especially your children in school. Responsibilities will not only give your boy a chance to earn your approval and contribute to his self-esteem, but they will also allow him an opportunity to make a real contribution to your family.

Here is a list of responsibilities that are appropriate for a six- to eight-year-old boy. It's not a complete list. Some of them require your help and guidance at first, but gradually your boy should be able to manage them almost completely on his own.

- Getting up on time in the morning.
- Getting dressed in school or play clothes.
- Washing his hands and face before meals.
- Brushing his teeth after meals.
- Putting dirty dishes in the sink or dishwasher.
- Picking up clothes from the floor and putting them on the bed or in a drawer.
- Picking up books and toys and putting them away.
- Putting on boots and outer clothes.
- Taking off boots and outer clothes.
- Asking you if there is anything he can do to help.
- Doing his homework (usually begins around grade two or three).
- Putting out all his school things the night before.
- Putting out his clothing for the next day.
- Getting into his pajamas when he's supposed to.
- Taking a bath or shower.
- Coming home right after school unless otherwise arranged.
- Always telling you where he is going.
- Giving you all written information sent home by the school.
- Going to bed at the appointed time.

Here, also, is a list of some of your responsibilities to your six- to eight-year-old boy. It's not a complete list. Some of them are obvious, some are difficult, and some are easy. But all are important in helping your boy grow up in a positive, loving atmosphere.

- Loving, hugging, and praising your boy for all his attempts and accomplishments at home, in school, and in the community.
- Modeling the kinds of responsible behavior you expect from him.
- Helping him with his responsibilities.
- Not expecting perfection.

- Praising him for his willingness to try.
- Never hitting him or fighting with him.
- Helping him with homework when he asks, but not doing it for him.
- Monitoring his work at school.
- Going to all parent-teacher interviews.
- Giving his teachers the respect you expect your boy to give them.
- Getting to know your boy's school principal.
- Not leaving your boy alone in the house.
- If you can't be home when your boy comes home from school, making some arrangement with another adult to be there for him in some way.
- Always making your home a place where your boy and his friends feel welcome.
- Showing your boy that increased responsibility goes with increased freedom.

Three Things You Must Do

1. Give your boy responsibilities suited to his age and abilities.
2. Love and praise him for his willingness to try to fulfill these responsibilities, not just for his successes.
3. Model responsible behavior for him.

Things to Say and Do

Talk to your boy about the things he thinks he can do for himself. Even if some things seem too much for him, let him try, and help him along. Say such things as:

- What kinds of jobs do you think you can do around the house?
- Do you have any little jobs you do at school for your teacher?
- What does your teacher expect you to be able to do for yourself, and what does she help you with?

Sit down with your boy and draw up a list of things that he would like to try to do himself. Say such things as:

- Why don't we list the things you would like to help out with?
- What should we put on the list?
- What things could you do if I helped you, at least at the beginning?

Praise your boy's attempts to do things for himself, even if he fails. Say such things as:

- Tying shoelaces is still pretty hard to do. But you really gave it a good effort.
- Can you reach the hangers in your closet and hang up your shirt? I think they're still too high, but good for you for trying.
- I'm really impressed with the way you can put the dishes in the dishwasher. Well done.

Talk to your boy about the new privileges that go along with new responsibilities. Say such things as:

- Now that you're so helpful around the house I think you deserve a reward. What would you like?
- You're getting to be such a big boy and doing things for yourself that I think you deserve to stay up later on Friday and Saturday nights, since there's no school the next day.

Model responsible behavior for your boy. Say such things as:

- See how I try to keep my room as neat and clean just like I ask you to do.
- I blamed you for something you didn't do. I apologize.
- You can ask me to help you with a job just like I sometimes ask you for help.

Words, Phrases, and Actions to Use

- Please.
- Thank you.
- Well done.
- That's your responsibility.
- Can you do it?
- Do you want to be responsible for that?
- I think it would be a good responsibility for you.
- Try.
- I'll help.
- Don't give up.
- Try again.
- I'm so proud of you.
- Good try.

Things Not to Say and Do

Don't continue to treat your boy as a baby. Don't belittle his ability to take on responsibility. Don't say such things as:

- I could never let you do that at your age.
- You're just a baby.
- You're not coordinated enough.

Don't be a poor role model. Don't say such things as:

- Do as I say, not as I do.
- Don't worry about what I do. Just do what I tell you.
- I don't care if I forgot to do it. That's my business, not yours.

Don't expect perfection. Don't say such things as:

- You'll never get it right.
- If you can't do it properly there's no point in my giving you that responsibility.
- You're just too young to get it right.
- The world doesn't reward people for trying, only for success.

Don't give your boy unrealistic responsibilities. Don't say such things as:

- I want your room to be spotless. That's your responsibility.
- You can fix your own dinner tonight. I'm too tired.
- I want you to look after your little brother while I nap.
- When you get home from school I want you to vacuum the living room.

Words, Phrases, and Actions to Avoid

- You're a baby.
- Get it right or don't bother.
- You failed.
- When will you grow up?
- It's not too much to ask.
- You've got to give me more help.
- Doing your chores is more important than doing your homework.

RIGHT AND WRONG

◆

You've always tried to teach your boy right from wrong. This moral dimension of his upbringing is very important to you. You realize that it doesn't matter whether or not your boy turns out to be a religious person, but he must still make moral decisions in his everyday life that will affect not only himself but those around him. You've tried to teach him the right thing to do from the day he was old enough to start doing things on his own. But now that he's a young schoolboy, you've noticed that he comes home with lots of new ideas, new ways of talking, and new questions about why he must do one thing rather than another. He seems generally to have more of a mind of his own. While you recognize these changes as a normal part of his growing up, you don't want to lose control of his moral education.

Things to Consider

We are all born with a "me first" attitude. It's a natural and necessary part of being an infant and, according to the experts, it is the first stage in the moral development of children. As a parent you have the job of helping your boy move through stages in his moral development from the self-centeredness of his infancy and very early childhood to the adult man who has well-developed ideas of justice and human dignity. You will see that as a young schoolboy your son will stop when you say, "Don't do that!" because he knows that your rules say that that's the wrong thing to do. But he probably doesn't yet understand why those rules are there.

Learning to follow rules is the second stage in moral development and your boy will go through that stage right into early adolescence. The third stage of moral development, understanding right from wrong, good from bad, moral from immoral, according to some experts, really develops during adolescence when your boy gains a sense of individuality. The fourth stage, recognizing and cherishing himself and others with a fully developed sense of justice and humanity, comes as your boy reaches adulthood.

These stages are just general approximations and you should not let them interfere with your attempts to teach your boy your ideas of right and wrong. However, you must realize that there are limits to what your boy's brain can make sense of at this age. Your boy, to really act from an understanding of right and wrong, as distinct from just following rules has to have a highly developed sense of empathy. He needs to be able to put himself in someone else's place. At his age this empathetic sense is still developing, and it will continue to develop as you repeatedly ask your boy to think about how his actions may make others feel.

Help your boy learn right from wrong by talking about things that happen in his life at school, in the family, and in the neighborhood that have consequences for him or others. Any time your boy has to make a decision, and it's important that he has the opportunity to make his own decisions about some things, ask him how he will decide what to do. Start him questioning his own motives and actions and thinking about what he did and why he did it. Ask him what he thinks is fair, and why.

Let him experience the consequences of his actions, as long as these consequences are not too harmful or hurtful to himself or others. Given his age and immaturity you still have an obligation to protect him from harming himself or others with his actions. But he needs to know that his actions have consequences and that he needs to think about them before he does or says something.

Three Things You Must Do

1. Recognize that your boy has a very limited understanding of the abstract concepts of right and wrong.
2. Let your boy make some of his own decisions.
3. Listen for your boy's intuitive sense of right and wrong and work with it.

Things to Say and Do

Give your boy the opportunity to talk about things that bother him. Use that talk to discuss specifics of right and wrong. Say such things as:

- Why do you think your allowance isn't fair?
- I didn't know your teacher was mean to you the other day. What did she do?
- "Johnny" got a new bike. Do you think that's a good reason for you to get one too?

When you reprimand your boy for doing something wrong, tell him why it's wrong. Repeat the message as often as you find it necessary to remind him of what he did wrong. Say such things as:

- That was not a nice thing to do because you hurt his feelings.
- You took more than your share. That doesn't leave enough for your brother. That makes him feel very sad.

- When you start crying and fussing in the store that makes me feel very embarrassed because other people will think I don't have a well-behaved boy.

Encourage your boy to talk about his feelings of right and wrong, tied to specific situations. Say such things as:

- You think your school report isn't fair. Why not?
- Your friend has new sneakers, and you don't. Why do you think that's unfair?
- You want me to let you stay up late to watch a TV program. Do you think that's the right thing for me to do?

Model good behavior for your boy. Talk to him about why you choose to do the things you do. Say such things as:

- Not buying you a new bike when I know you wanted one was a hard thing for me to decide. This is what I thought about it.
- Sometimes I do the wrong thing unintentionally, but I hope I never choose to do the wrong thing.

Words, Phrases, and Actions to Use

- . . . rules . . .
- . . . consequences . . .
- That was good.
- That was bad.
- That was right.
- That was wrong.
- That's fair.
- That's unfair.
- Think about the other person.
- How would you feel?
- Why did you do that?

Things Not to Say and Do

Don't expect your boy to understand the concepts of right and wrong at his age. Don't tie your talk to abstractions. Don't say such things as:

- Don't you know the difference between right and wrong?
- You should know better than to do that when you know that's wrong.

Don't let your boy make decisions that have serious consequences. Don't say such things as:

- You know right from wrong, so you decide.
- You have to decide whether or not you're going to do your homework.
- It's up to you whether or not you tell me where you're going after school.

Don't expect your boy to know right from wrong in every situation. Don't punish him for making the wrong decision. Don't say such things as:

- How could you have done that?
- That was the wrong choice. You have to be punished.
- There's a right and wrong in every situation and you chose the wrong. That's unforgivable.

Never hit your boy for making the wrong choice.

Words, Phrases, and Actions to Avoid

- You're a bad boy.
- You're no good.
- You're stupid.
- You're terrible.
- You're nasty.
- There's no right and wrong.
- Whatever you do is right.
- You deserve a beating.

SCHOOL

◆

Your boy is starting elementary school and you're nervous for him. You know that boys have more problems in school than girls. Especially in the early grades, boys have more difficulty sitting still, they don't read as well as girls, they are generally less verbal, they are less mature, they have more trouble concentrating on tasks, they learn better through seeing and doing than hearing, and they are reprimanded for bad behavior on average at least five times more than girls. But your boy doesn't know all this and he's very excited. He's going to a real school, not just another playschool, and he feels like he's really grown up. You want him to like school, to fit in with the other children, to be liked, and to do well. You have investigated all the schools in your community, both public and private, and you have chosen to send him to the one you think is most appropriate. But you are worried you might have overlooked some important things that will affect your boy's success in school.

Some Things to Consider

If you are like most parents you want the best school experience for your boy that he can have because you know that success in school will give your boy options in life that he won't have if his schoolwork is poor. There is much you can do to help your boy have a great experience in school, to learn and excel in his studies, and to earn the praise and respect of his teachers and classmates. Much of what you must do includes understanding the differences between boys and girls that give girls who are beginning school considerable advantages over their male counterparts.

Whatever the innate intelligence and ability of your boy may be, he will be at a disadvantage compared to girls of the same age because of differences in male and female brains and different rates of maturation. As Michael Gurian points out in his book *The Good Son*, because of the structural and functional differences in male and female brains, boys tend to be more oriented toward the space that is outside of them and girls toward the space that is inside.

Boys beginning school at age six will not be very good at doing what most teachers demand of them—keeping quiet, sitting still, listening, reading, writing neatly, and remembering what they are told to do. Boys need to be active, to move around, to run, to be outside, to build, to roughhouse, to touch, and to climb.

But most schools reward the opposite kind of behavior. In elementary school girls have an advantage over boys both socially and intellectually in every area except spatial perception and reasoning. In the elementary years girls also have a physical advantage over boys in height and growth rate, are better in tasks requiring fine motor skills, like writing, and have better balance and control in their movement.

Boys who begin school at age five or six may have poor social skills. That combined with the frustration they experience when they can't easily follow the teacher's instructions or understand what is expected of them will often lead them to antisocial behavior. Thus begins a vicious cycle of bad behavior and bad performance during the most critical years of schooling. At the very time when boys should be learning to read, write, and do arithmetic skills that are the foundation of all later work in school, they may be spending most of their time being reprimanded by the teacher or principal.

You can avoid or at least mitigate many of these problems by judging your boy's readiness for school, not forcing him to start school before he is ready, giving him school experience by putting him into play groups or playschool before he starts first grade, and, once he has begun school, by monitoring his work and behavior very carefully. As a rule of thumb the older your boy is when he starts school, the better. He will have had that much more time to mature. Even a few months can make a big difference.

I've heard of at least one school district that has recognized the importance of school readiness, especially for boys. They have a two-year kindergarten so that children who are not ready after the first year can stay for a second with no stigma attached. The lesson for you is, don't push your boy to start school early if he's not ready socially. Keep your boy in kindergarten, even if he is old enough for first grade, if he is not mature enough for first grade. Remember that his chances of school success and happiness can be damaged if he starts grade one before he's ready.

Your boy is ready for first grade if he can do the following:

- Sit still and concentrate on a single task for at least twenty minutes.
- Listen to a set of directions and understand and follow them successfully.
- Understand and follow a set of rules.
- Play with other children without losing his temper or fighting.
- Listen to an adult when she asks for his attention.
- Stop what he is doing when he is asked to do so.
- Put his toys away neatly in their proper place.
- Dress and undress himself reasonably well.
- Make new friends easily.
- Respond to and seek praise.
- Avoid negative attention-getting behaviors.
- Use a pencil.

- Use a pair of scissors.
- Know when to say please and thank you.
- Care about others' opinions of him.
- Ask politely for things rather than just taking them.
- Know his own address and phone number.

Three Things You Must Do

1. Prepare your boy socially for school in play groups or playschools.
2. Start your boy in kindergarten or grade one when he is ready, and not before.
3. Carefully monitor your boy's schoolwork and behavior in first grade and beyond.

Things to Say and Do

The most important thing in deciding your boy's readiness for school is your knowledge of his social skills. Hopefully, you've had many chances to see how he gets along with other children and with adults. Use these observations to decide if he's ready for school where he will have to get along with many new children and adults.

Talk to your friends and your friends' children if you're not sure how your boy behaves when you're not around. Above all, talk to his other caregivers, like baby-sitters, play group monitors, and playschool teachers. Say such things as:

- I'm trying to decide if "Sam" is ready for school. What do you think?
- How does "Sam" behave when I'm not around?
- Do you think "Sam" is socially mature enough for grade one?

Some of your boy's readiness will depend on his attitude toward school. Ask him what he thinks. Say such things as:

- What do you think about going into first grade?

If your boy is already in school, be sure to talk regularly to his teachers. Don't wait for parent-teacher interviews. Ask his teacher if you can volunteer in her class. Meet with her to talk about any problems your son may be having.

Talk to your boy regularly about his school experience. Help him with his homework. Ask to see the work he's been doing. Say such things as:

- Do you like school?
- What do you like best?
- What do you like least?

- Can I help you with anything?
- Do you have some of your work that I can see?

Watch for any signs of behavioral changes in your boy that may indicate some kind of problem he's not telling you about. Look for the following:

- Change in appetite.
- Change in desire to go to school.
- Mysterious disappearance of items like electronic games, skates, or money.

Words, Phrases, and Actions to Use

- ... school ...
- You're becoming so grown-up.
- Are you ready for ... ?
- Are you excited for ... ?
- School is fun.
- Good work.
- Do you want to go?
- Who is your best friend?
- Are you happy?
- What a good teacher.
- Show me your work.
- Are you afraid of anything?

Things Not to Say and Do

Don't push your boy into starting school when he's not ready. Don't say such things as:

- If you don't start school at your age people will think there's something wrong with you.
- Even if you're not ready you have to go.
- You'll learn to cope.

Don't ignore your boy's schoolwork. Don't say such things as:

- You're doing okay. I don't have to meet your teacher.
- You'd tell me if things weren't going okay, wouldn't you?
- If you don't do well in school you'll be punished.

Don't ignore the differences between boys and girls. Don't say things like:

- Boys are better than girls.
- You can do as well as you want to. You just have to try harder.
- You should be able to do it as well as any girl.

Don't blame your boy's problems on his teachers without very good reason. Don't meet with his teachers to criticize, belittle, or yell at them. If you do think your boy has a problem teacher discuss it with the school principal. If the teacher is a problem there will likely be more than just your complaint.

Words, Phrases, and Actions to Avoid

- You stupid boy.
- What a stupid school.
- What a stupid teacher.
- You're a bad boy.
- I'm going to punish you.
- Do your work and don't give me any excuses.
- It's your fault.
- You'd better grow up.

PART 4

Older Schoolboys

(9–12 years)

ALLOWANCE

◆

You, like most parents, have money concerns. Your nine-year-old boy is also very concerned about money, mainly the fact that he doesn't have any to call his own. He depends on you for everything from clothes to food to skateboards. You realize it's time for him to learn about the responsibility of having money by giving him an allowance, money that he controls. You've waited a little longer than many other parents to give him an allowance. Some of his friends have had one since they started school three years ago. But you decided that grade four was a good time to begin. Now that you've decided to give him an allowance you have to decide how much to give him, how often, and whether or not he'll get it in return for doing some chores around the house. You're going to ask other parents what they do and then decide how you'll handle it. It will be up to your boy how much he spends, how much he saves, and what he spends his money on. You hope your boy will learn a good lesson about the value of money from having his own allowance.

Things to Consider

The gender differences show themselves when it comes to allowances. Girls at this age want money to spend on clothes, girls' magazines, music, and movies, probably in that order. Boys want to buy equipment like skateboards and snowboards, video games, electronic games, music, movies, junk food, and clothing, also in that order.

Boys become interested in money as soon as they start school or even before. Wise math teachers use real-life money issues as successful learning exercises. Some parents start their children's allowance at an early age. But others feel that a regular allowance is too much for very young children to be responsible for and leave it until they begin the last half of elementary school. They've given their boys spending money from an early age, but don't begin a formal allowance until around age nine.

Giving your boy an allowance is an important part of preparing him to be a responsible man. In this respect it's vital that you give him complete control over his money, even if you know he's going to waste it. The only way any of us have learned about the value of money is from having our own to do what we wanted, and to have wasted it. That experience is worth one hundred lectures from you on the value of money.

Some parents tie allowances to chores, some don't. I don't think it really matters what you choose to do. It's simply a matter of your own values. But I can tell you what my wife and I did with our boys. First, we gave them each a weekly allowance for which no work was required. Second, we gave them some responsibilities around the house, like keeping the floor of their rooms tidy and clearing away their own breakfast dishes, for which no money was paid. We wanted them to have unpaid responsibilities simply as members of the family. We also had a third scenario. They could, if they wanted to, do special jobs for me or their mom, for which they would be paid extra, beyond their allowance.

We felt that these three things gave our boys a good range of experience, responsibility, and opportunity. They had a guaranteed weekly income, work for which there was no pay, and work for which there was extra pay. Our boys seemed to think this was fair, and both of them have turned out to be very responsible with their money.

Another thing to think about is what you want your boy to be responsible for buying out of his allowance. Do you expect him to buy any necessities with it? In this case you will probably need to give him more money than if you continued to pay for all his basic needs and he was responsible only for luxuries. You pay for his "needs," he pays for his "wants." Again, how you decide to do it depends on your family values and circumstances, because what might be a luxury for a boy in a low- or middle-income family can be a necessity for a boy in a family with lots of disposable cash.

The matter of how much to give your boy has to be decided within the context of your family circumstances. It must be enough to make it seem fair to your boy, who will compare his allowance to that of his friends. Talk to his friends' parents to get a good idea of the prevailing rate, and ask them if it's tied to chores and if their boy has to buy some necessities from it. Then look at your income and make a decision.

Finally, you can help your boy with his allowance if he asks you to. You can give him pointers on saving, budgeting, and investing, and you can get him to think about foregoing spending his money on little things in order to save up for a big thing. Also, it's a good idea to monitor your boy's spending habits to see how well he does handle his money. It will give you a good insight into his values and character.

Three Things You Must Do

1. Give him an allowance.
2. Give him complete control of his money.
3. Give him advice when he asks for it.

Things to Say and Do

Talk to your boy about an allowance. Ask him if his friends have an allowance, how much it is, and if they have to work for it. Say such things as:

- I think it's time you got an allowance.
- How much do you think would be fair?
- What do your friends get? Do you know?
- Do they have to do any work for their allowance?

Tell your boy why you're giving him an allowance and what he has to do for it and with it, if anything. Say such things as:

- We want you to learn the value of money and we think this is the best way. Your allowance will be yours to control. You can spend it on whatever you like, you can save it, you can invest it, you can give it to charity. It's up to you.
- We are going to give you an allowance but to get it you have to do some jobs around the house.
- We're going to give you an allowance but you have to buy your school supplies from it. And if you want a new game, you'll have to save up for it from your allowance.

If your boy wants your help in managing his money don't hesitate to help. Say such things as:

- What can we help you with?
- Do you want to open a savings account at the bank? We can help you.
- One of the things we do is work out our expenses for each week and see how much they will cost. We compare that to the amount of money we have.

If you want to, offer your boy money for jobs you need done around the house. Say such things as:

- If you will cut the grass each week I'll pay you for it.
- Helping me rake leaves and weed the garden can mean extra money for you.
- If you do the vacuuming on Saturday morning I'll pay you for it.

Words, Phrases, and Actions to Use

- . . . allowance . . .
- . . . money . . .
- . . . bank account . . .
- . . . saving up . . .
- . . . necessities . . .
- . . . luxuries . . .
- . . . needs . . .
- . . . wants . . .
- Save up for a rainy day.

Things Not to Say and Do

Don't refuse to give your boy an allowance. Don't say such things as:

- You're not getting any money from me. Any money you want you'll have to work for.
- You're not good enough with money. No allowance for you.
- I don't care if all your friends get allowances, we're not giving you one.

Don't tie all your boy's chores to money. You want him to learn that everyone in the family has work to do for the good of all, without being paid for it. Don't say such things as:

- I'll pay you to keep your room tidy.
- I'll pay you to do your homework.
- I'll pay you to walk the dog.

Don't control your boy's spending. Don't say such things as:

- I'll give you an allowance but you can't spend it without my approval.
- You're bad with money so I'm going to keep control of your spending.
- You waste your money on such stupid things. I'm cutting off your allowance.

Words, Phrases, and Actions to Avoid

- . . . wasted . . .
- You're irresponsible.
- You're untrustworthy.
- You'll never learn.
- That's not a necessity.
- You're stupid.
- You're unreliable.

BOOKS AND READING

◆

You've always encouraged your boy to read. You started reading to him when he was a baby. Every day there was story time. When he was a year old he began "reading" books for himself, but you still had a special time each day when the two of you sat down and read together. By the time he was in second grade he was really reading for himself. You didn't care what he read as long as he was reading. You figured that imposing your tastes, or the tastes of "experts," on your boy's reading habits would have one result: it would turn him off reading. So your policy has always been that within reason he chooses what he reads—comics, Harry Potter, sports magazines, or anything else. You welcomed his interest in computers and the Internet because boys who wanted them needed to read and write (type). As your boy has grown he has never shown any signs of giving up his habit of reading. His good schoolwork is a tribute to the importance of reading in school success. You know that his love of reading will be an asset for him for his whole life.

Things to Consider

When it comes to reading girls have an advantage over boys from the beginning. Research shows that reading uses both brain hemispheres. Girls are principally left-brained and boys right-brained, but girls are better able to use both halves of the brain because the nerve connections between the two are much larger and more developed in girls than in boys. So girls typically read better and start reading at an earlier age than boys do. The data also shows that boys have reading problems at three times the rate of girls.

Because reading is the most important factor in school success, reading problems are more than likely the principle cause of boys having a reported three times the learning problems that girls have. Therefore, you can never give your boy too much encouragement and practice in reading.

Wonderful books are continually being written. You can buy these books for your boy as birthday and holiday presents. Or you can buy them just because you think your boy will enjoy reading them. When our boys were young we told them that we would not buy them every toy they asked for, but we would never refuse to buy them a book they wanted.

Although you should let your boy choose his own reading material, you do need to keep in touch with his tastes. Know what he's reading. Ask him to tell you about it. Ask if you can read it when he's done. If you think he's getting misinformation, or dangerously slanted or prejudiced views of people from it, you need to discuss it with him and make sure he understands how to be a critical reader. Show him how to ask questions of what he reads, to look for evidence that supports what it claims to be true, and to compare it to his own experience. Encourage him to talk to you about any ideas or facts that he finds surprising or disturbing. There's no better way of developing and carrying on a good communicative relationship with your boy than reading the same things your boy reads and then discussing them with him.

Talking with your boy about what he reads helps him develop verbal fluency that will help him in school. Boys, being naturally less verbally proficient than girls, need more time and practice in expressing ideas in speech and in writing. Other ways to use reading as a means to develop this connection between having thoughts and expressing them is to encourage your boy to draw pictures of the stories he reads, to make up games using the characters and plots from novels, and to write his own stories.

The enjoyment of books and reading is a critical part of your boy's education, both at home and at school. Help your boy along this path in every way you can.

Three Things You Must Do

1. Surround him with reading material suitable for his age and ability.
2. Let him choose his own things to read for his own pleasure.
3. Discuss his reading with him and teach him to be a critical reader.

Things to Say and Do

Encourage your boy to read. Have lots of books around the home. Subscribe to magazines he likes to read. Get a daily newspaper. Say such things as:

- Here's a book you might like to read.
- Did you read that story about schoolboys in today's paper?
- If you like I'll get you a subscription to that magazine you enjoy so much.

Read some of the things your boy likes to read, then discuss them with him. Say such things as:

- I've just read that book you liked so much. What did you think about that boy who was really a wizard?

- Do you ever wish you could be like that boy in your book?
- What did you think of that teacher who was always mean to some of the kids?

Tell your boy that within reason you don't mind what he reads as long as it makes him want to read. Say such things as:

- I know lots of teachers and parents tell their boys what they can and cannot read. I don't agree. As long as you like something I'm happy for you to read it.
- Reading is the most important skill you can have because it helps you in everything you do. That's why I don't mind what you read as long as you read.
- Read whatever you want as long as it's something you can understand and know how to handle.

If you agree to let your boy read what he likes then it's even more important that you teach him to be a critical reader. Say such things as:

- Never believe everything you read.
- When you read novels and short stories you know that someone has made up the stories and they're generally not real life.
- When you read things in books, in magazines, in newspapers, and on the Internet you must always question whether or not it's true because people write lots of things that aren't true.

Encourage your boy to write his own stories. If he's artistic, have him draw pictures about the things he's read. Say such things as:

- You like reading so much, how about writing some stories of your own?
- Why don't you make up a story about a boy like yourself?
- Draw some pictures that tell the story you just read.

Be a good reading role model for your boy. Show him how much you like to read.

Words, Phrases, and Actions to Use

- Reading is great.
- Don't believe everything you read.
- Be a critical reader.
- Read whatever you want.
- Let's talk about what you read.
- Can I read your book?
- Who did you like?
- Who didn't you like?
- Who's your favorite writer?

Things Not to Say and Do

Don't censor your boy's reading unless you have very good reasons for doing so. Don't say such things as:

- I won't have you reading such trash.
- You're not allowed to read about wizards and witches.
- I don't want you reading anything without asking me first.

Don't discourage your boy from reading. If your boy says he's reading, don't say such things as:

- Then you're not really busy. Please take out the garbage.
- Reading is such a waste of time. You should be doing something useful.
- You read too much. Go out and play with your friends.

Don't criticize your boy if he doesn't read well, as long as he tries. Don't say such things as:

- Why can't you read like your sister?
- You're a poor reader. I don't know why you even bother.
- You'll never get any better. You might as well give up.

Don't be a bad role model. Don't say such things as:

- Reading is a waste of time. You can't believe anything you read anyway, so why bother.
- I don't ever read novels. They're useless.
- If I spent as much time reading as you do I would never get anything useful done.

Words, Phrases, and Actions to Avoid

- That's stupid.
- That's a waste of time.
- Books are boring.
- Do something useful.
- Reading never did anything for me.
- You'll read what I tell you to read.

CLOTHES

◆

You have discovered that a preoccupation with the right clothes and the "right look" is not just a girl thing. Your boy has reached the age during which his clothes really matter to him. He wants the right labels and the right styles. He wants to look like his friends. The only problem is that being in style costs a lot of money. You wonder what you can say to your boy to make him realize that you can't afford to keep him in the style to which he would like to become accustomed. You find yourself wishing that your boy's school had school uniforms so the clothing problem would solve itself, at least on that front. Whenever you attend parents' meetings at your boy's school, some parents and school administrators inevitably raise the issue of appropriate school clothing. The school principal urges you to make sure your child dresses appropriately, which means neutral (no gang affiliation), clean, and untorn clothes for boys, and modest, unexciting clothes for girls. These discussions make you wish even more for school uniforms. You know your boy doesn't like the idea, but you're sure he'd get used to it.

Things to Consider

Your boy is a preadolescent and he's reaching an age during which the clothes he chooses to wear will make an important statement about who he is. Even now, you can see the beginnings of self-assertion in his choice of shirts, T-shirts, jeans, trousers, and shoes. They say, "Look at me! This is who I am." Girls in his class have already matured far beyond him, both physically and socially. By grade six many of the twelve-year-old girls have reached puberty. It's hard for your boy, whether he's nine, ten, eleven, or twelve, to ignore the sexual messages that these girls innocently send out. Whether he's aware of it or not, he wants to wear clothes that girls find attractive.

Although he doesn't yet have a strong, conscious sexual desire, or all the social skills he needs to begin thinking seriously about relationships with girls, he wants to dress in a way that girls will notice. But he still needs approval from the boys in his group. He wants them to know by his clothes that he's one of them. He shares their tastes, their values, their attitudes, and the need to be part of them. He dresses to show that solidarity, to differentiate himself from boys in other groups, and to differentiate himself from girls.

As your boy gets older this need will increase until in high school it reaches its peak. The period between the ages of nine and twelve is a prelude to this. And you have to live with it.

If your boy's school requires uniforms you're in many ways fortunate. You only have half the problem that other parents have. You only have to worry about clothes for play and going out. If you're unfortunate you also have to worry about school clothes. However, be thankful you have a boy rather than a girl. Although boys are very clothes conscious, even at this age, girls are more so, and the choices among girls' clothes are greater, more expensive, and more problematic. With boys you don't have to worry about the problem of short skirts, see-through blouses, low-riding jeans, and high-riding blouses and sweaters. Boys' fashions don't offer the same opportunities to go beyond the limits of decorum and good taste in the clothes as girls' fashions.

Most schools will have a dress code, even if they don't have uniforms. These typically prohibit clothes that are too revealing, too gang related, too dirty, or too distracting for others. This makes your job a bit easier.

These are the big clothing issues for your boy:

- Cost—how much are you willing and able to spend to keep your boy in fashion?
- Style—do you approve of the styles your boy wants to wear?
- School dress code—do you know your school's dress code and how you can enforce it in your boy?
- Age appropriateness—do you insist that your boy dress like you feel he should for his age and not like his teen idols?
- Self-expression—do you believe that your boy should be allowed to express his individuality through his clothes in whatever form that might take?

Three Things You Must Do

1. Make sure your boy's clothes are clean, neat, and appropriate for the occasion.
2. Recognize that your boy's view of what is clean, neat, and appropriate may differ from yours.
3. Pick your battles and don't get upset about the small things.

Things to Say and Do

Talk to your boy about his taste in clothes. Ask him what he wants and why he wants it. Say such things as:

- Do you like what that boy is wearing?
- What's the latest thing for boys your age to wear?
- Why is that so cool?

Go shopping with your boy and see the styles available. Keep a lookout for what other boys are wearing. Say such things as:

- Let's go shopping. I want to see what kind of clothes the stores have for boys your age, and I want to see what they cost.
- What do you want?
- How much does it cost?

Talk about the cost of clothes and what you can afford. Let your boy save up from his allowance for clothing that you don't think is a necessity. Say such things as:

- This is what we can afford and this is what we can't.
- We want you to be able to dress like your friends, but we have a limited budget.
- If you really want that you'll have to save up from your allowance.

Tell your boy what your standards are for his clothes. Say such things as:

- I don't like it when you dress like that. As far as I'm concerned it seems to say you don't care about other people.
- You can't wear clothes that are dirty and torn.
- You can wear that, but you know there are limits. My limits and your school's limits and our community's limits.
- When you go out with us we'd like you to dress appropriately. We want people to see that you know the right thing to wear to go to a restaurant or to our church/synagogue/temple/mosque.

Words, Phrases, and Actions to Use

- ...cost...
- ...limits...
- ...dress code...
- ...for school...
- ...for play...

- ...for going out...
- ...our standards of dress...
- Be clean.
- Be neat.
- Be appropriate.

Things Not to Say and Do

Don't tell your boy that you don't care what he wears. Don't say such things as:

- Wear whatever you like.
- I don't care if you look like a slob.
- Just don't tell people you're my boy.

Don't let him violate his school's dress code. Don't say such things as:

- Schools have no place in telling you what to wear.
- I don't care what the school will do to you, you can wear whatever you like.
- You'll get into trouble, but I don't care if you don't care.

Don't buy your boy whatever he wants, no matter how wealthy you are. Don't say such things as:

- Let's go shopping. I'll buy you whatever clothes you want.
- Price isn't important. Let's get it.
- You're rich so you should dress like a rich kid.

Don't refuse to buy your boy the clothes he needs. Don't say such things as:

- I can afford it, but you're not getting it because I don't think you need to dress like your friends.
- You can wear the clothes I bought you last year. They're only a little too small.
- Your clothes may be dirty and torn and don't fit, but that's okay with me. I'm not buying you any new stuff.

Words, Phrases, and Actions to Avoid

- Wear whatever you like.
- Until you can afford to buy your own clothes you'll wear what I tell you.
- I don't care what your friends wear.
- Dress codes stink.
- I don't care about what others think.
- You look awful in everything.

COMPUTERS, VIDEO GAMES, MOVIES, AND TV

◆

Although your boy has been using computers since he began school (and for some boys, before that), he is now hooked on the Internet and spends time exploring Websites and playing video and computer games. He uses the computer at school as well as the one you have at home. His friends have computers. He e-mails them, and goes into chat rooms for boys. He wants to create his own Website. You take him to the movies when there's something special to see and you let him watch movies on television as well as on the VCR or DVD player. His TV viewing consists of cartoons on Saturday and Sunday mornings and other kids' shows. But most of the time he's playing games on the television or the computer. You wonder how much you should control and monitor his doing all of these things.

Things to Consider

Most boys love things electronic. Computers, TV shows, movies, and electronic games can hold your boy's interest for hours. You know he has more sources of electronic information and entertainment than you ever had. Although much of what's available from TV and computers has positive entertainment and educational value, there are also many unacceptable or harmful sites and programs. Although you can't completely protect your boy from encountering these, you can go a long way toward making your home a safe environment for his electronic viewing and playing.

Know what your boy is watching and playing and whom he is talking to via the Internet. You can control this by preventing him from watching extremely violent movies, playing video and computer games that reward killing and destroying people and animals, or visiting pornographic sites on the Internet. You can warn him of Internet chat rooms and bulletin boards where he might be talking to adults pretending to be young boys in order to establish relationships with them. Encourage him to visit Websites that you know provide good educational viewing and entertainment.

Keep your computer in an area of the house where you can monitor it. You can buy computer programs called filters that will allow you to prevent your boy from logging on to specific sites and to generic sites that are or could potentially be harmful to him. You can also program your TV, if you subscribe to cable or have a satellite dish, to prevent him from watching specific programs. At this age your son should not have the use of a credit card, which most pornographic sites require for access. But if you have any suspicions, carefully check your statements each month.

Don't allow violent video and computer games and movies into your house. It's important to know your son's friends. Talk to their parents to see if they have rules and values similar to yours regarding kids' movies, games, and Internet use.

On the other hand your son needs to share the experiences of his friends. Even at his young age it's important for him to know what they know and be able to talk about the movies, TV programs, and video and computer games that they talk about. Be strict and careful in your supervision, but be fair and realistic. You can't shelter him from everything. If you are doing your job and teaching your child the right values you can begin to trust him to make good decisions, with your guidance.

That's where good communication comes in. Nothing is more important than having a good communicative relationship with him so that you can talk freely about values and the good and bad TV programs, movies, games, and Internet sites. You have gained your son's trust by your habit of listening to him and not harshly judging what he tells you. You have taught him good values through your words and deeds. He knows that he can discuss anything with you, and you with him. You are always there for him and he understands and appreciates that.

Three Things You Must Do

1. Have rules about what is, and is not, acceptable material.
2. Monitor your boy's viewing, surfing, and playing.
3. Talk regularly and without judging.

What to Say and Do

Know what your son and his friends like to do with computers. Say such things as:

- What are your favorite Internet sites?
- What sites do your friends like to visit?
- Have you got any sites bookmarked? Can I see them?
- Do you like to surf the Web or play games?

Know the games and movies your son and his friends like. Say such things as:

- I know the games we have for you on our computer. What games do your friends have?
- Do you play computer games at school?
- Do you ever watch movies at your friend's house? What do you watch?
- I'd like to know what movies you're going to watch before you watch them.

Know what computers your son has available to him. Say such things as:

- Do you use your friends' computers?
- How often do you get to use the computers at school?

Talk about restricted sites on the computer and TV. Say such things as:

- You know that I try to restrict what you see on the computer and TV because there are things that are too violent, too sexual, or too hateful for a boy your age.
- Can your friends watch anything they want on TV?
- Do they have any restrictions on what they do with their computer?

Sit down with your son and work on the computer together, play games together, visit Websites that you think are good for him. Let him show you Websites he likes. Talk about them. Say such things as:

- Do you know how to get onto the Internet?
- What do you think of this Website?
- Show me the Websites you like.

Watch movies together and talk about them afterward.

Words, Phrases, and Actions to Use

- Would you show me your Internet?
- ... bookmarks ...
- ... games ...
- ... movies ...
- ... World Wide Web ...
- ... surfing the net ...
- ... my approval ...
- I'd like to know ...
- Let's talk about ...
- What do you think?
- That's inappropriate.

What Not to Say and Do

Don't give your son total freedom to surf the Internet. Don't say such things as:

- You can look at whatever you want. It's good for your education.
- As long as your friends can go there it's okay with me.

Don't shirk from your responsibility to monitor or control what video or computer games your son plays and what movies he watches. Don't say such things as:

- These video and computer games are harmless.
- Kids can always tell the difference between fantasy and reality.
- All movies are fake, so they're all right for you to watch.

Don't miss an opportunity to talk about what's appropriate for a boy his age and what isn't. Don't say such things as:

- I don't want to waste my time talking about those things. Do what you want.
- You'll do whatever I say so we don't need to talk about it.
- I don't have time to talk now. We'll do it later.

Words, Phrases, and Actions to Avoid

- Don't bother me.
- How could you watch/play such crap?
- I don't want to talk about it.
- Just do as I say.
- No more computer/TV for you for a month.
- That's trash.
- You sneaky little devil.
- I don't care.
- Look at whatever you want to.

DISCIPLINE

◆

Your boy, like all boys, sometimes gets into trouble at home or at school. He's not a bad boy, yet you sometimes worry about his behavior. You don't want little mistakes to grow into big ones. You wonder about the best way to discipline him now that he's a preadolescent. You ask yourself questions like: What do I want to achieve by disciplining him and how can I best achieve it? Which methods work and which don't? Is punishment the right way to think about teaching him to do the right thing? Should I really be thinking about how to teach him self-discipline? Does grounding him really make him realize that what he did was wrong? Do time-outs work? Does withdrawing privileges or cutting off his allowance work? Will that stop him from repeating the misbehavior? You wonder what the best way is.

Things to Consider

Brain differences between boys and girls show themselves in many ways. We see that boys are more likely to take risks, more competitive, more aggressive, quicker to react to threatening situations, less likely to put their feelings and thoughts into words, and more likely to put them into actions. All of these differences, and more, mean that you need to give more attention to how best to discipline your son.

To begin you must ask yourself what the larger context is for disciplining your boy. What's the big picture? Are you simply reacting to each thing your boy does as a onetime thing, or are you building in him something like *a system of self-discipline* that he can draw upon to sustain himself whenever he's confronted by choices that he has to make about what to do or not do?

Of course you have to do both. You must teach your boy why he shouldn't have done what he did. You must also help him realize how to fit this experience into this self-guidance system that you want him to internalize.

What does this system of discipline and self-discipline really mean? It means to help your boy:

- Love himself and others.
- Value his own opinion of himself as well as the opinion of others.

- Learn to put his feelings into words or other ways of expressing himself, rather than into physical violence.
- Respect the legitimate authority of others.
- Respect the rights and property of others, including their bodies.
- Empathize with others.
- Do unto others as he would have others do unto him.

This is not a complete list of all the components of such a system, nor is it the way you might want to express it in terms of your own personal, social, or religious philosophy. But it can be a starting point from which you can develop your own plan for disciplining your son. Michael Gurian suggests a system of his own in *The Wonder of Boys*. His list of ten elements includes consistency, leadership, respect, variety, recrimination, spiritual context, choices, respect for feelings, authoritative structure, and early, ongoing, and adaptive use.

You can see that there is more than one way to understand discipline. But there is a common thread. Your system of discipline is for your boy's sake, not yours. It's to help him be a good person who relates well to himself, his friends and family, the whole community, and any situation in which he finds himself.

How do you implement your system? You can do the following:

- Stop your boy from doing anything hurtful or destructive to other people or property.
- Remove him from the situation.
- Ask him if he knows that what he did was wrong and why.
- Ask him to tell you if he knows how it affects others.
- Ask him if he knows what the consequences of his actions will be for himself.
- Talk to him about those consequences.
- Enforce those consequences consistently.
- Make those consequences things that will positively reinforce the system of self-discipline you're teaching.
- Tell your boy that you love him, not for what he has done, which was wrong, but because he is your son.
- If you ever blame or discipline your boy by mistake, admit your error and apologize.
- Monitor your boy's behavior and see if there are any patterns that need to be changed.
- Acknowledge and reinforce your boy's good behavior with praise and love.
- Model good self-discipline for your boy.
- Never hit your boy.

Three Things You Must Do

1. Have a consistent, fair system of discipline.
2. Make that system for your boy's sake, not yours.
3. Help your boy develop good self-discipline.

Things to Say and Do

Stop your boy from doing anything hurtful or destructive to other people or property. Say such things as:

- You know that's the wrong thing to do.
- You must stop that immediately.
- That's unacceptable behavior.

Once you've stopped him from doing what he's doing, remove him from the situation. Ask him if he knows that what he did was wrong and why. Say such things as:

- Can you tell me what you were doing wrong?
- Why were you doing that?
- You know that what you were doing was wrong. Why is that?

Ask him to tell you if he knows how it affects others. You're testing his empathetic sense, which may be lacking under the circumstances. Say such things as:

- How do you think what you've done makes "Mary" feel?
- Do you care about how "Robby" feels?

Ask him if he knows what the consequences of his actions will be for himself. Talk to him about those consequences. Say such things as:

- What do you think is going to happen to you now? What do you think should happen?
- What can we do to make sure you don't do this again?
- Here is what is going to happen now and this is why it's going to happen.

Enforce those consequences consistently. Make those consequences things that will positively reinforce the system of self-discipline you're teaching. Discuss the behavior and what was wrong with it. Say such things as:

- Do you know why what you did was wrong? Let's talk about it.
- Let's talk about what the world would be like if everyone behaved the way you just did.
- Why am I unhappy about what you did?

Never hit your boy. Tell your boy that you love him, not for what he has done, which was wrong, but because he is your son. Say such things as:

- You know that I will love you in spite of what you do. But you also know that what you did was very wrong.

If you ever blame or discipline your boy by mistake, admit your error and apologize. Say such things as:

- I know now that you didn't do it, and I'm sorry I blamed you and didn't believe you.

Monitor your boy's behavior and see if there are any patterns that need to be changed. Acknowledge and reinforce your boy's good behavior with praise and love. Say such things as:

- That was a wonderful thing to do.
- I'm so proud of you.
- You are a good boy.

Take every opportunity to encourage your boy to express his feelings. Say such things as:

- I know you were angry. Next time try talking instead of fighting.
- Let me show you how to move around when you're angry.
- What kind of noises would you make if you were angry?
- Can you draw a picture that tells me what you're angry about and what you want to do about it?

Be a model of good self-discipline for your boy.

Words, Phrases, and Actions to Use

- ... consequences ...
- ... empathy ...
- Do you know why?
- That's unacceptable.
- I need to be able to trust you.
- Explain.
- Understand.
- Let's talk about it.
- You can think it or say it but don't do it.
- Like yourself.
- Like others.
- Have respect.

Things Not to Say and Do

Don't let your boy get away with being mean or hurtful to others. Don't say such things as:

- Do what you like.
- I don't care.
- It doesn't matter to me.

Don't let your boy be physically aggressive in anger. Don't say such things as:

- If he bugs you hit him.
- She deserved what she got.
- I'd have hit him too.

Don't be inconsistent in your discipline. Don't say such things as:

- I know I said you could do it, but I changed my mind so now you're going to be punished.
- I think I'll give extra punishment this time.
- You're grounded for a week. What happened last time doesn't matter.

Don't refuse to discuss the problem or the discipline. Don't say such things as:

- I don't want to discuss it.
- There's nothing to discuss.
- Just do what I say and don't ask any stupid questions.

Don't threaten to cut off your relationship with your boy because of his misbehavior. Don't say such things as:

- You're not my boy anymore.
- I can't love you anymore.

Never hit your boy.

Words, Phrases, and Actions to Avoid

- You're a loser.
- Keep your feelings to yourself.
- I'm going to beat you.
- You'll regret you ever did that.
- I'm not interested.
- You liar.
- I don't care.
- Do what you like.

EMPATHY

◆

The older you get the more you think that developing a good empathetic sense is one of the most important things your boy can do. Too often you see people going about their lives as though they were the only ones in the world who mattered. They seem to give no thought to the effect of their actions on others. They seem so inconsiderate. You see no sign that they can escape their own self-centeredness and put themselves in others' shoes. You don't want your boy to turn out this way. You will work to constantly remind him to think about the effect anything he might do will have on others. Above all you want him to understand what others might be thinking or feeling when they do something, and not judge them from only his own selfish perspective. You want to realize that others do what they do, feel what they feel, and think what they think for good reasons, even if that isn't the way he sees it. You think a good empathetic sense is one of the best attributes a good man can have.

Things to Consider

Many people, both men and women, believe that when God handed out the genes for empathy, he forgot to give them to the male of the species. Males are stereotyped as relatively unfeeling, insensitive, and unperceptive. It goes even farther than that. We identify sensitivity and empathy as feminine traits so much that we question the masculinity of men who have them. So, like most stereotypes, this one is self-fulfilling because we notice men who reinforce it and choose to ignore those who don't, saying they aren't real men.

The first thing I want to do is dispel the notion that boys aren't capable of empathy. It is true that the level of the male hormone, testosterone, is, on average, twenty times higher in boys than in girls, while the levels of estrogen and progesterone, the female and the bonding hormones, are relatively low in boys and high in girls. This hormone difference makes it more difficult for boys to be empathetic since their first reaction to a problem tends to be aggression. As a result, boys need more education and practice in empathy.

Your boy is now old enough at age nine or ten to have a well-developed empathetic sense, to be sensitive and to care deeply about others. He just may have inadequate ways of showing it because, as a boy, he has less facility with expressing his feelings in words rather than actions. Girls certainly seem to find it easier to talk to others about their feelings. Boys find it easier to express their feelings in physical activity, but even there they are less likely to express empathetic feelings like love, caring, sympathy, and understanding with hugs and kisses. Social norms tell us that girls are allowed to hug and kiss boys and girls. Boys are allowed to hug and kiss girls but not other boys.

The job of teaching your boy to be empathetic is more difficult than if he were a she. You not only must teach your boy to pay attention to the needs and feelings of others, you also must show him how to show others that he's doing it.

Michael Gurian points out in *The Wonder of Boys* that boys' task-oriented, problem-solving nature affects their empathetic responses to others. Boys need to see a problem-solving, social, or practical purpose in empathy, otherwise they will redirect their energies toward the task at hand. Not all boys are like this, but enough are so that we see this behavior as characteristically male.

To help your boy develop his empathetic sense you need to use his natural predisposition toward aggressive behavior by encouraging him to act out his feelings of understanding, concern, and sympathy for others. Show him that that's as much of a worthwhile task as winning a game, race, or fight. In other words teach your boy that empathy is a worthwhile task in itself.

Part of this training involves showing your boy, through your own words and deeds, that he has a responsibility for the well-being of others, not just himself. Involve him in charity work, for example, or in volunteering to raise money for others less fortunate. Ask his teacher to let him help teach other children in the class when he's good at something that they are not. You can encourage him to do the same thing in any sports in which he's involved.

The other part of this training involves giving your boy the words to use to express his feelings for others. Encourage him to put his feelings into words. Doing this accomplishes two things: it teaches him to have feelings for the situation of other people, and it gives him a means to express those feelings.

Three Things You Must Do

1. Teach your boy to put himself in other's shoes.
2. Show him that empathy is a worthwhile feeling in itself.
3. Teach him how to express his feelings and concern for others in words and actions.

Things to Say and Do

Be a good role model for your boy. Show him that you feel responsible for others and that you have a concern for their well-being. Say such things as:

- Isn't it sad that so many children in this world grow up poor?
- I think we should do something to help them. What do you think?
- I feel that we are all responsible in some way for everyone else. Do you ever feel that way?

Encourage your boy to join groups that help others. He can become a scout, become a member of a youth group at your place of worship, or join a community group that does charity work. Say such things as:

- If you want to help others you can become a Boy Scout.
- Would you like me to help you find some group in town that works at helping poor kids?
- What do you think you could do to make a difference in the lives of kids who don't have as much as you do?

Teach your boy to express his empathetic feelings in words. Say such things as:

- If you feel sorry for someone you ought to say so.
- If you love someone you can say, "I love you."
- If someone gets hurt you can say, "That looks like a bad cut. Let me help you."
- If you think that your friend hurt himself in a game, what would you say to him?

Talk to your boy about the value of empathy as a worthwhile feeling in itself. Talk about it in language that he'd understand. Say such things as:

- It's a good thing to feel concern about other people.
- I'm so proud of you. You stopped what you were doing to help that boy.
- How does it make you feel when you've tried to help someone else? I know it makes me feel really good.

Words, Phrases, and Actions to Use

- . . . responsibility for others . . .
- . . . empathy . . .
- . . . sympathy . . .
- . . . feelings . . .
- . . . concern . . .
- . . . love . . .
- . . . understanding . . .

- Good work.
- How do you feel?
- Can I help?
- What's wrong?
- Let me fix it for you.
- I'm here for you.

Things Not to Say and Do

Don't discourage your boy's natural instinct to be empathetic. Don't say such things as:

- "Me first." That's my motto. It should be yours too.
- You don't have to worry about anyone but yourself.
- Why should you help anyone else? What have they done for you?

Don't discourage your boy's desire to help others. Don't say such things as:

- Winning is the only important thing.
- You have to beat out everyone else, so don't help them beat you.
- Life is a race. In order to win you have to beat the others. So you can't win by helping them.

Don't be a bad role model for you boy. Don't say such things as:

- I don't care about anyone but myself.
- People only need your help because they're lazy.
- I don't help others because they wouldn't help me.

Words, Phrases, and Actions to Avoid

- It's okay to be selfish.
- Watch out for yourself.
- They don't need help.
- Help yourself.
- Nobody cares about you.
- You're on your own.
- You come first.

FRIENDS

◆

You noticed that your daughter started making close friends years before your son did. Now that your son has a close friend you see that the relationship is different from your daughter's relationship with her friend. Hers involves talking and sharing thoughts and feelings. His revolves around doing activities together like building things, playing sports, and competing in electronic and computer games. You realize that there is nothing more important to your son and your daughter than their friends. You see that he has reached that stage in his development where he can have strong feelings for the welfare of someone other than himself. Experts say that these early feelings for someone else mark the beginning of your boy's ability to create a relationship, which ultimately expresses itself as love between two people.

Things to Consider

Girls form same-sex friendships earlier than boys do. Girls may be genetically wired to do this. From a young age they have excellent role models in their mother and other women to nurture relationships with others. Young boys tend to do things in packs. Around age nine they begin to show a developing capacity for single friendships with other boys. Relatively few boys have girls as close friends until adolescence when their desire to have close relationships turns from other boys to girls.

It seems that late-maturing boys may do better in relationships later in life because their sexual interest in females is delayed while they form strong and lasting friendships that have no strong sexual content with both boys and girls. However, it is hard to expect preadolescent boys to ignore the sexual aspects of relationships with girls when they are bombarded with programs and magazines full of sexual content. Your job as a parent is to help your boy keep sex out of friendship until your boy is emotionally, physically, and socially mature enough to handle it.

There are a number of ways you can help your boy with his friendships. First, when you notice that he has developed some early friendships, you can help him understand exactly what friendship means. Talk to him about how friends do things for each other, help each other, exchange dreams and wishes, share experiences, and care for each other.

Second, you can talk to your boy about your own friendships, past and present.

Describe your childhood friends. Tell stories about what you and your friends did when you were your boy's age. Most boys love hearing their parents tell stories about their childhood adventures (at least the first few times). Talk about the way your friendships developed and how they grew and changed over the years. Share the wonderful experiences you've had when you see an old friend after many years and can pick up from where you left off as though it were yesterday.

Third, encourage your boy to talk about his friends, about who they are, who their parents are, why he likes them, and what he likes doing with them. Make sure that your home is open to your boy and his friends. This will give you two advantages. You will get to know your boy's friends very well. And you will know where your boy is and what he's doing.

Parents always worry about their children's ability to make and keep friends. Any help you can give your boy in the art of friendship, without being pushy or intruding on his life, will be a plus for him and for you.

Three Things You Must Do

1. Encourage your boy to develop close friendships.
2. Talk to your boy about the meaning of friendship.
3. Make your boy's friends welcome in your home.

Things to Say and Do

Encourage your boy to make close friends. Say such things as:

- I'm glad to see you have a good friend.
- Having a few really good friends is just as important as having lots of friends.
- You really like "Joe," don't you? I think that's great. He's a good friend to you.

Talk to your boy about the meaning of friendship. Help him understand what friends mean to each other and how they act toward each other. Say such things as:

- Being a friend means listening to your friend talk about things that are important to him.
- Friends always stick up for each other.
- A good friend will know when his friend is in trouble and will try to help him.
- Good friends can trust each other, always.
- You can tell a good friend anything, and he won't get angry.

Talk to your boy about your own friendships over the years. Tell stories and explain your relationships. Say such things as:

- Let me tell you about my best friend when I was your age.
- We used to do the craziest things. That's why I'm not surprised when you do crazy things.
- One day my friend and I went on a hike and got lost. Boy, were we scared.
- I still have friends that I made when I was in grade six.

Tell your boy that he can always bring his friends home to his place. Say such things as:

- I like it when you and your friends come here and play.
- You can bring your friends here anytime you like.
- I am always happy to have your friends here, and they can sleep over if you want and they have their parents' permission.

Whenever your boy is going out to play with his friends make sure you know where he will be. Say such things as:

- I'll always let you play with your friends, but you must always let me know where you will be.
- The rule is that I must always know where you're playing with your friends.

Words, Phrases, and Actions to Use

- . . . friends . . .
- . . . close . . .
- Real friends are treasures.
- . . . like . . .
- . . . pal . . .
- . . . trust . . .
- . . . fun . . .
- Don't judge.

Things Not to Say and Do

Don't discourage your boy from developing good, close friendships. Don't say such things as:

- You don't need any friends; you've got your family.
- Friends always disappoint you.

- Don't think he's your friend just because he says so. Make him prove it.
- I don't see why anyone would want to be your friend.

Don't ignore your boy's friends. Don't say such things as:

- I don't care who your friends are, just keep them out of my hair.
- Do you have any friends? I don't think so.
- I'm not interested in your friends.

Don't prohibit your boy's friends from coming to your home. Don't say such things as:

- I don't want you and your friends here. You make such a mess.
- Keep your friends outside.
- No friends allowed.

Don't stop your boy from doing things with his friends, as long as they are safe. Don't say such things as:

- No, you can't go.
- No, you can't sleep over.
- No, you have to help me with the chores.

Don't refuse to talk to your boy about friendship. Don't say things like:

- I don't want to talk about it.
- Maybe later, I'm too busy.
- I don't think friendship is very important so I don't want to talk about it.

Words, Phrases, and Actions to Avoid

- You're worthless.
- You're untrustworthy.
- Don't bother me.
- You're stupid.
- You don't need friends.
- Friends are a waste of time.
- Who'd want you as a friend?

GIRLS

◆

Although your boy is only ten years old, you've noticed that his attitude toward girls seems to be changing. He's started talking about the girls in his class more than he ever did before. He seems especially interested in one pretty little girl. He seems interested in what she says about him, where she may be hanging out on the weekend, and who her friends are. You've seen your boy and others teasing this girl and others, pulling on their coats and backpacks, throwing snowballs at them, and chasing them. You recognize these actions as typical preadolescent sexual behavior. Your boy shows no outward signs of the onset of puberty, but this new and different interest in this girl, not just as a friend or playmate, but as a girl, makes you wonder if something isn't going on that you can't see. You think you better start talking to him about girls, if you haven't already done so, so that he has a good sense of what the opposite sex is really like. You want him to develop a realistic, wholesome, and positive attitude toward girls before he reaches adolescence and the full blast of hormones starts running through his veins.

Things to Consider

It may be that the most important thing you can teach your preadolescent boy about girls is thoughtfulness. Teach him to think about and behave toward girls with respect, consideration, empathy, and appreciation of the differences between the sexes. It's likely he already knows about most of the obvious physical differences between boys and girls, and between pre- and postpubescent girls. You can add to his knowledge by talking about some of the differences he's observed but may not quite understand.

Your boy may say, even at his age, that he has fallen in love. It's not unusual. On Valentine's Day in middle and junior high school cards fly fast and furious between boys and girls even though puberty may still be years away for most of the children in grades five through seven. Aside from the natural feelings your boy may have about girls in general, or one girl in particular, what would you like your boy to know about girls?

Here are a few things that you might want to consider when you talk to your boy about girls. Knowing them will help you understand some of the more important differences between boys and girls, as well as your boy's feelings about girls and their feelings about him. (The following generalizations, taken from a variety of sources, don't take specific individual differences among girls and boys into account, which is something you and your boy must do.)

- Girls are not helpless or fragile.
- Girls are strong.
- Girls are determined.
- Girls are competitive.
- Girls are ambitious.
- Girls cooperate with each other.
- Girls value sharing.
- Girls like to talk things through.
- Girls value emotional and physical closeness.
- Girls value intimacy in relationships.
- Girls value security in relationships.
- Girls value commitment.
- Girls are not victims.
- Girls are good listeners and talkers.
- Girls do not value risk-taking the way boys do.
- Girls look beneath the surface of a boy to find the real person.
- Girls value aggression in boys, but not violence.
- Girls like sex but have different views about it than boys.
- Girls have different kinds of sexual urges than boys.

Talk to your boy about these things on a regular basis as he becomes more and more girl conscious. Don't think that a onetime mention of the differences between girls and boys will teach him what he needs to know. Monitor his talk and relationships for his own attitudes and actions toward girls and make sure they meet your standards. You want your boy to have a healthy regard and understanding of girls so that he will grow up to have a healthy regard and understanding of women.

Three Things You Must Do

1. Accept your boy's growing interest in girls as girls.
2. Let this transition happen naturally, don't push it.
3. Talk to your boy about the differences between boys and girls.

Things to Say and Do

Talk to your boy about treating girls with the same respect and consideration that he would use with boys. Say such things as:

- You would never push or hurt girls, would you?
- Girls need respect and consideration, just like boys.
- Do the girls you know get teased a lot?
- How do your friends act toward the girls in your class?

Talk to your boy about how he feels about girls. Say such things as:

- You have some nice friends who are girls. Are they as good friends as boys?
- Do you have a crush on that girl in your class?
- Do you like girls differently from the way you like boys?

Talk to your boy about his views on how girls and boys are the same and different. Say such things as:

- I'm interested in what you think about girls. Do you think girls are the same as boys?
- How are they the same?
- How are they different?
- What differences matter to you?
- Do you like the differences?
- Do you think girls are as good as boys? Why?

Talk about the differences between boys and girls that you want your boy to know and understand. You can use the list from the earlier part of this chapter. Say such things as:

- Let me tell you some of the differences between boys and girls that you might not have thought of.
- You know that girls seem to like different things than boys. Let's talk about these differences.
- Girls value lots of things differently than boys do. Tell me what you think they like differently and I'll tell you what I think.

Model respectful, sensitive, and caring talk and behavior regarding girls and women.

Words, Phrases, and Actions to Use

- . . . love . . .
- . . . respect . . .
- . . . differences . . .
- . . . similarities . . .
- . . . less aggressive . . .
- . . . less violent . . .

- Be sensitive.
- Be caring.
- Listen.
- Share.
- Be gentle.
- Girls are different but equal.

Things Not to Say and Do

Don't dismiss your boy's feelings about girls. Don't say such things as:

- You're too young to feel that way about girls.
- Don't be silly. You don't know what love is.
- Stop saying that. Girls aren't interested in boys your age.

Don't pretend there are no differences between boys and girls, even in preadolescent children. Don't say such things as:

- At your age boys and girls are the same.
- At your age there are almost no differences between boys and girls.

Don't encourage your boy to be aggressive toward girls. Don't say such things as:

- If a girl doesn't do what you want her to do, just make her do it.
- Sometimes girls need to be put in their place.
- You can hit a girl if she's bigger than you are.

Don't demean or belittle girls or women. Don't say such things as:

- Females are a different species and not as good as males.
- Women and girls should do what men want them to do.
- Females were created to be the servants of males.
- Males are bigger and stronger and better than females.

Words, Phrases, and Actions to Avoid

- The man's the boss.
- Girls are no good.
- Females are frail.
- Girls are teasers.
- They don't know what they want.
- Females are meant to serve men.
- Girls are different and unequal.

GOOD AND BAD

◆

You want your boy to grow up to be a good man. He's reached an age during which you can begin to discuss moral issues with him and you will because you find it interesting to hear him talk about what he thinks is right and wrong, good and bad. You are constantly surprised to learn what a strong sense of this he has. He can tell you when he's been bad and has no problem being disciplined for his behavior as long as he thinks it's fair, and as long as you're consistent. Your boy often seeks your opinions on what is good and bad about many things, but mainly about what goes on in his life in school. He thinks his teacher is pretty good. She treats her students fairly, he says, and she never loses her temper at someone in front of the rest of the class. If she's angry, she takes the boy or girl into the hall and tells them off there so she's not embarrassing them in front of everyone. He thinks that's a really good thing. He doesn't think it's good that some kids seem to get everything they want from their parents, and others get very little. You and he have disagreements about what games, movies, and friends are good for him, but you're able to talk about it pretty easily and you don't get angry at each other. You often tell him he's a good boy, because, compared to a lot of other boys you hear of, he is. You hope he'll turn out to be a good man.

Things to Consider

Biology seems to work against boys being as "good" as girls. Girls seem less naturally aggressive and better at empathizing with others and developing and valuing relationships. Christine Hoff Sommers in *The War Against Boys* reports on some recent surveys that show that girls seem more inclined to be honest than boys. Seventeen percent more boys than girls said they were willing to cheat on tests and twelve percent more boys said they had shoplifted more than once in the past year.

It's certainly true that boys get into much more trouble than girls in school and in the community. Almost three quarters of children between ten and seventeen arrested for property crimes in 1993 were boys, and boys accounted for almost 90 percent of those arrested for violent crimes. Hopefully your boy isn't part of these statistics.

How do you teach a boy good from bad and how do you help him behave well at home, in school, and in the community? First, it is clear that boys need more discipline and rules than girls. Their natural aggression and competitiveness, and their need to act things out rather than talk them through and verbalize their feelings, means that they need help controlling their behavior. You must help him learn how to do this.

Second, boys respond better to a concerted effort to teach them good, moral behavior. You, his teachers, his coaches, his priest, rabbi, or other spiritual leader, the police, and neighbors, as well as the person in the street, all need to send the same message: think before you act, realize that your actions have consequences, and empathize, putting yourself in the other person's place before you do anything that might anger or hurt them.

Your boy is a preadolescent. He is still young enough for you and the community to teach him how to decide between good and bad for himself, how to avoid being caught up in any macho cult of cool, irresponsible, and sometimes hideously violent and senseless male behavior. It is your responsibility to ensure that your boy is getting the same message from the adults in all areas of his life.

Never allow your boy to be abusive or cruel without stopping him, disciplining him, and getting him to tell you why he did such a thing. Be sure to say nice things about your boy's good behavior whenever you see him being kind, gentle, caring, or helpful without being too "gushy" or "syrupy," which will only embarrass him. Make sure your boy understands the rules of good behavior and that you monitor him to make sure he lives by those rules. When he doesn't talk to him about what he's done, why he's done it, and what the effects of his actions will be on himself and others.

Watch your boy's behavior, what he says, and what he does and see what kinds of values it shows. Talk to him about what you see. With boys at this age it's always best to talk about specific good and bad behaviors. Abstract discussions of morals don't work. Specific cases do.

At this age your boy still wants your approval. When you see him do good things give it to him. Make sure your boy doesn't seek approval from the wrong group of kids. Kids with self-esteem problems often seem to seek others who will approve of bad behavior.

Model good values for your boy. Your boy will give a certain amount of respect simply because you're his parent. But the rest has to be earned. Hopefully you've been a good parent and your boy knows it. If your boy respects you and you've behaved badly you can tell your boy about it and use it as an example of the mistakes we all make. Tell him that you don't expect him to be perfect, but you do expect him to try. If you are a good parent and a good person chances are your boy will be good too.

Three Things You Must Do

1. Have rules of behavior for your boy and discuss them with him.
2. Monitor his behavior for the values it expresses.
3. Model good behavior for your boy.

Things to Say and Do

Your boy needs help to develop sound notions of good and bad. Talk about his life and experiences in these terms, including current events that he might know about. Say such things as:

- What do you think about those boys fighting in your school? Do you think that's a good way to settle arguments?
- I've heard the way some of your friends tease other kids, especially girls. Do you ever do that kind of thing? Is it a good thing to do?
- You remember us talking about The Golden Rule? How would you feel if someone took away your Halloween candy the way you took your little brother's?

Talk to your boy about the rules he needs to know good from bad. Say such things as:

- Let's talk about the things you see on your video game where people fight and hurt one another. Would you ever do a thing like that? Why not? What's the rule?
- When you think about the right thing to do, why is it a good idea to ask yourself how it will make others feel?
- Do you always try to treat others the way you would like them to treat you?
- You know our rules for behavior: think before you act, realize that your actions have consequences, and empathize, putting yourself in the other person's place before you do anything that might anger or hurt them.

Talk to your boy about anything he's done that you think is bad behavior. Get him to tell you why he did it. Ask him how he thinks it might affect others. Say such things as:

- I don't think that was a very nice thing to do. What do you think?
- Why did you do that?
- Do you think anyone else would think what you did was a good thing to do?

Help your boy put his thoughts about good and bad into words. Say such things as:

- Does that make you angry? Why is that?
- Tell me what you think about what your teacher did to you.
- If you think that was unfair can you tell me why?

Model good behavior for your boy. In your relationship with him, with the rest of your family, and in the community, try to be kind, generous, thoughtful, patient, and forgiving.

Words, Phrases, and Actions to Use

- Be loving.
- Be thoughtful.
- Be empathetic.
- Be considerate.
- Be good.

- Be honest.
- Be helpful.
- Be trusting.
- Be gentle.
- Be caring.

Things Not to Say and Do

Don't ignore your boy's moral education. Don't say such things as:

- You're a good boy. You can do whatever you want.
- There's no such thing as good and bad—only what's good for you or bad for you.
- All that talk about good and bad is just softhearted, soft-brained nonsense. It's the law of the jungle in real life. Eat or be eaten.

Don't ignore any bad actions your boy may do. Don't say such things as:

- I don't care what you do as long as you're all right.
- You only did what any real boy would do.
- Don't think about good and bad. Only think about you versus the other guy.
- I'm not bothered by what you did. Most boys would have done the same thing.

Words, Phrases, and Actions to Avoid

- Do what you want.
- Rules are made to be broken.
- Think of yourself first.
- There's no good and bad.
- Do what's best for you.
- If it feels good do it.

PREJUDICE

◆

You have tried to be a model of tolerance and understanding for your boy since he was a toddler. You firmly believe that prejudice against groups of people is wrong and you don't want your son to be that way. You haven't tried to shield your boy from instances of prejudice, because you want him to know what it's like to be the object of hatred, stereotyping, and intolerance so that he won't do it to others. You have, on many occasions, talked to your boy about the problem of prejudice against racial, religious, cultural, national, and social groups, and against males or females. Your conversations have drawn on examples that he has seen in his school, in his community, or in movies. You have talked about the subtle ways in which some groups of people get labeled as somehow unworthy or less human than others. You have talked about discrimination in sports, in jobs, in countries, and in politics. You have made your views quite clear to your boy and you have tried to get him to tell you his.

Things to Consider

It is natural and necessary for boys to see differences among people as well as to generalize and stereotype. We all put people into pigeonholes of one sort or another. We couldn't cope with life if we had to treat every situation and every person as unique, even though they are in many ways. Generalizations make our world manageable. However, it is not natural to be prejudiced, intolerant, or racist.

Thinking that some people are lesser human beings, or not worthy of our understanding and respect, because they are a different color, a different religion, come from a different country, have a different sexual orientation, or are the other gender serves no good purpose and simply makes life miserable for people who we label as bad, evil, un-American, sinful, or unhuman.

Boys, even more than girls, like to travel in groups. It's important for your boy to be a member of some group. But membership in these groups is almost never open to everyone. Some boys are accepted and some are rejected. The need for membership in a group can turn even the most liberal young boy into someone with strong prejudices.

Your preadolescent boy can sound very prejudiced at times, even if you've worked very hard at trying to teach him to embrace rather than to reject differences. Your boy has a strong need to be a member of his group and that includes identifying and excluding those kids who don't fit in. One of the most picked on groups of boys are those who seem effeminate, or obviously homosexual. These boys have a very hard time and in adolescence have a much higher suicide rate than normal for teenage boys.

You must work with your boy to overcome his prejudices. Ask him what kinds of prejudice he has seen at school or in the community. Does he have friends who are different? Do you have friends who are different? Don't let him get away with telling racist jokes, or making sexist comments. Don't let his friends get away with that either.

If you think your boy may be a victim of prejudice, talk to him about the possibility. Ask his friends if anything like that happens in or out of school. Be on the lookout for any changes in his behavior. If his appetite changes or if he seems reluctant to go to school, go outside to play, or go to places he used to enjoy, it may be that he is afraid of something.

You need to help your boy in two ways. First, you need to ensure that he doesn't feel superior to any other boys or girls or groups for any arbitrary reason. Go out of your way to emphasize the similarities among all people. Second, you need to help your boy feel proud of his own background, race, religion, or culture, not to the detriment of others, but to build his own confidence and to combat the negative stereotypes that feed prejudice, intolerance, and hatred.

Three Things You Must Do

1. Reject prejudice in all its forms.
2. Monitor your boy closely for signs of prejudice, both against others or against him.
3. Be a good role model for your boy.

Things to Say and Do

Talk to your boy about prejudice in his school or community. Ask him what he has seen. Say such things as:

- Do you see any kids being picked on at school? Why does it happen?
- You have lots of kids who are different at school. Do other kids do mean things to them?
- Have you seen anybody get picked on in town because they're different?

Ask your boy what he thinks about prejudice. Say such things as:

- What would you do if you saw kids being picked on just because they were a different color, or a different religion?
- Would you tell the kids to stop?

- Do any of your friends do that kind of thing?
- Have any of your friends ever been picked on?

Ask your boy about his own experience. Say such things as:

- Has anyone ever said hateful things to you?
- Have you ever been picked on because of the way you look or what you believe?
- Do kids ever tease you or bully you or pick on you?

Talk to your boy about possible prejudice in the practices of any of the groups at school or in the community. Say such things as:

- You belong to a club. How do you decide who gets in and who doesn't?
- Do you have any gangs at school that make trouble for kids who are different from them?
- Can anyone join the groups you know about?

Tell your boy your own views on prejudice. Say such things as:

- You know where I stand on this matter of prejudice.
- I won't tolerate intolerance.
- People who are prejudiced are not very nice people and I wouldn't want them as friends.

Make sure your boy has a good, positive self-image. Say such things as:

- You should feel really good about who you are.
- I hope you never feel you want to be anyone else because you are great the way you are.
- Don't ever wish you were a different color or a different religion. That would be wrong. There is nothing wrong with being exactly who you are.

Words, Phrases, and Actions to Use

- . . . tolerance . . .
- . . . equality . . .
- Be good.
- Be accepting.
- Love one another.

- Be open.
- Be understanding.
- Accept difference.
- Don't stereotype.
- Celebrate the differences.

Things Not to Say and Do

Don't be a bad role model for your boy. Don't say such things as:

- I hate those people.
- You're right not to like those people.
- Those people don't deserve to be treated like normal people.

Don't encourage your boy to be prejudiced. Don't say such things as:

- Everyone is a little bit racist. I know I am.
- People have to earn your respect and those people haven't.
- You can call those people anything you want because they deserve it.

Don't ignore your boy's prejudiced comments or jokes. Don't say such things as:

- That's a good one.
- You're right on about those people.
- Let me tell you a great joke I heard the other day.

Don't encourage your boy to feel superior to any group. Don't say such things as:

- You're a lot better than those people.
- Those people are just thieves and druggies.
- I don't want you hanging around with any of those kinds of people.

Words, Phrases, and Actions to Avoid

- They're rotten.
- They're thieves.
- They're evil.
- That's unnatural.
- They're perverts.
- They're criminals.
- They're drug traders.
- They're less than human.
- They don't deserve respect.

RESPONSIBILITIES

◆

Your boy is truly at an age during which he needs to take on increasing responsibility for some of his life. You want him to take care of some things for himself because it will help him along on the road to becoming an adult, and because it will make your life a little easier. You don't plan to load him up with too many responsibilities because you realize he's still very young in many ways, but he can certainly handle some things that relate to his personal care, his membership in the family, and his work in school. He's been responsible since he was seven for keeping the floor of his room free from clutter so you can vacuum it, and the surfaces clear of clothes, books, magazines, and paper so you can dust them. He's also been given a few chores to do at dinnertime like helping to set and clear the table. Now that he's ten you want him to help load the dishwasher, walk the dog, and take out the garbage. He's also responsible for bringing his dirty clothes to the laundry room and putting his newly washed clothes in their proper place. You also expect him to tell you about school, show you what his daily homework assignments are, and let you review them when he's finished. These are just a few of his new responsibilities.

Things to Consider

Your boy wants responsibility and he wants to please you. He wants to get it right. You must give him the opportunity to succeed in his responsibilities and the freedom to fail. Don't expect him to always get it right the first time. You probably didn't when you were his age.

Your boy is now old enough to understand his responsibilities to himself and the family in different ways than when he was younger. He should begin to feel a strong sense of obligation to you and to himself to do what is in everyone's best interests, although he will often find it difficult to decide what that is. With luck he has come a long way from the time he was a little boy thinking only about himself.

Michael Gurian in *The Good Son* gives us a nice list of responsibilities for the preadolescent boy, which he calls "Rules to Live By." I'll summarize the more important rules in Gurian's very sensible list with some of my ideas thrown in as well. The responsible preadolescent boy should:

- Tell his parents where he will be and what he's doing when he's not at home.
- Speak respectfully to all adults.
- Avoid obvious displays of selfishness.
- Talk about problems in appropriate ways.
- Respect the feelings, wishes, and beliefs of others, including younger siblings.
- Act like an adult in adult situations like mealtimes, visits to other people's homes, and visits to restaurants and other public places.
- Accept his responsibilities willingly and with a good attitude.

You want to help your boy become this kind of responsible person. What should you do? Here is my list of things that you must do to help your boy along this important road to adulthood:

- Talk to your boy about your expectations so he knows what you're thinking.
- Ask your boy what responsibilities he thinks he's ready for.
- Have a trial period during which you both can see if he's ready for a particular responsibility.
- Treat your boy as an adult in regard to these responsibilities. He is more likely to act like a responsible adult if you treat him like one.
- Add responsibilities gradually according to your boy's maturity.
- Praise your boy for his attempts as well as for his successes.
- Expect and accept imperfection.
- Trust your boy to carry out his responsibilities unless he proves he's consistently untrustworthy.
- Be flexible. Allow for time off from some responsibilities. We all need vacations from work.
- Know your boy, his strengths and weaknesses, and give him responsibilities that will help him in both areas.
- Keep track of your boy's responsibilities to others. Know what's expected of him in school, in sports, in scouts, and in religious or community youth groups. Help him fulfill those responsibilities.
- Talk to your boy about his obligations to himself and others. Discuss his own sense of responsibility and how he feels about what he's doing.
- Ask others about your boy's willingness to accept responsibility. Talk to his teachers, your clergyman, his scout leader, his coach, and your community leaders.

These are a few ways to help your boy learn to be a responsible citizen in the family, at school, and in the community at large.

Three Things You Must Do

1. Give your boy increased responsibilities appropriate to his age and to what kind of boy he is.
2. Praise him for attempts as well as successes.
3. Don't expect perfection.

Things to Say and Do

Talk to your boy about the responsibilities you would like him to take on and what he thinks he would like to do. Say such things as:

- I've made a little list of the things I think you could do for yourself. What do you think?
- I know what I'd like you to be responsible for. What about you? What do you think you can do?

Have a trial period for each new responsibility. Say such things as:

- Let's try having you make your bed each morning before you leave for school. Do you think this is a reasonable thing for you to do at your age?
- Would you be willing to do this chore? We can try it and see if it's too much for you.

Talk to your boy as an adult about his new responsibilities. Say such things as:

- What do you think about all these new responsibilities? Do you think you're up to it?
- You're getting to be such a responsible guy.
- Pretty soon you'll be grown up and doing everything for yourself.

Praise your boy for his attempts as well as for his successes. Say such things as:

- That was a good try. I don't mind if it's not perfect. Just keep trying to do it better.
- I'm very impressed by all the effort you're putting into your schoolwork.
- Good work. You're really helping me out and that means a lot to me.

Be flexible. Allow for time off from some responsibilities. Say such things as:

- I think you need a rest from this. I'll do it for the next week.
- It's time for your sister to take over this responsibility from you for a while.

Know what's expected of your boy in school, in sports, in scouts, and in religious or community youth groups. Help him fulfill those responsibilities if he needs help. Talk to your boy about his obligations to himself and others. Say such things as:

- You seem to be more responsible for yourself these days. Have you noticed that?
- How do you feel about all these obligations you have? Are you having any problems with them? Which ones?
- Everybody notices how mature you're getting. Do you see how you're becoming more responsible for things?

Ask your boy's teachers, clergy, scout leader, coach, and community leaders about his willingness and ability to accept responsibility.

Words, Phrases, and Actions to Use

- . . . responsibilities . . .
- . . . obligations . . .
- . . . maturity . . .
- . . . help . . .
- . . . attempts . . .
- . . . successes . . .

- Is it too much?
- Try.
- Good work.
- Thank you.
- You owe it to yourself.
- You owe it to others.

Things Not to Say and Do

Don't expect perfection. Don't say such things as:

- You've failed again. Can't you do anything right?
- What's wrong with you? Can't I trust you to do anything?
- You're really "responsibility challenged." You never get things done.

Don't avoid giving your boy responsibility for things. Don't say such things as:

- I don't think you're mature enough to do things for yourself.
- I'll do it, honey. Don't you even think about doing it for yourself.
- I love doing things for you. You don't have to lift a little finger.

Don't let your boy ignore his responsibilities outside the home. Don't say such things as:

- That doesn't matter.
- Do whatever you like.
- Don't let those obligations get in your way.

Don't simply order your boy to do things. Don't say such things as:

- This is your responsibility whether you like it or not.
- I don't care what you want to do. You'll do as I say.
- Here is a list of things you have to do. I made it up and I'm not prepared to discuss it with you. It's not negotiable.

Words, Phrases, and Actions to Avoid

- Just do it.
- I don't care what you think.
- You'll do what I tell you.
- You're a loser.
- You can't do anything right.
- I can't trust you to be responsible for anything.
- You always do it wrong.
- What's wrong with you?

RULES

◆

You know your boy needs rules at every age. The only difference now is that your boy is older and rules become more complicated because he recognizes that there are competing sets of rules. And one of those competing sets is his own set of rules that he is building for himself. Your boy has moved from an early stage of moral reasoning during which he believed that following rules was the way to make the world good and right to his present stage during which he has begun to recognize the complications that life continually throws at all of us, complications that make understanding the rules more difficult than following them. This is all the more reason for you to talk to your boy about some of the rules you expect him to follow as well as the rules all people have to try to follow simply to make the world a safe, livable place. You want him to understand the more sophisticated notion of rules, not as simple guides to behavior, but as the way we have of recognizing the rights and responsibilities of all people to themselves and to others.

Things to Consider

Because boys are naturally more aggressive and active than girls, because they are much more likely to take risks, because they often react too quickly to situations that really need some thought before action, because they still rely on acting out their feelings as much as, or more than, talking about them, your boy needs a good set of rules to help him do the right thing. But this is much more complicated now that he is a preadolescent because simple rules like "don't touch" or "that's not good for a boy" are no longer enough. You find that your boy is not as willing to accept your rules as the last word on his behavior.

Now, as he gets closer to puberty and adolescence, your boy questions your authority to make the rules. "Why shouldn't I do that?" he now asks when you tell him you don't want him to ride his bike to a friend's house. "Because it's too dangerous," you answer. "I can take care of myself, I'm not a little kid anymore" is his reply. You then resort to that time-honored response of parents, "As long as you're living in this house you'll do what I tell you." End of discussion!

Obviously, you don't see this as a happy resolution to the issue of rules. You want your boy to follow the rules at home and when he's at school or in the community for his own sake as well as yours because you know how much pain and grief can come from not following them. On the other hand you don't want to stifle your boy's spirit, creativity, or boyish enthusiasm for exploring new things. You want him to develop his own rules.

The most important thing to understand is that rules don't explain themselves. You and your boy have to make sense of them in each new situation. Your job is to give your boy examples of how he can apply the rules to these new situations. You're not always there to tell him what to do, nor would you want to be. You want your boy to have the skills and good sense to know what the proper thing to do is when he has to make choices. And he always has to make choices such as calling home to tell you where he is, doing what the teacher asks in school, avoiding that shopping mall, practicing his musical instrument, not trying that cigarette, not tasting that beer, and not harassing those girls.

You've spent eight or more years working to instill in your boy a working sense of right and wrong, good and bad, yes and no. You've tried to model good behavior for him by showing how you follow certain rules in your life, especially in your relationship with him. You hope that talk and modeling will pay off in having a boy who generally tries to follow the rules, even if he doesn't always succeed.

Now that your boy is a preadolescent you are giving him rules at a higher level and want to help him understand how to apply them to specific circumstances in his life. Here are some of those rules:

- Think before you act.
- Imagine yourself in the other person's place.
- Don't break the law.
- Respect the authority of your teachers in school.
- Live up to your promises and commitments.
- Never lie, steal, or cheat.
- Never hit another person in anger.
- Respect other people's bodies and your own.
- Always be polite.
- Never be unkind to an animal or other living creature.
- Respect other people's property.
- Always do your best.
- Never be cruel to another person.

These are not a novel set of rules. You try to live by them yourself. You don't always succeed. Part of that is due to the nature of life and all the things that are beyond your control. So you know that trying to do the right thing is as important as succeeding in doing it. Remember to teach that to your boy.

Three Things You Must Do

1. Give your boy rules to live by.
2. Expect some resistance to your rules.
3. Encourage your boy to create his own set of rules.

Things to Say and Do

Talk to your boy about the rules you have for him and why they're important. Say such things as:

- Let's talk about what I expect of you and what you expect of yourself.
- You know you have some rules that I gave you. Do you think they're fair?
- How do our rules for you compare to the rules your friends have?

Ask your boy if he has any rules that he uses in his life at home, at school, or in the community. Say such things as:

- How do you decide what to do in school when the teacher asks the class to do something and you don't want to?
- Do you have rules about your brother's things, when you can look at them and when you can't?
- If a store in town doesn't like too many kids in it at the same time, do you keep out?

Talk to your boy about the different kinds of rules there are. Some rules are very specific and some are much more general. Say such things as:

- You know we have rules about the TV, the computer, bedtime, washing your hands and face, brushing your teeth, keeping your room clean, and lots of things like that. That's one kind of rule. What other kinds of rules do you have to obey?
- Do you think it's ever right to hit your sister?
- Do you know that I have to follow rules just like you? Do you know what some of them are?

Talk to your boy about the consequences of disobeying rules. Say such things as:

- Why do you think it's so important to obey rules?
- Are all rules just as important?
- Are there any rules that it's okay to disobey?

Ask your boy about the reasons for rules. This will help him think about why all those rules exist that stop him from having fun and doing what he wants. Say such things as:

- Why do you think we have rules that we're supposed to follow?
- Do you think we could live without rules? What could happen if we didn't have them?
- What rules do you have that you think you don't really need?

Words, Phrases, and Actions to Use

- . . . rules . . .
- . . . proper behavior . . .
- . . . your rules . . .
- . . . everybody's rules . . .
- . . . good rules . . .
- . . . bad rules . . .
- . . . consequences . . .
- Does it make sense?
- Why do we have rules?
- Rules help you live.
- Rules help you make choices.

Things Not to Say and Do

Don't let your boy do whatever he wants. Don't say such things as:

- Rules are for sissies.
- You should do whatever you think is best for you.
- Rules are made to be broken.

Don't give up giving your boy rules. Don't say such things as:

- Now that you're nine years old, I don't have any rules for you. Do whatever you like.
- You don't need rules anymore.
- Big boys don't have little boy rules.

Don't give your boy all the responsibility for making up his own rules. Don't say such things as:

- You make up your own rules.
- Your rules are the only important rules.
- I want you to make up all your rules.

Don't be too restrictive with rules. Don't try to have rules for everything. Don't say such things as:

- You shouldn't have moved that chair. We have a rule about that.
- You know there are rules for everything in this house.

Don't expect perfection. Don't say such things as:

- You better follow the rules, otherwise you'll be severely punished.
- Don't ever break any of my rules or you'll regret it.
- I don't care about trying to follow the rules. I expect perfection.

Words, Phrases, and Actions to Avoid

- Can't you ever follow the rules?
- You're a failure.
- Follow the rules or I won't love you.
- I'm going to hit you for breaking the rules.
- You live in my house, you follow my rules.
- Rules don't matter.
- Make up your own rules.
- Rules keep you from doing what's fun.

SCHOOLWORK AND BEHAVIOR

$\diamond$

Your boy is between the ages of nine and twelve. If he's on schedule then he's in one of grades four through seven. You know how important school is for your boy's future and you try to keep track of his schoolwork and behavior. Your boy knows that you expect him to do his best to achieve good marks and to behave appropriately. You are also rightly concerned about the school your boy attends. Some of the things you worry about are the quality of your boy's teacher and your boy's relationship with him. Does he seem sensible, likeable, well-educated? Does he seem happy in his work? Does your boy like him, or not? Does he seem to like your boy, or not? Does he seem to know how to relate to preadolescent boys? You have made it your business to get to know the school principal. You have been watching how she runs her school and especially her relationship with her staff, students, and parents. You are pleased that she allows parents to volunteer in the classroom and you have done this in your boy's class. You realize that boys and girls learn differently and you are anxious to see if your boy's school makes any allowance for this in the organization and methods of teaching.

Things to Consider

Boys and Girls Learn Differently, by Michael Gurian, is an excellent new book available to parents who want to know how the latest research on brain differences between boys and girls translates into how schools and teaching should be organized so that boys and girls can learn to their highest potential. Gurian suggests many structural and teaching innovations that schools can use to recognize the different cognitive strengths and weaknesses of boys and girls. He looks at the advantages of the following changes:

- Year-round schooling with breaks three to four times a year.
- Making the school day coincide with parents' work times.
- Reducing teacher-pupil ratios to the optimal one teacher/teacher aide/parent volunteer to fifteen students.

- Having students stay with the same teacher all day from the first grade through the sixth grade for the sake of good bonding.
- Keeping the total number of children in each school small.

These are but a few of the structural changes he believes would take advantage of the developmental needs that both boys and girls have to learn best. It seems clear from brain research as well as the evidence from our experience that boys have more problems in school than girls. Boys are more impulsive, and have more discipline, reading, writing, verbalizing, motivational, and learning and behavioral problems.

What can you do to help your boy overcome any problems in these areas that he may have? Here are a few general guidelines. You will have to tailor them to your boy's specific needs. If your boy has more than occasional learning and behavioral problems you may need to seek professional help.

- Encourage your boy to talk about his school experiences every day.
- Tell your boy about your own school experience.
- Be a parent volunteer in your boy's classroom and/or school.
- Get to know your boy's teachers and school principal.
- Get a copy of the curriculum guide for your boy's grade level.
- Know what teaching materials, gifts, or presentations your school accepts from outside organizations, businesses, and corporations.
- Know what, if any, special consideration your boy's school gives to the effect of brain differences on how boys and girls learn.
- Be willing to research and discuss the relative advantages and disadvantages of single-sex classes.
- See if your boy's teacher channels boys' high energy levels, competitiveness, and aggression into productive work in the classroom.
- See if your boy's teacher gives boys time and space for physical activity.
- See how your boy's teacher helps boys to develop their reading, writing, and verbal skills.
- See how your boy's teacher encourages boys to learn through doing.
- Be an active member of your school's parent council/association.
- Know what standards your school or school board uses in hiring new teachers.
- Know the salary grid for teachers in your district compared to others.
- Know your school's discipline policies and practices for bullying, harassment, violent behavior, gang membership, and general misbehavior.
- Reject zero-tolerance policies as too simplistic, rigid, and unrealistic.
- If you think your boy's teacher is a good teacher trust her evaluation of your

boy's abilities and achievements more than that of standardized IQ or achievement tests.

- Encourage your boy to read by letting him choose his own books and magazines.
- Read some of the books and articles your boy reads and discuss them with him.
- Encourage your boy to write down his reactions to what he reads.
- Give your boy any help he needs with schoolwork, but don't do the work for him.
- Talk with your boy about your expectations for his schoolwork and behavior.
- Praise and hug your boy for all the good effort he puts into his schoolwork.

Three Things You Must Do

1. Be involved in your boy's school.
2. Know what he's supposed to be learning.
3. Know what the latest brain research tells you about how boys learn differently from girls.

Things to Say and Do

Encourage your boy to talk about his school experiences every day. You can also tell him about your daily experiences at work. Say such things as:

- How did that assignment you were doing this week turn out?
- What's your homework for this evening?
- Let me tell you how I did on that report I was writing for work.

Be a parent volunteer in your boy's classroom and/or school. But make sure your boy knows that you'll be doing it. Some boys find having their mom or dad in their class very embarrassing. Say such things as:

- You wouldn't mind if I was a volunteer in your class, would you?
- I know you have a lot of kids in your class. I'm going to be coming in to help your teacher out a few days each week. Is that okay with you?
- Do you have parent volunteers in your class? Would you like it if I did that?

Get to know your boy's teachers and school principal. Ask your boy's opinion of them. Say such things as:

- What do you think of your teacher? Do other kids like her? Is she as good as "Mrs. Jones" last year?
- Do you like your principal? Do the other kids like the principal?
- Do the teachers like the principal?

Ask your boy if his teacher does anything differently with boys and girls. Say such things as:

- Does your teacher ever just teach the boys or just teach the girls?

Ask your boy what he thinks about having single-sex classes for some things. Say such things as:

- Would you like a class of just boys? For what things?

Encourage your boy to read by letting him choose his own books and magazines. Say such things as:

- Let's go to the bookstore. I'll buy you whatever you want to read.
- What's your favorite book you've ever read?
- You like to read those magazines, don't you? I think that's great.

Read some of the books and articles your boy reads and discuss them with him. Say such things as:

- I'm going to read that book when you're finished and then we can talk about it if you like.
- I just read that book you read. I think it's great. What did you think?

Talk with your boy about your expectations for his schoolwork and behavior. Say such things as:

- You know that I want you to do well in school. Do you know why?
- What do you think are the most important things that you learn in school? Do you want to know what I think?
- I think you can do very well in school and I want you to always do your best. Do you think that's fair?

Give your boy any help he needs with schoolwork, but don't do the work for him. Make sure your boy will always come to you with any problems he's facing in school. Say such things as:

- I'm always glad to help you with your homework.
- If you ever have any trouble at school I know you'll tell me, won't you?
- I sometimes had trouble at school when I was your age so I know what it's like. I'm here to help you anytime you have any trouble.

Words, Phrases, and Actions to Use

- . . . homework . . .
- . . . good behavior . . .
- Well done.
- Boys and girls learn differently.
- Let's talk about it.
- School is so important.
- You're doing a great job.
- How can I help you?
- Do you like what you're doing?
- Do you like your teacher?
- Does your teacher like you?

Things Not to Say and Do

Don't ignore your boy's schooling. Don't say such things as:

- I don't care how you're doing in school. You'll be okay.
- School's not that important.
- I hated school.

Don't always take your boy's word for things about school. Investigate any allegations against his teacher carefully. Don't say such things as:

- I hate teachers.
- I don't trust teachers.
- Your teacher is probably as bad as mine were.

Don't ignore teacher's notes from school or avoid parent-teacher interviews. Don't say such things as:

- Tell your teacher she's got no business telling me what to do about your education.
- I'm not going to parent-teacher interviews. It's a waste of my time.

Don't discourage your boy from reading. Don't say such things as:

- I don't like reading either.
- Reading is a waste of time because everything you read is a pack of lies anyway.

Don't ignore your boy's learning or behavior problems. Don't say such things as:

- Boys will be boys.
- You'll grow out of it.
- It's not such a big deal.

Words, Phrases, and Actions to Avoid

- School stinks.
- Teachers stink.
- School's a waste of time.
- You listen to me, not your teacher.
- Your teacher can't tell you what to do.
- You can do everything in school better than girls.
- Your teacher doesn't know what he's talking about.

SELF-ESTEEM

◆

You're confused. You want your boy to feel good about himself and you've tried to give him lots of praise and positive reinforcement for everything he's ever done. Even when he's done some things you'd rather not remember, like cutting off the legs of his sister's favorite doll when he was six years old, you praised him when he apologized and offered to give his sister all his savings to help her buy a new doll. You love your boy and want him to think highly of himself. Your own experience tells you that when you feel good about yourself you feel good about other people too. But now you've read about some psychologists who say that building high self-esteem isn't all it's cracked up to be, what people really need is self-discipline and a realistic assessment of their accomplishments, not some "feel good about yourself no matter what" attitude. You wonder if you worry too much about self-esteem. Should you change your way of talking to your boy about who he is and what he does and be completely honest in your judgment of his successes and failures without worrying if it will lower his self-esteem?

Things to Consider

Preadolescent boys have a different kind of problem with self-esteem than girls do. Girls have body image and lack of attention and recognition problems, especially in school. Boys have fewer body image problems but they have major attention problems. The problem is that much of the attention boys get, especially in school, is negative attention.

Boys also have self-esteem problems that come from their biological role as aggressor. Boys need to be members of the pack. They need to find a comfortable place for themselves among other boys. This dominance issue makes boys very sensitive to whom they are and their standing in their group.

The self-esteem issue for you and your boy is not for you to make him feel good about himself at all costs. You want him to be realistic. You want him to know his strengths and weaknesses. You want him to have good relationships with other children and adults. Relationships are one of the most important parts of good self-esteem. You want him to be able to cope with his share of failures and successes throughout his life so that no matter what happens he won't doubt that he is a worthwhile human being.

Remember when your boy was a toddler? You marveled at how much he learned, how quickly he understood things, and how observant he was. Even when he broke a figurine, or threw his food on the floor, you never lost your temper. You quietly and consistently tried to teach him how to do things constructively rather than destructively. You took advantage of the fact that your boy really wanted to please you. You loved him unconditionally. You did everything you could to make him feel safe and secure. These are the three pillars of self-esteem: feeling loved, feeling safe, and feeling secure about ourselves.

The fact that your boy is now a preadolescent doesn't mean that he has any less need for these pillars. Make sure they are there for your boy all the time, even when you are disciplining him, he has misbehaved at school, he argues with you, and he gets into all kinds of trouble. You are there to give your boy a secure base from which to venture forth into the aggressive, competitive world of other boys.

Giving your boy a high opinion of himself when others don't share it is not giving him good self-esteem. Good self-esteem needs to be honest and realistic. You want your boy to be able to see himself as others see him. Having an inflated view of oneself is a sure road to disaster.

Throughout his short life your boy has been looking to you for signs that he is doing things right. Think about your interaction with him. What do your words say to your boy about how you value him? What does your body language say? What do your facial expressions say? What do your actions say? Would you and your boy agree on your view of him? If you were in your boy's place what would you think your parents thought of you? Do you please them or are you a disappointment?

I can't emphasize enough how important it is to your boy's self-esteem that you have realistic expectations of him during these preadolescent years. Don't give him the idea that you expect him to be a star athlete, a brilliant scholar, a leader among boys, or a musical prodigy, if your boy is not physically, intellectually, or socially gifted. Let your boy show and tell you about his own gifts and how he wants to use them.

Boys often do better in sports than in school because competitive physical activity comes so naturally to them. Make sure you give your boy the chance to do some kind of athletics if he shows an interest, particularly team sports in which even a small contribution can help bolster a sagging self-esteem. On the other hand pushing him to be something he's not interested in will not help his self-esteem nor his chances for a happy life.

Your main job is to help him feel loved, safe, and secure for who he is, not for who you want him to be.

Three Things You Must Do

1. Accept your boy for who he is and help him to accept himself for himself as well.
2. Praise your boy for his attempts and his successes.
3. Recognize that boys may hide their real feelings about themselves.

Things to Say and Do

As a preadolescent your boy needs your love to help his self-esteem more than ever. You need to be there for him in every situation, yet you have to recognize that as a boy he may not admit to needing your love and support. Say such things as:

- I love you.
- Let me hug you.
- Whatever happens I'm always here for you.

Be realistic. Help your boy to see himself as others see him. Say such things as:

- "Jonah" is your best friend, isn't he? What are the things you like about him? What are the things he likes about you?

Show your boy you love and value him in what you say and do. Do such things as:

- Tell your boy he's a good boy.
- Wrap your boy in your arms.
- Smile at your boy when you talk to him.

Be realistic in your expectations of your boy. Don't expect him to be a star at something if that's not his thing. Let your boy show and tell you about his own gifts and how he wants to use them. Say such things as:

- What do you really like doing?
- What makes you feel really good about yourself?
- Is there anything you'd like to do that you haven't told me about?

Give your boy the chance to do sports if he shows an interest, particularly team sports.

Words, Phrases, and Actions to Use

- You're a good boy.
- I love you.
- Just be yourself.
- You're good at lots of things.
- You have nice friends.
- Do you ever wish you were someone else?
- What would you like to do?
- I'm always here for you.
- Always do your best. That's all anyone can ask of you.

Things Not to Say and Do

Don't tease your boy about himself. At his age it may not go over very well. Don't say such things as:

- You're a little fatty.
- Not very good at that, are you?
- What do the girls say about you?

Don't push your boy in directions he may not want go. Don't say such things as:

- I want you to try out for that team. It will be good for you.
- You'll do that because I say so.
- I expect you to be outstanding at school.

Your boy needs good relationships with other children. Don't make it difficult for him. Don't say such things as:

- I don't want you to bring your friends here.
- I don't like your friends.
- How come you have so few friends?

Don't compare your boy to his siblings or friends. Don't say such things as:

- Why can't you have more friends like your sister?
- You're not doing well in school. Why can't you be more like your brother?
- All your friends seem to do better in school than you do.

Words, Phrases, and Actions to Avoid

- How come you're not better at that?
- You'll never get that right.
- You're a really slow learner.
- You're going to lose all your friends.
- I wish you had more friends.
- Why don't people like you?
- You're not a likeable boy.
- You always get everything wrong.

TRUST

◆

You know the best relationships are built on mutual trust. You've told your boy many times that you trust him. More important, you have *shown* him that you trust him. You don't ask him questions to which you already know the answer, like "Where have you been?," knowing very well that he's been somewhere you'd rather he hadn't. Trying to catch him in a lie is one of the best ways to destroy trust. If you've built a trusting relationship between the two of you, you will trust him to have good reasons for what he's done, even if they are not your reasons. You've explained to him that trust works both ways. When you ask him to do something he needs to trust that you have his best interests at heart even if that may not seem clear to him at his age. You're quite open about it and never defensive. You don't discourage him from asking you questions about your rules for him. Your boy trusts you and you trust him because you have built that trust over the years. You both know that because some things are private and better left unsaid that you needn't always be open and honest with each other. But that has never damaged your relationship because you trust each other to do the right thing and never intentionally do anything that would violate that trust.

Things to Consider

You and your boy need to show that you trust each other. It's not good enough to say you trust him and then show that you don't by your actions. At this age boys are starting to show the need for more independence. They question your authority and want to make more of their own decisions. In spite of this apparent need boys don't really want to be left on their own. They still trust you to make the important decisions and to be there for them when they are confused, afraid, or in trouble.

Your boy might say that he doesn't want to be treated like a little kid, that he's more grown up now and soon will be a teenager. You may find that he's becoming quite sensitive to the way you talk to him, telling him what he can and cannot do, where he can and cannot go, and with whom he can and cannot be friends. You've got to show your boy that he can trust you to recognize his growing maturity and give him more room to make his own choices, while being there to protect him from the serious consequences of bad choices.

Issues of trust include issues of fairness. Your boy needs to trust you to treat him fairly. The context for this is how you treat his brother or sister, and how his friends are treated by their parents. Your boy trusts you to give him appropriate freedom, responsibility, allowance, and discipline, and to trust him to try to do the right thing as he sees it. He trusts you to love him, keep him safe, and defend him against others as well as to be consistent in your treatment of him and to always be there for him.

Contrary to what some TV commercials suggest, young children are born trusting their caregivers. How could it be otherwise? You then nurture this trust in you by providing the essential love, food, and shelter that your baby needs. But you can lose it if you can't give him the love, food, shelter, and respect that he needs to sustain himself and grow.

Similarly, your boy should have your trust until he shows by his actions that he doesn't deserve it. Show him that your trust depends on how he behaves. It's also important that he grows up feeling that he is trustworthy. That is an important part of his self-esteem.

Finally, you want your boy to be a trusting person. Even though you worry about what might happen to him if he trusts too easily, you are better off with a boy who trusts than a boy who mistrusts. The simple matter is that all relationships are built on some measure of trust. Your boy will have a much easier time in his relationships now and in the future if his first instinct is to trust rather than mistrust, even if it turns out that that trust is misplaced.

Help your boy be a trusting person by telling him the truth about things in ways that he can understand; by making promises and keeping them; by being there for him on important occasions like sports events, school events, birthdays, and holidays; by being fair to him; by being reasonable and consistent; by trusting that he has good reasons for what he says and does; and by giving him the love, care, and security that he needs to grow up to be a loving, trusting man.

Three Things You Must Do

1. Show your boy that he can trust you.
2. Show your boy that you trust him.
3. Encourage your boy to be a trusting person.

Things to Say and Do

Show that you trust your boy. Talk about trust and about what you both do that shows this trust. Say such things as:

- I never say no to you unless I have a very good reason, which I'm always willing to tell you.
- You've shown me that you're a trustworthy boy.
- I think we have a good relationship of trust between us, don't you?

Show that you recognize your boy's need for more independence and to make more of his own decisions. Show that you trust him to do this in areas where he has competence appropriate to his age. Say such things as:

- I trust you to make good choices in friends.
- I trust you to do your best in school.
- I trust you not to lie or cheat.

Explain why, even though you trust him to make some decisions, he needs to trust you to make important decisions for him and to be there for him when he's confused, afraid, or in trouble. Say such things as:

- You're growing up fast and it's important to decide some things for yourself, but not everything just yet.
- You know I'm always here for you to help you when you need it.

Your boy doesn't want to be treated like a little kid anymore and he's becoming quite sensitive to the way you talk to him. Tell him that you recognize this and will try to be careful in what you say. Say such things as:

- You're growing up fast and I'll try to treat you like a young man. But remember that you have to act like one as well.
- If I say something that bothers you, you can tell me.
- If you think I'm treating you like a baby just say so.

Talk to your boy about issues of trust. Say such things as:

- You know I try to treat you fairly. If you think I'm being unfair please tell me.
- I try to give you as much freedom as your friends have.
- Do you think I should give you more responsibility? What for?
- Do you think the way I try to teach you the right thing to do is fair?

Show your boy that your trust in him depends on him. Say such things as:

- I trust you because you've always shown that you're a trustworthy boy.
- I hope you trust me for the same reason.
- Everyone I know thinks you're a trustworthy boy.

You want your boy to be a trusting person. Talk to him about the importance of trusting others. Say such things as:

- Everything we do depends on trust because we can't check up on everything people say. We have to believe most of what people tell us.
- The world wouldn't work unless we trusted most people to do the right thing and to be honest.
- Do you think you can trust most people? Is there anyone you know that you don't trust? Why not?

Help your boy trust you. Show him that you're honest, you keep your promises, you show up for his important events, you treat him fairly, you're consistent in your love and care for him, and you keep him safe and secure.

Words, Phrases, and Actions to Use

- ... love ...
- ... care ...
- ... trust ...
- ... truth ...
- ... reasons ...
- ... attention ...

- Don't lie.
- Don't cheat.
- It works both ways.
- It's better to trust than mistrust.
- Trust makes the world possible.

Things Not to Say and Do

Don't lose your boy's trust by your words or deeds. Don't say such things as:

- I know I promised but I couldn't do it for you. That's life.
- I don't trust you so why should you trust me?
- I know I lied but I couldn't help it.

Don't automatically mistrust your boy. Don't say such things as:

- I won't trust you unless you show me you're worthy of my trust.
- You have to prove to me that you're trustworthy.
- I never assume I can trust you.

Don't encourage your boy to mistrust others. Don't say such things as:

- People are generally liars, cheats, and totally untrustworthy.
- I don't trust anyone and you shouldn't either.
- It's better to mistrust than to trust.

Don't assume your boy is always out to deceive you. Don't ask him test questions. Don't say such things as:

- You're a liar.
- I asked you where you were and you lied to me. I already knew where you were and I was just testing you.
- Watch out. I'm always checking up on you because I can't trust you.

Words, Phrases, and Actions to Avoid

- . . . liar . . .
- . . . cheat . . .
- . . . untrustworthy . . .
- Never trust anyone.
- I don't trust you.
- Fair is what I say is fair.
- I don't care if you don't like it.
- I don't care if your friends' parents trust them.

PART 5

Young Teenage Boys

(13–15 years)

ALCOHOL, DRUGS, AND CIGARETTES

◆

All potential threats to your young teenager worry you. You keep a close watch on newspaper reports of the ever-present danger of consuming alcohol, doing drugs, and smoking among teens in your community, and you talk to your boy's principal about the state of these things in his school. You know the pressures on your boy to be one of the guys and to do what his friends do. So you keep close tabs on who he "hangs" with, reminding him that his friends are always welcome at your home. You have, over the years, taken the time to have conversations with him about the legal and health issues involved with consuming alcohol, taking drugs, and smoking cigarettes. You talked about how they could seriously affect his ability to do the things he likes to do, like mountain biking, skateboarding, and even playing electronic games. You told him that drinking, doing drugs, or smoking cigarettes would also reflect badly on his intelligence and the respect he has always had for himself. One thing you did, which you almost overlooked because you had taken his knowledge of this for granted, was to show him pictures of what the different drugs looked like. It turned out that he didn't know, and initially, neither did you.

Things to Consider

Every family has its own beliefs and rules about drinking, smoking, and doing drugs. Alcohol, in my opinion, is the least dangerous of this group because it can be done in moderation and needn't be addictive, while drugs and cigarettes most certainly are.

The drug of choice these days seems to be either marijuana or ecstasy. Alcohol is usually beer or wine, and cigarettes will just be cigarettes. In all likelihood your son will at least experiment with one or all these things. The first question is when, where, and how much? The second question is what can you do about it?

The answer to the first question is that he will probably do it as soon as the raw materials are available. He will do these things at parties, raves, concerts, and just hanging out with his friends. How much he will do it depends a lot on him and on you. It will depend on how much he needs to be a member of his group, how much pressure his friends put on him to try these things, how well he can resist these pressures, and how much he wants to resist them. It will depend on his self-esteem, how comfortable he is with himself, or how much he depends on others' opinions of him to justify himself. It also depends on his other commitments to school, sports, and family.

What can you do? With drinking you might want to let him have a little glass of wine or beer on special occasions so that he learns to drink in moderation at a very early age. You can model that for him with your drinking habits. And tell your boy your own attitudes toward drinking. If you don't allow alcohol in your home and don't drink yourselves, you may have a more difficult time with your boy because it becomes "forbidden fruit." At this age your boy won't yet have a driver's license so drinking and driving isn't an issue. You must still, however, teach him that he is never to ride in a car with anyone who has been drinking.

Drugs are a bigger concern to most parents because drugs are so potentially harmful and addiction can lead to a life of crime. According to some estimates 15 to 20 percent of teens have tried marijuana, starting as young as age twelve or thirteen. But some studies report that just under 30 percent of eighth graders say they have used illicit drugs.

Why do boys use drugs? All their friends talk about drugs and they want to know what it's really like. Boys will use drugs to show their independence from parents or to show they belong to their gang. Some boys will use them for the euphoric feeling they give to relieve the stress and tension of school or home life, or simply as an escape.

What can you do to keep your boy off drugs? First, be a model for him. Don't use drugs to solve your problems. Don't have a supply of mood-enhancing pills that he can sample. Make sure he doesn't have the money for drugs. "Hard" drugs are expensive. Monitor his behavior for signs of moodiness, listlessness, incoherence, or loss of appetite. Keep a close lookout for drug problems at his school. Know his friends. Talk to him about the dangers of drugs, particularly their addictiveness, their destructiveness, and the legal consequences of his being caught using them.

Smoking is the third addictive threat to your boy. One survey reported that almost 20 percent of eighth graders reported having smoked a cigarette within the last month. Boys seem to start smoking for different reasons than girls. Boys want to show they're mature and masculine. Boys also want to do what their friends do. Girls seem to use smoking for weight control (although medical reports show it doesn't work).

You should be able to tell if your boy smokes because his breath, hair, and clothes will smell of it, and his fingers and teeth will have nicotine stains. If your boy is determined to smoke it will be hard for you to stop him unless you can guarantee that he never has the money to buy a pack or friends from which he can "bum" one. You can only hope that he's just experimenting at his age and will not develop a taste or need for it. Once he's addicted the job of stopping is immense. So an ounce of prevention is worth more than a pound of cure. One grandfather offered his grandchildren the price of a pack of cigarettes a day until they reached the age of twenty-one if they agreed not to smoke. The money was deposited in an education fund. It worked!

Another approach is to sit down with your boy and list the pros and cons of smoking. Talking about the health problems smoking seems to cause might not work very well with your young boy because he probably thinks he's immortal, as most kids do. A better approach is to have him surf the Internet for the latest information about the dangers of smoking. Have him check the antismoking and lung cancer sites.

Most important, be a good model for him. Don't smoke yourself, or if you do, give it up for his sake and the sake of the rest of your family.

Three Things You Must Do

1. Teach your boy your attitudes toward drinking through conversation and by example.
2. Reject recreational use of addictive or behavior-altering drugs.
3. Set a good example by not smoking.

Things to Say and Do

You can try to teach your boy to abstain from alcohol for personal or religious reasons by telling him what those reasons are and what you expect of him. Say such things as:

- I can't be around all the time to keep you from drinking but I trust you to do the right thing.
- You may think you know better than I do about what's good for you but I think you'll find out that drinking isn't good for you.

If you approve of social drinking, say so. Say such things as:

- Doctors say that a drink or two a day, especially red wine, can be good for you. But you're a bit too young to start.
- You can have a little wine or beer with us on special occasions.
- Alcohol is okay in moderation when you reach legal age. But drunkenness at any age is unacceptable.

Let your boy know your attitude toward all kinds of drugs. Say such things as:

- We all use certain kinds of drugs, but even medicines should only be taken when absolutely necessary.
- Drugs are never a good substitute for love, understanding, or feeling good about yourself.

Talk to your boy about his knowledge and experience with drugs. Say such things as:

- Have you seen any of these drugs?
- Do any of your friends or other kids at school do drugs, or sell them?
- Are drugs available at your school?
- Have you ever tried marijuana? I did when I was in college, and I didn't like it.

Know your boy's habits, friends, and attitudes toward smoking. Say such things as:

- What do you think about smoking?
- How many of your friends smoke?
- You'd tell me if you smoked, wouldn't you?

Talk about your attitude toward smoking. Say such things as:

- I'm against smoking for adults as well as kids.
- It seems to me that it's impossible for someone to smoke without hurting themselves, others, or both.

Words, Phrases, and Actions to Use

- . . . alcoholism . . .
- . . . drunkenness . . .
- . . . moderation . . .
- . . . maturity . . .
- . . . responsibility . . .
- . . . addiction . . .

- . . . health . . .
- . . . harm . . .
- . . . cost . . .
- . . . cancer . . .
- . . . smell . . .
- . . . effects on others . . .

Things Not to Say and Do

Don't make drinking a bigger issue than it needs to be. Don't say such things as:

- If I ever learn that you've had a drink I will throw you out of the house.
- Drinking is sinful.
- Alcohol is evil. If you drink it you are evil too.

Don't encourage your boy to drink. Don't say such things as:

- Don't be a sissy. A little drink never hurt anybody, even at your age.
- You need practice in drinking. Try this.

- Be a man.
- I had my first drink in a bar when I was twelve.

Don't ignore your boy. Demands for attention can be a cry for help and a sign that drugs are already a problem or about to become one. Don't say such things as:

- I don't have time for you just now.
- You're old enough to cope with your own problems.
- I'm busy.

Don't refuse to discuss the issue of smoking. Don't say such things as:

- I don't care if your friends smoke. There's nothing to discuss.
- It's not open for discussion.

Don't be extreme in your threats of punishment for smoking. Don't say such things as:

- If I find out you smoke you're in big trouble.
- No child of mine will ever smoke, or else.

Don't be a bad role model.

- Don't be a heavy drinker.
- Don't do drugs.
- Don't be a smoker.

Words, Phrases, and Actions to Avoid

- You can never get enough of a good thing.
- It's good to get drunk every so often.
- You're never too young to start drinking.
- Drugs are my way of coping.
- Marijuana is good for you.
- Don't bother me.
- Take a pill and you'll be fine.
- Smoking is cool.
- I smoked when I was your age.
- There's nothing better than the first cigarette of the day.

APPEARANCE

◆

Your boy wants to be just like the other boys in his group. He's thankful he's a member of that group and he doesn't want to risk being left out because he doesn't fit in. A big part of fitting in for your teenage boy is to look cool, whatever looking cool means among his friends. You wish it meant dressing nicely in clothes that fit and didn't jump out at you trying to make a statement. Unfortunately, your boy's fashion statement includes pants that are big enough for two boys his size and shirts that would be too big for his father. His hair is spiked and he desperately wants an earring. You long for the good old days when you would buy him clothes that you thought looked so cute and he would happily wear them without a fuss. Now he wants nothing to do with your tastes or choices. He wants to look like his friends and nothing less than that will satisfy him.

Things to Consider

Your boy needs to fit in. Everyone knows that about teens. He still needs you for love and support, but he always looks toward his friends for role models and approval.

His appearance is his statement of who he is. For boys, even more than girls, appearance means more than words because boys are less articulate than girls at every age, even though girls may be less willing to speak up than boys. Your boy shows the world who he is by his clothes, his hair, his physique, and his demeanor. It's no accident that gangs in Los Angeles identify themselves through colors and tattoos. They want to be immediately recognizable for who they are.

Your boy also wants people to recognize him for who he is from his appearance. He may be a jock, a computer geek, a skater, or a student academic and social leader. Whatever he is he needs to dress the part. You may think he looks awful and his appearance may embarrass you. But you have to realize that he is no different from you in that regard. But what can you do about it? What is the best course of action to take with your young teenager? Here are some guidelines that may help you through this difficult time:

- Pick your battles wisely. Don't fight him over clothes as long as they're clean, legal, and relatively in one piece. He'll eventually grow out of this phase and you really don't want to damage your relationship over this issue.

- For clothes make price, not fashion, the issue.
- If he wants over-the-top fashions tell your boy he has to buy them for himself.
- Hair, thank goodness, grows back in its natural, pristine state no matter what's done to it. Let your boy dye, cut, spike, gel his hair as he wishes. He'll grow out of this too, eventually, as will his hair.
- Don't let him pierce his body or get tattoos. He's too young to make a reasonable decision about these permanent disfigurements. Tell him he has to wait until he's sixteen.
- He's not too young to learn that his appearance will affect others' impressions of him. He must already see that it affects how you see him. He's still young enough for people to pass it off as what young boys do. But as he gets older he'll need to realize that the way he looks has consequences.
- As far as possible ignore your boy's fashion fads. We've all been through it at his age.
- Judge his appearance in the context of *his* peer group, not yours.
- Put your foot down when it comes to his appearance with you at restaurants, the theater, concerts, weddings, or other special and public occasions. Make sure his appearance shows respect for the place, the people, and the occasion.

Three Things You Must Do

1. Realize that your teen's appearance expresses his view of himself in the context of his friends.
2. Prohibit permanent changes to his appearance.
3. Pick your battles wisely.

Things to Say and Do

If your boy wants a special haircut or hair color don't make a big thing of it. Say such things as:

- My only rule is that you have it done professionally.
- Why don't you use that temporary hair color that washes out?
- I don't mind what you do with your hair as long as you keep it clean.

Laugh about the things you really disapprove of while telling him what you really think. Say such things as:

- I'm happy to let you dress the way you want but I still have to tell you that I don't like it.
- If I ever dressed that way when I was your age my parents would have had a fit.
- You're lucky you have such liberal and understanding parents.

Tell your boy that certain aspects of his appearance are still your responsibility. Say such things as:

- Everything you wear has to be clean and not ripped up.
- Whatever you wear has to be legal.
- You cannot get a tattoo or a nose stud.

Tell him your rules for public appearances with you. Say such things as:

- When we go out together to special occasions you have to dress appropriately by my standards.
- When we go to parties together, or concerts, or nice restaurants, or the theater, you have to show respect in your appearance for the other people, the place, and the occasion.

If you are the parent of a boy who doesn't care about his appearance you can offer to help him with his choices. Say such things as:

- Let's go shopping.
- That's a nice haircut you got last time. I think we should go back there again.
- Do you ever think about what you'd like to wear?

Words, Phrases, and Actions to Use

- . . . your choice . . .
- . . . clean . . .
- . . . in one piece . . .
- . . . washed . . .
- No permanent changes.
- Be respectful.
- Your responsibility.

- My responsibility.
- Like.
- Don't like.
- Different.
- Unusual.
- Consequences.

Things Not to Say and Do

If your boy is a grunge skater realize that his clothes are specifically designed for this kind of statement and sport. Don't tease him about his appearance because it will only antagonize him. Don't say such things as:

- I could make you two pairs of pants with that much cloth.
- What size do you wear in those, XXXXXXXL?
- Have you lost a lot of weight?

Say nothing about your boy's appearance unless it's unlawful or so far out that you think he's lost his mind. Don't say such things as:

- I hate the way you look.
- I wouldn't be caught dead with you.
- You look awful.
- Either you change into something respectable or you're not going out.

Don't ignore the importance of him looking like his friends. Don't say such things as:

- I don't care how your friends look. You're not looking like that.
- Your friends don't matter to me. Only you do.
- What your friends think is less important than what I think.

Words, Phrases, and Actions to Avoid

- You look terrible.
- You look stupid.
- That's criminal.
- Never let me see you dressed like that again.
- Do what I say.
- You're still a child.

BULLYING AND TEASING

◆

It worries you that bullying and teasing are two of the biggest problems in your boy's school. You know from experience that teasing goes on in every school classroom, every school corridor, and every schoolyard. Bullying is almost as common, and much more serious. Your boy has never complained about being bullied but occasionally he tells you that he can't wear that shirt, or those pants, or that sweater anymore because it's not what his friends wear and they'll tease him about it. You realize that saying to him that he has to rise above that kind of teasing is the wrong approach. Teasing can be a serious problem for boys because they are constantly jockeying for position in the group, looking to move up the ladder. Your boy must avoid any vulnerability or he will be verbally assaulted. Even more serious is bullying in which your boy may be the object of threats, extortion, and even physical assaults. You also worry that your boy may be the teaser rather than the teased, or the bully rather than the bullied. What, if anything, can you do to make your boy teasing proof and bully proof? And keep him from doing either to other boys or girls?

Things to Consider

Bullying and teasing are so common in schools that one begins to think that many kids, especially boys, are hardwired to act this way. Research reports show that boys, by the time they are four years old, naturally begin to realize that people differ from one another in many ways, including physical characteristics. As they grow older they become more aware of how these differences translate into who is friends with whom and who socializes with whom. They see these relationships in their own family circles as well as at school. Sometimes boys will use these differences to justify teasing and bullying other children. They will pick out children who are physically different, socially different, smaller, new to the school or neighborhood, or from a minority ethnic group for special attention and teasing and bullying.

Another important fact about boys' bullying and teasing comes from the need for boys to organize themselves in some hierarchy. Male animals in virtually every species seem to need to fit into some kind of "pecking order." Such hierarchies seem to prevent the need for constant battles for dominance. Boys learn where they stand in their group and don't have to fight each other every time they meet to decide who follows whom.

But boys, as much as they may be following the natural order of things, still can't be allowed to hurt others through teasing or bullying.

Teasing is not always malicious. Sometimes it is simply part of the pubescent, adolescent sexual dance. Boys show affection or interest in girls by pulling their hair and clothes, throwing snowballs at them, chasing them, making comments about them, and showing off in front of them by teasing or bullying other boys. These actions can be misunderstood if the teaser and the teased don't feel the same way toward each other. But it's important always to try to see the intent of the teasing rather than automatically condemn it.

Bullying, on the other hand, is always malicious. There is no good reason for bullying. The biggest problem for you is to know that bullying is happening to your boy, or that your boy is a bully, and what to do about it. Dr. Eli H. Newberger points out there is a code of "cool" that prevents boys from telling their parents or other adults about being badly teased or bullied. Boys know that they're not supposed to tell or they'll be bullied and teased more than ever. They also know that telling doesn't always guarantee protection. Teachers, and parents, confronted with a "your word against his" situation don't know what to do. Even if they do, boys know that there won't always be an adult around to protect them.

Feelings of shame and inadequacy can also prevent a boy from telling anyone else he's being bullied. It's part of the "Why me?" syndrome. Boys are not proud of the fact that they're being picked on rather than someone else. They certainly don't want to share these feelings with others, especially not their parents.

What should you do? If you have a good relationship with your young teen you might at least be sure your boy will tell you if he is being badly teased or bullied. If he is a bully you're less likely to find out about it from your boy. Here is a list of things you can do to help prevent, stop, or treat bad cases of teasing and bullying:

- Keep good lines of communication open between you and your boy and your boy's friends and teachers.
- Watch for signs of avoidance behavior regarding school, play, places, or friends.
- Watch for changes in sleeping habits, eating habits, personality, or physical appearance.
- Watch for any unexplained loss of valued possessions or money, or requests for money.
- Watch for changes in behavior patterns at home, after school, or on weekends.

If you notice any of these things ask your boy about them. Don't give up if he refuses to discuss them. Check with his friends and teachers. Keep talking about your need to know if anything is bothering him. Once he opens up and tells you about the problem you can do the following:

- If the problem is teasing find out why he's being teased and see if you can fix that.
- Talk to your boy about the problem of mean teasing and why he mustn't accept it or why he mustn't do it to others. Explain how nice teasing may be misunderstood or undesired.
- If the problem is bullying you might need to get some evidence that this is happening. See if your boy can give you the names of potential witnesses. Keep a written record of who's involved, when and where it happens, and what the bully does. If extortion is involved make a detailed list of what's being demanded and given.
- Talk to your boy's teachers and school administrators about the problem. Make these talks confidential so your boy won't be branded a "squealer" or "sissy."
- Find out your school's policy on bullying and teasing and what action can be taken on your boy's behalf.
- If you know the name of the bully you can call his parents and discuss the problem. It helps a lot if you have evidence to support your claim, but even if you don't you can risk a call since the parents of the bully may have already had other problems with their son.
- If you get no satisfaction from any of these sources and the bullying is serious, contact the police.
- Help bully proof and tease proof your boy by helping him have high self-esteem and encouraging him to react to teasing with laughter rather than hurt. Laughter often disarms the teaser. You can also, if possible, help and encourage your boy to find an older "protector." One of the best ways is to get your boy to join a sports team and to have one of the older boys act in that way for him. Teams and clubs also can offer him good group support.
- If nothing works and your boy continues to suffer from teasing and/or bullying you might need to change schools. This seems like a drastic action, but it's quite common and can work very well.
- If your boy turns out to be a serious bully himself you may need to get professional counseling for him.

Three Things You Must Do

1. Keep good communication lines open.
2. Know your boy's school policies on bullying and teasing.
3. Stop your boy from being bullied or bullying, or being maliciously teased or maliciously teasing.

Things to Say and Do

Keep communication open. You want to be the first to know if your boy is being bullied or badly teased. Say such things as:

- Are you having any problems at school?
- Do you get along all right with your friends?
- Are any kids at school bugging you?

If you find your boy is being teased or talked about find out why he's being teased and see if you can fix that. Say such things as:

- What do they say?
- Who does it to you? Are they your friends?
- What do they tease you about?

Talk to your boy about why he mustn't tease others in a mean way. Also explain how nice teasing may be misunderstood or undesired. Say such things as:

- Do you tease other kids? Why do you do that?
- How do they react? Do they get angry or do they laugh and tease you back?
- If you're teasing someone and they ask you to stop, do you stop?

If your boy is being bullied talk about evidence that this is happening. Ask for the names of potential witnesses. Say such things as:

- Who's doing this to you?
- What are they doing?
- Are there any other kids he's doing this to? Do you know any kids who know this is happening to you? Can we work together to deal with it?

Talk to your boy's teachers and school administrators about the problem. Ask them about the school's policy on bullying and teasing and how they can help your boy. Help bully proof and tease proof your boy. Say such things as:

- You're a pretty strong boy. The bullying and teasing is tough but I know you can cope with it until we can make them stop.
- If someone teases you just laugh. It's the best defense.
- Whatever they say, you know you're a wonderful boy.

If you think your boy may be a bully confront him with it and see what he says. Say such things as:

- I've heard rumors that you've been bullying some kids. Is that true?
- Why do you think they'd say that if it weren't true?
- Do older kids bully you and that's why you're bullying younger kids?

Words, Phrases, and Actions to Use

- . . . bullying . . .
- . . . teasing . . .
- . . . evidence . . .
- Bullying isn't fun.
- . . . good intentions . . .
- Some girls like to be teased but others don't.
- That's mean.
- That's malicious.
- That's unacceptable.
- That's dangerous.

Things Not to Say and Do

Don't ignore any signs of bullying and mean teasing. Don't say such things as:

- Everyone gets bullied and teased. It's no big deal.
- You better learn to live with it.
- Don't be a sissy.

Don't blame the victim. Don't say such things as:

- You must be asking for it.
- It's your own fault.
- You're probably to blame for what's happening to you.

Words, Phrases, and Actions to Avoid

- It's your fault.
- That's harmless.
- That's life.
- Fight for yourself.
- You're a coward.
- You're a sissy.
- You're a tattle-tale.
- You're a loser.
- You're a weakling.
- You have no guts.

CURFEW

◆

Opposite of people who think teens become a serious threat to society after the clock strikes ten at night, you believe your boy's curfew is a question of health and safety. You need to make sure your boy is getting enough sleep at night during his adolescent years when he's using up so much psychic and physical energy at school, at play, and in coping with all the changes he's experiencing in his life. You also need to know where he is, who he's with, what he's doing, and when he's coming home. He needs to know your rules and expectations. You and he disagree on these from time to time, but that gives you a chance to talk about it and exchange points of view. You and he together work out a reasonable curfew for school nights, a second one for weekends, and a third one for special occasions. He's always mostly concerned that his curfew is earlier than those of his friends. You're mostly concerned that he gets home early enough to stay out of trouble and to get enough rest for the next day's activities. But you find that flexibility is the best approach. You know he needs to be like his friends and you're sympathetic to his pleas.

Things to Consider

Politicians and others make much noise about the need for strict controls on children of all ages, but especially on teens. For them, curfews are the best way to prevent teen crime and vandalism, and to some extent they are surely right. If your teen is at home he can't be "up to no good" someplace else.

But you know your teen. He's basically a good, law-abiding citizen, and so are his friends, even if they occasionally do things that give you a few more gray hairs. Yet, the way people talk you would think that every boy over the age of twelve is ready to commit murder and mayhem.

You know that teen crime is falling, not rising. And you know that all the curfews in the world won't prevent a small number of teenage boys from getting into serious trouble. You also realize that parental abuse of children is the main cause of teenage delinquency. Parental supervision is important, but without a home full of love and care and trust, parental supervision and curfews will not keep some kids out of trouble.

You need to work out curfew times with your boy that suit him and his circumstances. You have to decide if he needs an early curfew because he always looks tired, he has important work to prepare for school, he has a football game the next day, or because his past behavior shows he can't always be trusted.

His curfew will be earlier on school nights than weekends. You'll take his friends' curfew times into account by talking to his friends and their parents. You'll also vary his curfew time when he's going to a party or a concert or some other special occasion. Finally, his curfew will be later when he's fifteen than when he's thirteen, although not that much later since teenage boys rarely get enough sleep these days. Unfortunately, high school schedules are made for adults, not teenagers.

Finally, you and your boy have made a pact that if he's going to be late, he must call you. You won't get angry because you're just happy to know that he's not going to be home on time. As long as your boy can trust you to be reasonable about making curfews he will more than likely be reasonable about respecting them. And remember, a curfew is not a substitute for love, caring, and trust.

Three Things You Must Do

1. Have reasonable curfews for your boy.
2. Make them flexible enough to account for his needs, your needs, the night of the week, and his friends' curfews.
3. Be reasonable so that he is never afraid to call and say he'll be late.

Things to Say and Do

Discuss your boy's curfew with him so that he knows your needs and you know his. Say such things as:

- Let's talk about when you have to be home school nights and weekends.
- I always need to know where you are and who you're with.
- What do you think is a reasonable time for you to be home?

Talk about your boy's friends' curfews to make sure you or they are not way out of line. Say such things as:

- I want to make your curfew reasonable. When do your friends have to be home?
- Do all your friends have the same curfew?
- Do your friends have what you think are reasonable curfews?

Make your concerns about a curfew for him clear. Say such things as:

- You need to be home in good time at night because you need to get enough sleep.
- You're going through a time of growth and you need all the sleep you can get.
- My first priority for you is to keep you healthy. You need a good sleep every night.

Talk about the rules that surround a curfew. Say such things as:

- You know you have to be home by nine o'clock on school nights and eleven o'clock on weekends. If you are ever going to be late you must call.
- My responsibility is to keep you safe and healthy. Your responsibility is to help me do that by trying your best to respect your curfew.
- Regardless of your curfew we always need to know where you are, who you're with, and what you're doing.
- As long as you're good about getting home on time we'll be good about understanding why sometimes you're late.

Words, Phrases, and Actions to Use

- . . . curfew . . .
- . . . getting enough sleep . . .
- . . . reasonable . . .
- . . . the same as your friends . . .
- . . . good health . . .
- . . . responsibilities . . .
- Call us.
- It will change as you get older.

Things Not to Say and Do

Don't be rigid and refuse to listen to your boy's needs. Don't say such things as:

- I don't care what you want. I'm the parent and I make the rules.
- This is when you have to be home. I won't discuss it.
- This is your curfew. You either obey it or you're not going out.

Don't ignore your boy's need to be like his friends. Don't say such things as:

- I don't care what your friends' curfews are.
- Don't talk to me about your friends. I'm your parent, not theirs.
- Your friends' parents have their rules, I have mine.

Don't overreact if your teen is occasionally late. Don't say such things as:

- I told you if you were ever late you'd be punished.
- I don't want to hear excuses. You have a responsibility to be home exactly on time.
- I'm not interested in why you were late. You're grounded.

Words, Phrases, and Actions to Avoid

- You must never be late.
- If you're late your curfew will be earlier next time.
- I make the rules, not you.
- I'm not interested in your ideas.
- Shut up and listen to me.
- You'll do as I say.

DATING

◆

Do you let your boy start dating before he's sixteen? That's always a tough question to answer. You've given it lots of thought and are trying to put the question in the context of who your boy is and what the normal thing seems to be among his schoolmates. If he were a girl it would be an easier question to answer. Girls mature faster. You would expect your daughter to want to go out with a boy on her own by the time she was fourteen, even though you'd prefer her to wait until she was sixteen. With your boy it's a different matter. You're even surprised that he wants to go out at his age. He's a somewhat immature fourteen year old, as are most of his friends. You wonder what girl his own age, or even younger, would want to go out with him? Another part of this whole thing is the shock of realizing that your little boy actually has an interest in girls. He's always been such a boy's boy. Could it be that sexual urges are finally making themselves felt?

Things to Consider

Nature has programmed boys to be sexual aggressors. Dating is a sexually aggressive activity and boys take the lead in it. Even today boys usually ask girls for a date, not the other way around. Sex is probably the most important issue in dating.

You may think that if you allow your boy to start dating at this age, the sexual issues won't arise because he and the girl are too young. But the fact is that once boys reach puberty, and for some, even before, the sex drive takes over. Dating is their way of organizing sexual pursuit, making it socially acceptable and giving it some rules.

Adolescent boys want sexual intimacy of some kind. Kissing, holding hands, hugging, and fondling girls are, for boys, a prelude to intercourse. For some boys this prelude lasts a long time and intercourse may never happen during dating. For others intercourse is their prime reason for dating and nothing short of that will satisfy them.

There is a wide range of dating experience and practice among young teenage boys. By age sixteen many boys will have had lots of dates and even intimate sexual experience. But many other boys will have never been on a solo date and will have had no physical sexual experiences with a girl. You have to decide which group you want your boy to belong to. If you're like most parents you'd probably like your boy to be in neither group. You would like him to have girls for friends and to go out with girls in a group, but not one on one.

Don't hesitate to talk to your boy about your feelings. Encourage him to go out on group dates, but discourage him from forming a relationship with only one girl. It may not do any good when he and a girl find each other mutually attractive, but it's worth a try. Sometimes knowing your wishes will make your boy think twice about what he does.

More important than when he actually starts to date is for you to talk to him about how to behave toward girls, both in groups and individually on a date. Here are some things to talk about:

- Sex—talk to your boy about the moral and health aspects of sex. He must know your views on sex and he must have a good grasp of what is safe and what is dangerous sexual activity.
- Respect—talk to your boy about the importance of his respecting his date's person and individuality. Make sure he understands his obligation to honor his date's wishes. If she says no, it means no!
- Self-worth—talk to your boy about the need for him to understand that his date must not be belittled, demeaned, insulted, or harassed.
- Kindness—talk to him about The Golden Rule. He should be as kind to his date as he would want her to be to him. No macho posing or violent threats or actions.
- Independence—talk to your boy about accepting that his date is her own person, even when she is his date. She has her own feelings, opinions, desires, likes, and dislikes, and he needs to recognize and respect them.
- Responsibility—talk to your boy about his responsibility for his date's safety. He must never put her in any situation in which she feels threatened by him, or by others.
- Fun—dating is supposed to be fun. Remind your boy that there's something wrong if he's having fun, but his date isn't.

If you feel your boy is ready to start dating remember that he's not going to be totally rational about his feelings. His desire to date is his way of expressing one of our most basic human drives, even though we have covered it over with many different kinds of social conventions and rules. Be clear with your boy about your values, beliefs, expectations, and rules. He may reject what you say but you must say it nevertheless.

Three Things You Must Do

1. Decide when you will let your boy start dating.
2. Make your views on dating clear to your boy.
3. Discuss his responsibilities to his date.

Things to Say and Do

Talk to your boy about dates you remember. Sharing such stories will help him to learn about proper dating behavior. Say such things as:

- Let me tell you about my first date. What a disaster!
- I started dating when I was sixteen. Before that I was too shy.
- When I was your age I used to think about girls all the time. But I didn't really know how to have girls as friends.

You might want to encourage your boy to go out with girls in groups of boys and girls rather than on single dates. Say such things as:

- I think you're still a bit too young to take a girl out on your own. But going out in groups is fine.
- Do you and your friends like going out with groups of girls?
- I'm glad to see you have girls as friends, not just as girlfriends.

Talk about dating etiquette, including the issues I've raised above. Say such things as:

- Let's talk about how you should treat a girl on a date.
- Tell me what you think about how a boy should behave toward a girl on a date.
- Do you and your friends know what girls like to do on a first date?

If you can, talk to your boy about the moral, emotional, and safety issues of sex because it may be an issue in his dating. Say such things as:

- Although you really like this girl, you need to realize that you are both too young for sex, however you may feel about each other.
- What have you learned about sex in school? Do you know the serious health issues in sex? What do you know about safe sex?

■ I know you have strong sexual urges but you need to control them for your sake and your date's.

Talk about your view that your boy should get to know lots of different girls. Say such things as:

■ At your age going around with lots of different girls is a good idea. What do you think?
■ You need to get to know lots of girls. It's important at your age.

Words, Phrases, and Actions to Use

■ . . . dating . . .
■ . . . safety . . .
■ You're too young.
■ This is how to behave.
■ Never be violent.
■ Never be mean.

■ Don't be unkind.
■ Show respect.
■ Have fun.
■ Do what's appropriate.
■ Let's talk about it.

Things Not to Say and Do

Don't ignore your boy's context for dating. Don't say such things as:

■ I don't care what your friends do. You can't date until you're sixteen.
■ Your friends' parents have their rules, I have mine.
■ You'll do as I say.

Don't avoid talking about dating. Don't say such things as:

■ I don't want to discuss it.
■ I don't care what you think or what you want.
■ I'm not discussing it. These are my rules and that's the end of it.

Don't stop your boy from talking to you about his relationships. Don't say such things as:

■ Your dating is your own business.
■ I'm not interested in hearing about your dates.
■ Keep it to yourself. I don't want to know.

Don't encourage your boy to be some macho fool. Don't say such things as:

- You've got to be tough with girls. If you're soft they won't like you.
- Girls are supposed to do what you say. You're the boss.
- If she doesn't want to do what you want to do then dump her.

Words, Phrases, and Actions to Avoid

- Be tough.
- Do what you want.
- Girls don't deserve your respect.
- It's okay to be mean to her if she won't do what you want.
- Fear is more important than respect.
- Maybe you'll get lucky.
- I had sex on my first date when I was thirteen.
- Go for as much as she'll give you.

HOMOSEXUALITY

◆

You don't want your boy to be homophobic. You want him to have a healthy regard for the different ways people feel about other people. You don't think homosexuality is a choice or a sin, but simply the way some men and women are made. You believe that brain and hormonal differences account for most homosexual feelings just as they account for most heterosexual feelings. You've often thought about how you would feel if your boy turned out to be gay. You know, if you're completely honest with yourself, that you'd be unhappy and disappointed. Not because being gay is bad, or wrong, but because you know how much discrimination and hatred exists for gays, and you also would have no grandchildren to look forward to. But whether your boy is straight, or gay, you want him to know how you feel on the issue, and you want to know how he feels.

Things to Consider

There are at least two issues here. The first is how you feel about homosexuality and how you communicate that to your boy. The second is how you find out if you suspect that your boy is homosexual and how you would feel about it if he were.

What do you think about homosexuality? Do you believe the scientific evidence we have that says sexuality isn't a choice, or do you believe that we can all choose our sexuality? What will you tell your boy when he tells you that he has a friend he thinks is gay? Will you say that homosexuality is a sin against God, the family, and all the traditional values of society? Or will you tell him that in your view God made people in many different ways and that two men or two women can love each other just as much as a man and a woman? Will you encourage him to be tolerant of homosexuals, or will you say it's all right to discriminate against them, to deny them legal rights afforded to heterosexual couples, and even to physically assault or abuse them? Will you tolerate "gay bashing" of any sort?

Your answer to these questions is very important. Assaults on gay students and the rate of suicide among gay boys are both much higher than you might think. Adolescent boys, struggling so hard to make sense of their own sexual urges, often take out their confusion on other boys who seem different, gay, or effeminate. William S. Pollack in *Real Boys* and Dr. Eli H. Newberger in *The Men They Will Become* have excellent discussions of the dilemma of homosexuality for adolescent boys. Both point out the difficulty of establishing the cause of homosexuality in boys, but both are equally vocal in their view that homosexuality is not a disease or some sexual disorder.

I have a childhood friend who knew he was not like other boys when he was in elementary school. After admitting to himself and others as an adult that he was gay he embarked on a course of psychological counseling to try and become straight. Of course it didn't work and he finally accepted who he was. It seems to be the case that boys as young as nine or ten have feelings they later realize were early manifestations of their homosexuality. If they hide their feelings and have no one with whom they can discuss them they feel isolated, confused, and guilty. From a sense of hopelessness they frequently see suicide as a solution. If they admit their homosexuality they face ridicule, hostility, and possibly physical assault, especially from other boys.

Do you have the kind of relationship with your boy that would allow him to tell you that he thought he was gay? This is really another way of asking if he feels safe with you. Or is he afraid to tell you the truth about himself for fear of your reaction?

If you suspect your boy might be gay, and want to find out if he is, you and your son will probably need to see a therapist. Your boy may know but he may just as well be confused and unsure. You will both be better off knowing and a therapist experienced in working with adolescents and adults will give you the chance of finding a good answer to your questions. The big question is, will your boy agree to go?

If it turns out that your boy is gay you need to revisit all the things I talked about earlier regarding your attitudes toward homosexuality because now they have a new and different meaning.

Three Things You Must Do

1. Know your own views on homosexuality.
2. Whatever your view teach your boy tolerance.
3. Know if your boy is homosexual.

Things to Say and Do

Find out if your boy knows any kids in school who are homosexual. Say such things as:

- Are any kids in your school gay?
- Do you have any friends you think are gay?
- Do you know any gay guys?

Talk to your boy about various views on homosexuality. Say such things as:

- What do you think about homosexuality?
- Do you think it's something boys choose to be? Or girls?

- Some people think that homosexuals are sick, that it's an illness. What do you think?

Tell your boy your own views. Say such things as:

- I think it's not a choice. I think we don't choose whether we love males or females. I certainly didn't choose. For as long as I can remember I liked girls.
- I don't blame people for being gay. It's just another way people are.
- I think homosexuality is just different, not sick, or a sin, or a crime.

Talk about gay bashing. Say such things as:

- Do gay kids in your school get hassled? Who does it? Do you do it?
- I think it's terrible when gay kids get harassed or abused. What do you think?
- Does your school protect the gay kids? How do they do it?

If it's appropriate talk to your boy about the possibility of his being gay, but you'll need to lead into it carefully. Say such things as:

- I have the feeling your friend may be a bit different from other boys. Have you noticed?
- I really like your friend. What do you think about him?
- Would you tell me if you were gay?

Words, Phrases, and Actions to Use

- . . . gay . . .
- . . . homosexual . . .
- . . . heterosexual . . .
- . . . different . . .
- . . . choice . . .
- . . . biological . . .
- . . . love . . .
- . . . lifestyle . . .
- That's normal in its own way.
- They deserve the same rights as heterosexuals.

Things Not to Say and Do

Don't preach hatred of gays. Don't say such things as:

- I hate gays.
- Homos are just perverts.
- Gays aren't human.

Don't blame them for what they are. Don't say such things as:

- It's their choice to be perverted.
- Gays could be straight if they wanted to be.
- Homosexuality is a sin against God.

Don't prohibit your boy from having gay friends. Don't say such things as:

- If you hang around with homosexuals you'll become one yourself.
- I don't want you hanging around with that kind of boy.
- Never bring a gay boy back to this house!

Don't discourage your boy from talking about homosexuality. Don't say such things as:

- I never want to hear you say that again.
- Those are sinful words. Don't ever use them in this house.
- I've told you how I feel about homosexuality. I don't want to discuss it anymore.

Don't make your boy afraid to tell you that he thinks he may be gay. Don't say such things as:

- If I ever found out you were homosexual I'd throw you out of the house.
- No son of mine will ever be homosexual.
- If you are gay I don't want to know. Just go away.

Words, Phrases, and Actions to Avoid

- . . . homo . . .
- . . . pervert . . .
- . . . sinner . . .
- . . . the devil . . .
- It's an abomination.
- It's evil.

MENSTRUATION AND CONCEPTION

◆

You want your boy to understand girls and to have a good knowledge of the natural wonders of sexuality. He's already had some sex education at school but you're not sure how much he really understands about the mechanics of a woman's monthly cycle and conception. So these topics are on your list of things to talk about, even though you realize that you may be repeating what he already knows. It's only through a good conversation about this topic that you'll really find out. But you wonder how to begin this kind of discussion with your thirteen-year-old son. He doesn't have an older sister or brother so he can't learn about it from them. You want him to know the facts but you're embarrassed to start talking about it yourself. How do you say to your son, "Do you know what a woman's menstrual cycle is? Do you know how that relates to conception?" And where do you say it? At breakfast, in the car, at the beach?

Things to Consider

Your boy has most likely already had discussions of menstruation and conception in sex education classes in school since fourth or fifth grade. When he was nine or ten years old it would have played to his curiosity about sex, but because a real relationship with a girl was still a few years away it would not have the same meaning that it does now. Your boy is now at an age, early adolescence, during which the information is truly meaningful and important for him. Now he needs to know the facts and their implications, and he needs to understand the moral and social issues surrounding reproduction.

Naturally you find it hard and embarrassing to talk about this with your boy. Even talking about a perfectly natural, normal, and nonerotic subject like a woman's menstrual cycle can be a tough conversation to have with a young teenage boy. It's easier to talk to a prepubescent girl about a change that will occur in her body that will make her able to bear children than to talk to a boy about the female cycle that enables a girl as young as twelve to be a mother. Yet it's something he needs to know about.

For your boy in junior and senior high school a girl's period is a fact of life. It's much better for him if you come right out and talk about it before his lack of knowledge embarrasses or totally confuses him. He's old enough to understand and, hopefully, still young enough not to be too embarrassed by the conversation.

How should you approach it? The best way is for him to bring it up. If you have a good communicative relationship with your boy he knows he can talk to you about almost anything. But this topic may be too sensitive for even him to bring up. So a good way is to use TV commercials for sanitary napkins as a lead into the discussion.

You're sitting together watching television and one of these commercials comes on. You can ask your boy if he knows what the commercial is selling. If he says yes then ask him to tell you in detail. If he says no then you can take the opportunity to tell him the details.

Ask him if he ever hears his girlfriends talk about getting their periods. Does he know that they are referring to a special time every month when girls ovulate. This means that each month they have eggs inside them, in their ovaries, which, if fertilized by sperm from the male, grow into babies. If these eggs aren't fertilized they are pushed out of the ovaries and come out of the female's vagina in the form of blood. This happens to girls and women every month from the time they get their first period, these days as early as age eleven or twelve, until they are past childbearing age, usually in their late forties or fifties. This happens every twenty-eight to thirty days, which is why it's called a period.

As I said, your boy may already have a good idea how this works but it never hurts to go over it in detail so that he knows. You can also use this conversation to begin talking about morality and possible consequences of sexual intercourse, and why boys and girls his age shouldn't do it.

Three Things You Must Do

1. Ask your boy what he already knows about the relationship between menstruation and conception.
2. Tell your boy, if he doesn't know or has misinformation, the mechanics and purpose of menstruation.
3. Talk about the moral and social aspects of sexual intercourse and conception.

Things to Say and Do

If your boy asks you about menstruation give him the facts. Say such things as:

- I'm glad you asked. Here are the facts.
- Where did you hear about it?
- I'm happy to tell you. This is what happens.

If your boy asks you about conception give him the facts. Say such things as:

- I'm glad you asked. Here are the facts.
- This is something you should know about. Let me tell you.
- I'll tell you. If there's anything you don't understand please ask.

If your boy doesn't ask about menstruation tell him anyway. Say such things as:

- I think you need to know about a woman's period.
- Have you ever heard girls talk about having their periods? Let me tell you what they're talking about.
- There's never a right time to tell you about this so why don't I do it now. I want to tell you what happens inside a woman when she gets what we call her period.

Ask your boy what he knows and doesn't know about the facts of reproduction. Say such things as:

- What do you know about how babies are made?
- Tell me the facts of reproduction.
- Can you tell me about how a woman's menstrual cycle and sexual intercourse work together to produce babies?

Talk about the moral issues involved in reproduction. Say such things as:

- You already know the facts so let's talk about why and when you should have sexual intercourse.
- Normally people have intercourse because they love each other. But that's not the only time and we have to talk about that to see whether it's right or wrong, good or bad, especially for kids like you.
- We believe that a man and a woman should only have sexual intercourse after they are married. Let's talk about why we believe that.
- I believe that sexual intercourse should only be between people who love each other and who are old enough to care for a baby in case a baby is produced.

Talk to your boy about the social aspects of sexual intercourse. Say such things as:

- Sexual intercourse can be very pleasurable for the man and the woman. But there are also dangers in doing it, especially dangers of disease. That's one of the reasons boys and girls your age should not have sexual intercourse.
- Boys and girls your age can't possibly look after a baby.

- You need to control your sexual urges until you are much older because of all the health problems and social problems sexual intercourse can cause.

Encourage your boy to ask you questions about menstruation and reproduction. Say such things as:

- Is there anything I've told you that you don't understand?
- What more can I tell you?
- Ask me questions about this stuff and I'll tell you if I know the answer, or we can go and find the answer together.

Words, Phrases, and Actions to Use

- . . . menstruation . . .
- . . . period . . .
- . . . cycle . . .
- . . . ovaries . . .
- . . . eggs . . .
- . . . reproduction . . .
- . . . love . . .
- . . . morality . . .
- . . . dangers . . .

Things Not to Say and Do

Don't discourage your boy from asking about menstruation. Don't say such things as:

- I won't talk to you about such a dirty subject.
- That's not a fit topic for us to talk about.
- Don't let me ever hear you talk about that again.

Don't discourage your boy from asking about reproduction. Don't say such things as:

- You shouldn't be thinking about that kind of thing at your age.
- I certainly won't talk to you about that. When you're old enough to do it then I'll tell you.
- What a filthy thing to be asking me.

Don't talk about it using slang. Always use the proper terms. Don't be irresponsible in your talk about a woman's period. Don't say such things as:

- It's a curse.
- It's filthy and dirty.

Words, Phrases, and Actions to Avoid

- That's dirty.
- That's filthy.
- I won't discuss it.
- Don't ever ask me again.
- Do whatever you like.

MONEY

◆

You want your boy to have good sense when it comes to making money, saving it, spending it, and investing it. You want him to know the value of a dollar. You're not poor by any means but you're not "rolling in dough." You're trying to save money for your boy's education and you can't be wasteful. You want him to realize that and yet you don't want to be stingy with him. You know that he has certain needs, many of which have to do with wearing the kind of clothes his friends wear, going to the movies and concerts they go to, having the same video and electronic games they have, and having the right sports equipment. You give your boy an allowance and from this money you expect him to buy his "wants" while you supply his "needs." You want him to realize the difference between wants and needs. You give him advice on money matters when he asks. You point out that if he wants something expensive he'll just have to save for it. You're quite happy to pay him for doing special jobs around the house but not for his normal chores.

Things to Consider

You don't expect ever to have as much money as you would like to have so you try to live within your means. You realize that you have much more disposable income than most people in the world. You value the things money can buy but you don't consider yourself greedy or a conspicuous consumer, buying things just to outdo your friends and neighbors. You think you know the value of a dollar. You hope you are setting a good example for your boy.

You want to pass on your attitudes toward money to your boy. Even in today's society men are the principle breadwinners so you want to prepare your boy for that responsibility. You feel your job is to teach him to work hard, spend less than he earns, and make his money work for him by investing his earnings sensibly. You believe that financial security lies in conservative, low- to medium-risk investments for the long-term and not in quick, get-rich-in-a-hurry schemes and high-risk speculation.

Your boy, at his age, is likely to be a risk-taker so you don't want him to have control over too much money. But you do want him to have a chance to learn from experience in handling money. Now is the time to start teaching him good money management when he's just beginning to have a real sense of what it costs to live the way he'd like to live, with always enough money in reserve to buy special treats for himself or gifts for family or friends. He's still quite young but it's good for him to start investing in a very limited way in bonds and the stock market. Talk to him about your investment strategy and show him how to make good choices by evaluating the options. Let him learn by doing.

If you've been giving him a weekly allowance for a number of years now that he's a teenager you might want to move to a monthly allowance to help him learn how to budget his money over a longer period of time. You need to talk to him about this and your purpose in doing it. You may offer to help him work out a budget of expenses and income over the month and see how they balance.

At first you and he can monitor his progress and see if he regularly runs out of money before the end of the month. Ask him to keep a list of what he spends his money on. Resist bailing him out. It may be a hard thing to do but it will help him learn to spend more wisely. Examining his expenditures will help you see if the amount of his allowance is really appropriate to his needs.

You can help your teen by being a good model of spending, saving, and investing. Show him how you budget your money. Help him work out a budget for himself. Even if your boy doesn't seem too thrilled by all of this detailed attention paid to money he will one day be grateful to you for giving him this foundation for good money management.

Three Things You Must Do

1. Give your boy control over some money.
2. Help him understand the difference between wants and needs.
3. Give him experience in budgeting, saving, and investing.

Things to Say and Do

Talk to your boy about his money needs. Let him tell you how he feels about his allowance and chores you pay him for. Say such things as:

- How are you making out with your money? Do you have enough for the things you need?
- How does your allowance compare with your friends'? Do they get more than you or less? Do they have to work for their allowance?
- You know you have certain jobs around the house that you have to do and then there are special jobs, which we'll pay you for. Is that what your friends have too? We want to be fair to you.

Talk to your boy about the difference between his wants and his needs. Make sure he understands your views and you understand his. Say such things as:

- Do you understand the difference between your wants and your needs? Let me tell you how I understand the difference for myself.
- What would you say are things you absolutely need to live an ordinary life at home and at school? What are the things you would like but don't really need? What's the difference between the two? I'd like to compare your ideas about this with mine.
- I think a parent's responsibility is to make sure you have your needs looked after. You take care of your wants with your allowance and what you earn from jobs.

Talk to your boy about budgeting. Show him how you do it. Say such things as:

- Here's how I control my spending each month in terms of my income.
- How do you work out how much you can spend on something?
- Do you sometimes have money left over when you get your next allowance?

Suggest that your boy start saving and investing his money, if you haven't already started him doing this. Say such things as:

- Do you think it would be a good idea to put some money in your savings account each month?
- If you save some money from your allowance over the next six months I'll match it and I'll help you choose a stock to invest it in.
- Let's talk about saving and investing your money rather than spending everything. Let me show you how I do it and you can see if you'd like to try the same thing.

Words, Phrases, and Actions to Use

- . . . wants . . .
- . . . needs . . .
- . . . budgeting . . .
- . . . the value of money . . .
- . . . saving . . .
- . . . investing . . .

- . . . greed . . .
- . . . reasonable . . .
- . . . value for money . . .
- . . . long-term . . .
- . . . short-term . . .
- . . . high-risk . . .

- . . . low-risk . . .
- . . . rate of return . . .

- Know your income.
- Know your expenses.

Things Not to Say and Do

Don't make your boy dependent on you for every penny he has. Don't be too controlling. Don't say such things as:

- If you need money just come and ask me for it.
- I will say what you can and cannot buy because I have the money, not you.
- I'm not giving you an allowance because you'll just waste it. And I won't pay you for working around the house because that's your responsibility. When you need money for something I'll decide if you get it or not.

Don't encourage your boy to expect to be paid for everything he does around the house. Don't say such things as:

- You don't have to do anything. If I need some chores done I'll pay you for them.

Don't be a bad role model for your boy. If you're not good at handling money don't pretend that it's not important. Don't say such things as:

- Money isn't important. I've always made out all right.
- Budgeting is for sissies.
- I just buy what I need and what I want.

Don't minimize the problems of being in debt. Don't say such things as:

- I'm always in debt and I don't find that a problem.
- If I really want something I just charge it to my credit card and then worry about how I'll pay for it.
- I always buy what I want even if I can't afford it. After all, I could die tomorrow.

Don't encourage your boy to become a gambler or a speculator in the stock market. Don't say such things as:

- No pain, no gain.
- If you want to make a lot of money you have to be willing to take big risks.
- I love gambling. It gives me a high. I love the risks.

Words, Phrases, and Actions to Avoid

- Spend, spend, spend.
- Budgeting is a waste of time.
- Here today, gone tomorrow.
- Risk is a good thing.
- You could be dead tomorrow.
- Live for today.
- I love to gamble.

PUBERTY

◆

You've found a copy of *Playboy* in your boy's room. He seems much more aggressive and moody than he used to be. He keeps his bedroom door closed when he's home. He's got dynamic energy one moment and lies crashed out on the sofa the next. Where he used to be unself-conscious about nakedness he is now shy and modest in your presence. You notice all these changes in your boy and you know that he's concerned about them. You think it's a good idea to talk about these to help him to understand what's going on. You can see he feels differently about himself and about girls, about you, and about others. He wants more independence and fewer rules and the freedom to make more of his own decisions. At times he seems confused as to whether he's a man or a little boy. He's confused by his new emotions and his new physical strength. Some of the girls who had been just friends now have a sexual attraction to him, even if he doesn't think of them as potential girlfriends. He's more impatient than ever when he can't solve a problem or things don't go his way. All these new experiences, feelings, and changes in his body and relationships mean that he needs your help now more than ever in finding his own way.

Things to Consider

What happens to a boy during puberty? His testosterone level increases by ten to twenty times the level of girls. His genitals increase to eight times their prepubescent size. His voice lowers and he begins to grow facial hair. His nipples swell in size temporarily. He becomes more obviously aggressive and feels an intense sexual energy. He spends much of his time thinking, fantasizing, and talking about girls and sex. He senses that he's in competition with other boys for girls and much of the way he talks, the clothes he wears, his hairstyle, and his activities in and out of school focus on making him attractive to the opposite sex. It is also the time when homosexual boys most clearly, and often most painfully, realize that they do not have the same feelings toward girls as their friends do.

You can be a great help to your boy by recognizing his changing needs and channeling his new energies and drives in socially acceptable directions. Don't think you can prevent him from feeling as he does. He is what his biological history has made him. Denial doesn't work. Look for ways in which he can release this tension.

Sports probably work best. The rough and tumble and controlled aggression demanded by sports, and the constant buildup and release of tension from them, are good substitutes for sexual aggression. If your boy likes sports now is the time to encourage full participation. But any activities that engage his body and energy will help. Working around the house or in the yard, building things, moving things around, biking, skateboarding, skiing, skating, running, hiking, rock-climbing, hunting, or horseback riding are only some of the suggestions. A part-time job will also help use up excess energy.

Talk to your boy about the changes and feelings he's having. Show him you understand his new energy and drives and needs and help him to understand them. Talk about testosterone, sex, girls, and how boys and girls are different. Make it clear that you accept him for the boy he is while helping him to understand what kinds of behavior are socially acceptable and what are not. It's a good time to talk about how he should behave toward girls, about not teasing them, not harassing them, and respecting their right to privacy.

Expect your boy to want instant gratification, to be impatient with you and with any problems he might run into, and to be aggressive, competitive, and wanting to take risks. These are male traits that have always been there but which become even more pronounced in puberty. Help your boy feel comfortable in his own male body. Don't expect him to be sensitive, caring, emotionally responsive, or nurturing in the same way girls are. Watch him express his sensitivity, caring, and concern for others in his own boyish way and love him for it.

Three Things You Must Do

1. Talk to your boy about the changes he's experiencing.
2. Help him find productive ways to release his energy and tension.
3. Accept and love him for his maleness while seeing it as a beginning, not an end.

Things to Say and Do

The first thing to do is make sure your boy knows what's happening during puberty. Given boys' natural reticence to talk about their bodies you needn't wait for him to come to you. Say such things as:

- Puberty's not an easy thing to go through, is it?
- Here's something you can read that will explain what you're probably experiencing right now. Read it and then we can talk about it.
- I know you're going through some pretty dramatic changes in your body. Would you like to talk about them?

Encourage your boy to be active in sports, if he's so inclined. Give him all the support he needs to participate in individual or team sports, organized or not. Say such things as:

- Why don't we go skiing this weekend?
- Are you going to try out for the team? I think it's a good idea.
- I'm glad you like playing basketball down in the park and at school.
- Let's go biking this afternoon.
- Want to go to the beach?

Recognize your boy's need for greater independence starting with puberty. Say such things as:

- What do you think about this?
- You decide for yourself.
- I think you need to make more decisions about your own life.

Talk about appropriate and inappropriate behavior toward girls. Let your boy know that you understand the strength of his aggressive, competitive, and sexual feelings and that he needs to understand and channel them appropriately. Say such things as:

- Tell me something about that girl you like at school.
- How do you behave around girls? Do you find it easy or hard to talk to girls?
- Do you ever see girls being harassed or mistreated at school? What do you think about that? Do you do anything to help them?
- You have stronger feelings for girls than you've ever had before, don't you?
- You know that you must always treat girls with respect and never violate their right to privacy.

Make sure your boy gets nutritious food and adequate sleep. He will eat everything in your refrigerator if given the chance so make sure it's well stocked with good food. Nine to ten hours of sleep each night is what he ideally needs at this age, but given most school schedules that's an unlikely event. So don't begrudge him sleeping in on weekends.

Words, Phrases, and Actions to Use

- . . . puberty . . .
- . . . testosterone . . .
- . . . sex . . .
- . . . tension . . .
- . . . release . . .
- . . . energy . . .
- . . . good food . . .
- . . . physical changes . . .

- ... emotional changes ...
- ... girls ...

- ... control ...
- Get enough sleep.

Things Not to Say and Do

Don't ignore your son's puberty. Don't be embarrassed by it or refuse to discuss it. Don't say such things as:

- I don't want to discuss it.
- That's your business, not mine.
- I don't feel comfortable talking about things like that with you.

Don't criticize your boy for feelings and actions that go along with puberty. Don't say such things as:

- You're too young to be thinking about girls.
- You're still a child. You don't know what love is.
- If you don't stop behaving like that I'm going to punish you.

Don't encourage irresponsible behavior. Don't say such things as:

- You're just feeling your oats.
- I was just as sex-mad when I was your age.
- Girls want sex as much as you do so go for it.

Don't reject your boy's masculine feelings. Don't say such things as:

- I don't know why you love sports so much.
- You better just calm down. Why can't you sit quietly like your sister?
- You're just another macho, insensitive male.

Words, Phrases, and Actions to Avoid

- ... stupid ...
- ... macho ...
- Any kind of sex is better than no sex.
- Girls are asking for it.
- Now you're a man so go for it.
- You're on your own.
- I don't want to talk about it.

RELATIONSHIPS

◈

You have concerns about two different kinds of relationships that your boy either has or will have. The first is his relationship with you, the other members of your family, and his friends. The second is any relationships he may have with girls. What can you say that will help him be successful in both these relationships? You have seen that many problems in family relationships, in friendships and in "love" relationships arise from poor communication and from people trying to make other people change into people they are not. There are many things you can tell your boy, and you will do that, but there are also things that you hope you showed him in your relationship with him and with the spouse you love. You firmly believe that being a good model in your relationships is the best way to teach your boy how to succeed in his. You also realize that it helps to make your approach to these relationships explicit by putting your methods into words. You intend to talk to your boy about relationships, yours and his, as a way of helping him through the inevitable problems that he will encounter.

Things to Consider

Boys are good at relationships in a different way from girls. Boys establish the best relationships through shared experiences and activities like sports, rough-and-tumble play, and doing "male things" together. Girls establish the best relationships through talking and telling stories, sharing feelings and practical knowledge, and listening and empathizing.

Fathers carry on relationships with their boys differently from the way mothers do. Fathers and boys work, play, watch television, and go to sporting events together. Fathers feel obligated to teach their sons how to be men through talk and example. They show the most concern for their boy's performance in school, in sports, and in doing "man's work."

Mothers and boys will talk about personal problems and relationships. Boys will tell their mom what hurts, what bugs them, what are their successes and failures, and what are their experiences of acceptance and rejection. Boys expect moms to listen patiently and understand, not judge them or blame them or try to immediately present solutions to complex problems. Moms are there to give boys a shoulder to cry on and enable them to express emotions that they would be afraid to express in front of their dads.

But whether you are a father or a mother, the best relationship you can have with your boy is one of trust, goodwill, and unconditional love. This kind of relationship comes from showing your boy over the years that he can trust you to listen to him and not have a knee-jerk reaction to things he has done wrong, mistakes he has made, and trouble that he has had. He learns that you reward truth regardless of how painful it may be. He learns that you and he can talk to each other about virtually any topic, and you both will listen sympathetically to the other's voice. He learns that you really want the best for him for his sake, not just for yours, and that you try to put yourself in his place and see his point of view.

If you have this kind of open, loving relationship with your boy, and he sees you also in this kind of relationship with your spouse, you are giving him a good model for his own future relationships. You want to show him, by example, that a relationship of love means wanting what is best for that person, not wanting to selfishly possess and control that person. You want to show him, by example, that physical violence and verbal abuse have no place in a good relationship. Arguments and disagreements get talked through and settled because you love, trust, and want the best for your spouse.

You know that your boy, as a young adolescent, experiences great spurts of testosterone-induced activity and feelings that affect his relationships with those around him. Your job is to accept the highs and lows that he experiences as an important part of the relationship you have with him. You will help him channel these rushes and releases in positive directions for himself and others. You will monitor his relationships with his boy- and girlfriends to see that they benefit all concerned. You will make sure that any relationship he has with a girl will be as good for her as it is for him.

Most mature adults will agree that relationships with loved ones are the most important things in life, more important than fame and financial success. You can do no better as a parent than to help your boy learn how to create and sustain these loving relationships.

Three Things You Must Do

1. Base your relationship with your boy on trust, goodwill, and unconditional love.
2. Explain that any good relationships he may have with girls as he gets older will be based on these same principles.
3. Model good relationships for your boy.

Things to Say and Do

Talk about the essentials of a good relationship. Use your own relationship with your boy as an example. Say such things as:

- I love you. That's the basis for our relationship as far as I'm concerned.
- I think we have a good relationship because I trust you and I think you trust me.
- How do we get along compared to what you see between your friends and their parents?

Talk about any existing or budding relationship your boy may have with a girl. Ask him to tell you about his feelings. Say such things as:

- How do you feel about "Mary"?
- How does she feel about you?
- Do you like having these feelings about one girl? How are they different from the way you feel about your friends?

Talk about what you think are the strengths of your relationship with your boy. Say such things as:

- I think we have a pretty good relationship because you can tell me almost anything about your life and I can talk to you about mine. Would you agree?
- I know that you have some private thoughts and feelings and things you do that you wouldn't feel comfortable sharing with your parents. We all do. But that's okay.
- I love the way we can talk to each other about things.

Talk about the different kind of relationship you and your spouse have with your boy. Say such things as:

- I think that you are more comfortable talking to me about some things than you are in talking to your dad about them. Let me give you some examples.

Words, Phrases, and Actions to Use

- . . . love . . .
- . . . trust . . .
- . . . goodwill . . .
- . . . unconditional love . . .
- . . . values . . .
- . . . truth . . .
- . . . selfishness . . .
- . . . control . . .
- . . . empathy . . .
- . . . girls . . .
- . . . respect . . .

Things Not to Say and Do

Don't set a bad example in your relationship with your boy or your spouse. Don't say such things as:

- I would never trust anyone, especially not you.
- I don't trust your dad.
- Relationships are a scary thing. I've never had any luck in them.

Don't be cynical about relationships. Don't say such things as:

- Never trust anyone.
- Saying you love someone is just an excuse for sex.
- I don't know of anyone who has a good relationship with their kids or their husband or wife.

Don't diminish any bond of love and trust you may have with your boy. Don't say such things as:

- I don't love you when you do that.
- You're so untrustworthy.
- You have destroyed our relationship.

Don't call your boy names that will destroy your relationship. Don't say such things as:

- You're a liar.
- You stupid kid.
- You're a rotten boy.
- I hate you.

Don't be cynical about any feelings he may have for a girl. Don't say such things as:

- Fat chance you'll ever have a steady girlfriend.

Words, Phrases, and Actions to Avoid

- You're a liar.
- You're a miserable boy.
- I hate you.
- You're no good.
- You're stupid.
- You're worthless.
- No one would want a friend like you.

RELIGION

◆

You want your boy to grow up to be a good man. You want him to have a sense of what's right and what's wrong. You go regularly to religious services and your boy goes with you, although more unwillingly each year as he gets older. Now that he's an adolescent he doesn't seem to have much interest in your religious practice, although he's happy to argue with you about religion and all the hypocritical people who call themselves religious but don't seem to love anyone but themselves. You think this is a stage he's going through and that he'll eventually come back to your religion. But you're not sure. You don't want to alienate him further by arguing about religion with him. But you also recognize that it's just as important to your relationship to talk about things that are uncomfortable for you as things that you enjoy discussing with him. How do you make sure that your boy will grow up to be a moral man when he seems more interested in playing football, playing video and computer games, or just hanging out on the weekends than going to religious services?

Things to Consider

First, a very pragmatic thought: boys at this age are either going at the speed of light, or close to sleep. They take off and fly high, then crash and burn. They have a very limited ability to sit quietly in a religious service for hours at a time listening to someone talk about things in which they have virtually no interest. Boys at this age care about girls, sports, games, and school, probably in that order. So in church they fidget, look around for their friends, sleep, and look generally uncomfortable, all the time wishing they were someplace else. In fact, you don't find many teenage boys who willingly go to worship on the weekends.

Take this into account when you think about how to get your boy involved. Also think about why you want your boy involved. What exactly do you want him to get out of religion? Is it morality, self-discipline, salvation, knowledge of the "word of God," the Truth, a sense of community? How much of this requires that he actually attend services every weekend?

You want him to get involved with the real work of your religion. Sitting through religious services isn't the only way, or even the best way, to make this happen. Perhaps a better way for you to proceed is to get your boy into some religious-sponsored programs. Get him to join a youth group or to do charity work. If he's got the interest study groups might work for him.

Boys, more than girls, need discipline and structure to help them order their lives. Religion can provide this but it has to accommodate a boy's need for action and problem solving. Show your boy how religion is, at its core, a spiritual discipline through which many of his questions can be answered. Make religion understandable to him as a spiritual quest. Talk to him about the power of prayer and love. Emphasize the freedom that unselfish, unconditional love brings to those who make it a fundamental part of their lives.

Use your boy's innate sense of right and wrong and his youthful, naïve idealism to his advantage and yours by showing him that that is what true religion is all about—a selfless concern for all of life. Talk to your boy about the mysteries of life and how to connect him to these mysteries through prayer, as a reflection on life's endless patterns and changes. You can model prayer for your boy, or have him join you if you do some form of meditation. It needn't be done in a formal, institutionalized setting.

As your boy has grown from infancy to adolescence you have had the chance to give him a sense of ritual and a sense of the sacred. Reading to him every night, saying bedtime prayers, saying grace before meals, going to religious services, celebrating your religious festivals, having special quiet times and places from which to escape the noise and rush of everyday life, talking regularly about his and your life's successes and failures, and problems and solutions are all ways you might have used to develop a sense of spirituality in your boy. If you haven't done any of these things you can start now.

In summary, don't make regular religious service attendance a battle. Think of religion as any attempt to reveal the spirit of love, compassion, and connectedness in all of life. Your role is to show that spirit in your own life and to help your boy recognize and develop that spirit within him.

Three Things You Must Do

1. Recognize that your boy is unlikely to enjoy religion in its formal setting.
2. Make developing a sense of spirit, not attending religious services, in your boy your first priority.
3. Use your boy's energy and idealism in doing good things for others.

Things to Say and Do

Your boy will most likely not enjoy going to religious services every weekend. Don't make it a big issue. Instead emphasize other kinds of connections with your place of worship. Say such things as:

- I'd love you to go to church with us this weekend. Would you like to?
- You know, the synagogue has a great social program for teens. I think it might be worth checking out.
- When I volunteer at the church food drive we could certainly use your strong arms to help us carry the donations of canned food.
- There's a meditation group for teens on Wednesdays. Are you interested? "Mrs. Ali" told me her son goes and really enjoys it.
- The church is organizing a teen choir. You have a nice voice. Why don't you join? I think you'd have a lot to offer them.

Talk to your boy about God, religion, spirituality, the mysteries of life, especially if he raises the subject. Say such things as:

- Do you ever think about God? What kinds of thoughts do you have?
- Do you ever find yourself praying? What do you pray for?
- I wonder about all the mysterious things in life, especially what I was before I was born and what happens after I die. Do you wonder too?
- I've learned some meditation practices that over the years have helped me work through some serious problems. Let me tell you about them.

Some religions seem quite exclusive. If you believe what they believe you are rewarded after death; if you don't you are damned. You need to talk to your boy about where you stand on this. Do you support or oppose religious exclusion? Say such things as:

- As you know our church believes that only those who believe like us will be saved. I want to talk to you about why we believe this.
- We believe in the promise of salvation after death. Does that make sense to you?
- I have trouble with religions that don't allow nonbelievers to be saved. Let me tell you why.

If you think your boy is in any danger of being approached or recruited by religious cults talk to him about it. Say such things as:

- Has anyone come up to you at school, or anyplace else, and started talking about religion?
- If anyone starts talking to you I'd like you to tell me what they say.
- Do you know what a religious cult is?
- Do you have any friends who have been asked to join a new religious group?

Emphasize the need for a quiet time of rest and reflection, even for teenage boys. Remind your boy of any little rituals you've had with him. Say such things as:

- I've always enjoyed that quiet time before you go to bed when I would come to your room and we'd talk or read together.
- Do you remember the special times we've spent together on the lake/walking in the woods/walking along the beach/working in the garden/going out for breakfast on Sunday mornings? Those times are really important for me. Are they for you?
- When I have a problem I have a little space inside me where I can go and work things out. Let me teach you how to do that for yourself.

Words, Phrases, and Actions to Use

- . . . prayer . . .
- . . . God . . .
- . . . holy . . .
- . . . spirit . . .
- . . . meditation . . .
- . . . mystery . . .
- . . . love . . .

- . . . compassion . . .
- . . . ritual . . .
- . . . birth . . .
- . . . death . . .
- . . . change . . .
- . . . interconnectedness . . .

Things Not to Say and Do

Don't force your boy to go to religious services. Don't say such things as:

- You have to go to church with us.
- I don't care if you want to play with your friends. Religion comes first.
- If you don't go to church you are committing a sinful act.

Don't ignore your boy's spiritual training. Don't say such things as:

- There is no God, nothing holy. It's just a lot of nonsense.
- Religion is just a lot of superstition and mumbo jumbo.
- I wouldn't waste my time with anything religious.

Don't be intolerant of other religions. Don't say such things as:

- We're the only true religion.
- Those who don't believe what we believe are damned to hell.
- I'm not interested in loving others, only in being right.

Don't encourage your boy to be selfish and greedy. Don't say such things as:

- It's every man for himself.
- You have to do what's best for you.
- Don't worry about the other guy because he's not worrying about you.
- Money is the measure of all things.

Words, Phrases, and Actions to Avoid

- There's no such thing as God.
- . . . superstition . . .
- That's nonsense.
- All religious people are hypocrites.
- Religion is stupid.
- I think all religions should be banned.
- We're the only true believers.
- You're damned to hell.

RULES

◆

Your boy needs rules as an adolescent just as he did when he was little. You can see that sometimes your boy is fourteen going on twenty-five and other times he is fourteen going on nine. He's a mixture of man and boy and you're never sure who is going to be sitting across the table from you at breakfast and dinner. You want to give him more control over his own life now that he's a teenager, but you want him to know that you still have certain expectations of him and many of these are best stated as rules of behavior. Many of them are also rules that you hope he has for himself and you hope that he won't reject them simply because they are also your expectations for him. You realize that self-discipline is really the only kind for a teen since he is much more on his own now than when he was younger. Although he's still dependent on you for most things he spends the majority of his time out of your sight and control. Unless he's got his own set of rules for what he should and should not do, all your rules won't matter much. So your approach to rules is to talk about the rules he has for himself.

Things to Consider

My theory of rules for teenage boys is much like my theory of the ten commandments. The ten commandments, I believe, are really an inventory of the bad things that people were doing and the good things that people were *not* doing long ago. Likewise, rules for teen boys are an inventory of the bad things that boys do and the good things they don't.

Of course the ten commandments don't tell us about the activities of all the ancient Israelites, and rules for teenage boys don't tell us about the activities of all boys. So the first consideration in talking about rules for your boy should be this: *rules for him should be based on who he is—his personality, history, behavior, trustworthiness, strengths and weaknesses, talents, and goals and ambitions—rather than on some stereotyped picture you might have of teenage boys.* This is the fair and realistic approach to creating rules that have a chance of succeeding and, more important, of helping him do the right thing for himself. The second consideration follows from this: *rules should be created for his sake, not yours. No matter what your feelings, fears, ambitions, hopes, and desires may be for your boy, these rules must be for his benefit, to make him the best person he can be.*

Having said this let's briefly look at why teenage boys need rules, how you can best create them, how you can best enforce them, and, finally, what these rules might be about.

Your young teenage boy needs rules more than ever because of the changes, conflicts, and confusions puberty create in him. Your boy needs guidance, advice, consistency, and stability in his life since the physical and emotional effects of puberty make his life much more complicated than it used to be. Rules are like a map for your boy. They tell him what path he should be taking to get where he wants to go. They help keep him on the right track and point out the dangers of straying off it. Rules can work as the "still point" in his life, as an anchor that helps keep him secure, and as a guidepost against which he can measure his own actions, thoughts, and desires.

A good way to create these rules for your boy is to get together with him and talk about the reasons for rules and what are some realistic rules to help him live his life to the fullest within the bounds of reason. Together, you and your boy should be able to come up with a sensible list of do's and don'ts that will cover many of the important issues he confronts in his young life at school, at home, and in the community. The advantage of creating rules together comes from ownership. With ownership your boy feels a greater responsibility for sticking to the rules than if you impose them on him.

Enforcing rules is the hard part. Realistically, you have to trust your boy to do the right thing because you can't always be there. If you and he have a good, open, caring relationship he will tell you when he's broken the rules and accept the consequences. But this will only happen if he believes you have treated, and will always treat, him fairly when he tells you he has done things that he knows you will not like. The best policy is always to reward him for being honest, while being fair and realistic in deciding on the consequences of the infraction. The discipline should be for his sake, not yours. Obviously, from what I've said in earlier chapters, any kind of physical punishment or violence is unacceptable.

Finally, what's a sensible list of topics to have rules about? This will largely depend on you and your boy, but here is a list from which you can choose whatever's appropriate in your family:

- School attendance
- School performance
- Homework
- Punctuality
- Knowing where he is
- Knowing whom he's with
- Knowing what he's doing
- Music lessons
- Sports practices
- Relationship with parents

- Relationship with siblings
- Relationship with other family members
- Relationship with neighbors
- Relationship with friends
- Allowance
- Saving money
- Spending money
- Buying needs
- Buying wants
- Care of sports equipment
- Care of his room
- Care of his clothes
- Care of his bicycle, skateboard, in-line skates, etc.
- Chores around the house
- Parties
- Curfew
- Bedtime
- Mealtime
- Food
- Language

These are a few areas in which you might find it appropriate to create rules with your boy. You can add or delete things as you wish. You can also make the rules formal or informal, rigid or flexible. They should also change over time as your boy and his needs change.

Three Things You Must Do

1. Jointly create rules for your boy.
2. Design them with him specifically in mind.
3. Remember they're for his benefit, not yours.

Things to Say and Do

Talk to your boy about the need for rules. See what he has to say. Ask him what kinds of rules might be helpful for him. Say such things as:

- You've always had rules to follow. Up to now do you think they've been okay?
- What kind of rules work best for you?
- Now that you're a teenager, I think we need to look at the rules you have, maybe create some new ones, and get rid of some of the old ones. What do you think?

Discuss how to create new rules and get rid of old ones. Say such things as:

- I think you need to tell me what kinds of rules you would find helpful and not and see if we can make some that work for you. Is that okay with you?

- What areas do you think you need rules in and what not? You give me your list and I'll give you mine.
- I think we need to work together on rules for you. And maybe we need to have some rules for me as well, things that will help us get along. Do you like that idea?

Talk to your boy about obeying the rules. Say such things as:

- I know you're good about doing the right thing. I hope you'd tell me if you found some of these rules impossible to follow.
- I think you're pretty good about obeying rules.
- Would you tell me if you broke an important rule?

Talk about the consequences of breaking the rules. Let your boy suggest what should happen. Say such things as:

- You're old enough to know your responsibilities. What should happen if you break an important rule?
- I'd like your views on appropriate discipline. For example, what should happen if you break curfew and don't call and tell me you're not going to be home on time?

Words, Phrases, and Actions to Use

- . . . rules . . .
- . . . discipline . . .
- . . . self-discipline . . .
- . . . consequences . . .
- . . . for your sake . . .
- . . . more and less important . . .
- . . . reasonable and unreasonable . . .
- Let's make the rules together.
- Let's make a list.
- What kinds of rules do your friends have about this?
- They must fit you.
- You take ownership.

Things Not to Say and Do

Although your boy needs rules, don't make rules for the sake of making rules. Don't be arbitrary. Don't say such things as:

- I make the rules and you follow them.
- These are my rules for you. I don't care what your rules for yourself are.
- I'm not interested in your opinion.

Don't exclude your boy from helping you create rules for him. Don't say such things as:

- I don't need your help.
- I don't want your help.
- This is my responsibility as a parent. Kids don't make their own rules.

Don't be unrealistic in your rules. Keep them in the context of your boy and his friends. Don't say such things as:

- I don't care what your friends' rules are.
- You'll do this whether you like it or not.
- I expect you to follow these rules to the letter. I want no excuses.

Don't be unreasonable if your boy breaks a rule. Don't say such things as:

- You broke that rule and I'm going to punish you severely. I don't care why you broke it.
- Maybe this punishment will ensure that you never break that rule again.
- You're grounded for a year.

Words, Phrases, and Actions to Avoid

- I'm going to beat you.
- You must never break a rule.
- You're a rotten kid.
- I can never trust you again.
- These are my rules for you and you must obey them.
- There's no such thing as a good excuse.
- I'm not interested in excuses.

SLEEP

◆

During puberty your boy needs at least nine hours of sleep a night. Is he getting it? Probably not. For one thing he's up late doing homework, watching TV, playing games on the computer, talking to his friends on e-mail, or surfing the Web. For another school schedules are not made to fit the needs of teens. They start too early and finish too early. Your boy is growing like a proverbial weed and the energy he needs to keep up is enormous. You try to give him a nutritious diet and you know that he needs a lot of sleep to regain all the energy he expends in physical growth each day. But getting him to go to bed early is tough. Not only does he get home late each day from school because of sports practices and club meetings but he has homework to do and needs time to relax. So he rarely gets to bed before eleven and is up at seven to get ready for school. Eight hours of sleep is good, but not good enough.

Things to Consider

According to some research experiments teenage boys who are allowed to create their own sleep schedules will go to bed around 1 A.M. and get up at 10 A.M. or later. These studies also show minimum alertness between 8 A.M. and 9 A.M. and maximum alertness after 3 P.M. There is no indication that schools recognize this. Their schedules typically have students starting school between 7:15 and 7:45 A.M., seriously affecting the sleep needs of all teens, but especially boys. Boys already have enough trouble with the verbal and written demands of most school subjects. Lack of adequate sleep only adds to this trouble.

Boys' academic and social behavior both suffer from a problem that it would seem simple to remedy. Have schools start their day later. Some people suggest another solution: make sure your adolescent boy gets to bed earlier. Unfortunately, this ignores two important aspects of the problem. According to the research reported by Michael Gurian in *Boys and Girls Learn Differently* hormonal and brain chemicals exert a strong influence on adolescent circadian rhythms (twenty-four-hour sleeping and waking patterns) and adolescents naturally stay up later at night than they did when younger. Second, the accelerated growth of certain brain structures at this age happens in the late evening. Trying to force your boy to go to sleep during this enhanced period of brain development doesn't work, as you probably know from experience.

Gurian recommends two solutions to the problem. First, and most obvious, is to lobby to have your high school start no earlier than 10 or 11 AM. Thus, even if your teen doesn't go to sleep until midnight or 1 A.M., he can still manage a minimum of nine hours of sleep.

The second solution is to timetable specific subjects to coincide with daily hormonal variations. Gurian gives the example of the relationship between spatial learning and testosterone (the male hormone) levels and verbal learning and estrogen (the female hormone) levels. Apparently, spatial learning is easier when testosterone levels are at their highest, which happens in midmorning. That's a good time to schedule math.

Although we know less about estrogen level cycles as we gain more knowledge we can schedule language, literature, and social studies classes when these levels are at their highest. Gurian also suggests that we schedule band and art, which encourage movement and whole brain activity, early in the school day. A logical addition to that would seem to be physical education.

In summary, you need to recognize that your teen's biological clock and brain development play a large role in his sleeping habits. If your teen is a normal, responsible teen help him to find his own patterns, although you must obviously place limits on his going to bed on school nights, even if he just lies there thinking, reading, or listening to music. On weekends and holidays let him sleep as much as he wants. Urge your school board to adjust high school start and finish time in tune to adolescent sleep patterns. Finally, try to avoid fighting with your teen about bedtime because you'll be fighting against his biological needs.

Three Things You Must Do

1. Explain to your boy the hormonal and brain influences on his sleep patterns.
2. Talk to your local school board about the possibility of adjusting its start and finish time to allow for normal teen sleep needs and to schedule subjects appropriate to hormonal patterns.
3. Talk to your boy about getting enough sleep.

Things to Say and Do

Discuss your boy's sleep needs. Help him understand how his brain and hormonal growth patterns affect him. Say such things as:

- I've been reading some interesting stuff on teen sleep needs. Are you interested in hearing about them?

- Do you know you need at least nine hours of sleep each night?
- Do you think you get enough sleep? How do you think you could get more?

Ask your boy about how he feels in school each day. See if you can see a pattern his sleep habits have on his schoolwork. Say such things as:

- Do you feel sleepy during some subjects more than others?
- When do you really feel awake at school?
- I usually feel sleepy during the day at around 2 P.M. What about you?

Talk about bedtime rules. Say such things as:

- I'm happy to let you decide when you are ready for bed, but remember you should really be getting nine hours of sleep each night.
- I don't mind if you stay up later now, but don't abuse the privilege.
- You're old enough to decide on lights out, but I'd like you in bed by 10 P.M. on school nights, even if you just lie there thinking, reading, or listening to music.

Lobby your school to adjust its start time. Talk to other parents about the start time. Talk to school administrators and the school board about research on teen sleep needs. Talk to your school about subject scheduling. And finally, if your boy has a choice of when to take specific subjects advise him, using the latest research on hormonal secretions, on the best times for each kind of subject.

Words, Phrases, and Actions to Use

- . . . brain research . . .
- . . . hormonal and brain chemical influences . . .
- . . . sleep needs . . .
- . . . reasonable . . .
- . . . school schedules . . .
- . . . spatial reasoning . . .
- . . . verbal and writing skills . . .
- . . . your body's daily rhythms . . .
- . . . lobby . . .
- . . . advocate new schedules . . .

Things Not to Say and Do

Don't fight with your teen about bedtime. Don't say such things as:

- You'll do what I say.
- I'm the boss. You'll go to bed when I tell you.
- You don't know what's good for you. Do what I tell you.

Don't completely ignore your boy's sleep needs. Don't say such things as:

- I don't care when you go to bed.
- It doesn't matter to me. It's your life.
- Do what you want.

Don't make your boy get up early on weekends if he doesn't want to. He probably needs to catch up on sleep he lost during the week. Don't say such things as:

- I don't care if it is Saturday, I want you out of bed by 7:30.
- You can't sleep in just because it's a weekend.
- If you didn't stay up so late you wouldn't have to sleep in so late.

Words, Phrases, and Actions to Avoid

- I don't care.
- Do what you like.
- No sleeping in on weekends.
- You'll do what I say.
- Bedtime is 9 P.M.

STUDY HABITS

◆

One of your biggest concerns for your boy is that he does well in school. Now that he's in junior or senior high school you're looking forward to his future, the kind of college he wants to go to, and the kind of work he might end up doing for his career. You know how difficult it will be for him if he doesn't do well in school. High grades mean he will have many options; low grades will severely limit those options. High grades mean the chance of a scholarship; low grades mean you will have to finance his postsecondary education. Your boy is bright but not a genius. He has to work to do well in school. You want him to have the best possible study habits so he will do his work well and efficiently. You know that developing good study habits in high school will help him have good study habits in college where they are even more important. You want to find the best advice you can on study habits for young adolescent boys so you can help your boy succeed in school.

Things to Consider

Boys have specific study needs in high school that arise from their biological as well as social makeup. First let's list adolescent boys' academic strengths and weaknesses. Remember that this is a general list and may not fit your boy in every case.

- Boys are better than girls at deductive reasoning, which is reasoning from a general proposition to a particular instance. This can make them better at multiple-choice tests, like the SATs.
- Boys are not as good at inductive reasoning, which is building generalizations from specific examples.
- Boys tend to be good at abstract reasoning, which includes subjects like philosophy, logic, and mathematics and occupations like architecture and engineering.
- Boys are not as good at language use and use fewer words than girls. They prefer jargon and technical language.
- Boys don't listen as well as girls and seek more evidence and logical explanation for what the teacher says.
- Boys get bored easily.

- Boys need more space than girls, spreading themselves out more into the available space.
- Boys need to move around more than girls and benefit from more frequent breaks in the work they're doing.
- Boys focus more on completing the assigned task and less on relationships with others in doing it.
- Boys seem more affected by their status within the group, such that the lower their status, the lower their academic success.
- Boys like working with symbols, diagrams, and graphs more than with written text.
- Boys benefit from working and learning in teams and groups and focus more on completing the task at hand.

What are the specific study habits that work for boys given these strengths and weaknesses? Here is a list of ways you can help your boy to study best:

- Make sure your boy reads well and has good comprehension because these are the core skills for any school success. If he is having any trouble get him a tutor or tutor him yourself.
- Be strict about setting aside a specific time and place for him to study each evening. Be there to make sure he's working. It should be quiet, cool, and well-lighted, with a minimum of distractions.
- Schedule breaks for moving and stretching.
- Help him work out a schedule of studying based on his weekly course schedule in school. You need to have a copy of his timetable to do this.
- Make it your business to have a copy of the curriculum guide in each subject he's taking and see to it that he masters the content for each unit.
- Encourage your boy to do his most difficult subjects first. Offer to help him in any way he may need, but don't do the work for him.
- Ask to see your boy's class notes and texts.
- Encourage your boy to make outline notes for all his readings.
- Encourage your boy to study with classmates who may understand the work better than he does, but make sure the studying is supervised by you or the other student's parents.
- Be aware of the work your boy is doing and try to find practical, everyday examples or uses for the knowledge, skills, or understandings entailed in that work. In other words help your boy make sense of it in practical terms.
- Encourage your boy to participate in school and community sports teams and service clubs and events. Boy athletes do better in school than nonathletes.

School and community service obligations serve two purposes: they force your boy to budget his time efficiently and they involve him in a network of students, teachers, and community members and activities that force him to develop and use social and academic skills.

- Help your boy with the verbal and written skills subjects where he may be weakest.
- Help your boy develop his inductive reasoning skills, working from the particular to the general.
- Monitor your boy's attitudes toward his school, classmates, teachers, and subjects to make sure that he is open and positive. Make sure he has the social and academic skills and knows how to use them to make a positive contribution in his classes and school.
- Know where your boy stands in his group's "pecking order."
- Help your boy put his current studying and schoolwork in the big picture. Talk to him about college and career plans and how his schoolwork will affect his options.
- Be positive about your boy's work and abilities, but be alert for any problems that may require professional help.

Tailor your help to suit your boy's strengths and weaknesses. Don't trust stereotypes or generalizations without putting them into the context of what your own boy is like.

Three Things You Must Do

1. Make sure your boy has the basic literacy and numeracy skills.
2. Know your boy's study needs.
3. Help him organize a strict study schedule, including a good time, place, and atmosphere.

Things to Say and Do

Talk to your boy about his attitudes toward studying. Ask him about his favorite and least favorite subjects to study. Say such things as:

- What do you like to study most? Can you tell me why?
- What do you like to study least? Can you tell me why?
- What do you think about studying in general? Do you like it?

Ask your boy about the areas he likes to do himself and those he thinks he most needs help with. Say such things as:

- Which subjects do you feel most confident about?
- Which are the subjects you think you'd like help with?
- Tell me what I can do to help you and I'll do it.

Talk about the importance of studying and what your boy thinks would help him the most. Say such things as:

- I'm sure you know why studying is so important. Let me tell you what I think and then I'd like to hear what you think.
- I know studying isn't always what you'd like to be doing, but what would make studying the easiest for you?
- What can I do to help make studying good for you?

Work out a study schedule with your boy. You'll need to know his school schedule. Say such things as:

- Let's set up a good study schedule for you. Tell me what subjects you have each day.
- You need a nice place to study. Let's see what we can do about that.
- What's the best time for you to do your studying each day here at home?

Suggest that your boy have a friend study with him when it might help. Say such things as:

- Since language is a little bit of a problem for you do you have any friends who are better and who you might want to have over to study with you?
- I used to study with a friend. I think it helped us both. Would you like to organize that here?
- Sometimes if you study with a friend who needs your help it helps you as well. Do you want to try it?
- If your boy needs specialized help in any subject ask his teachers about the availability of tutors.
- If your boy seems to have any learning disabilities seek professional advice.

Put your boy's study efforts into the larger context. Say such things as:

- You realize that learning good study habits now will help you later on when you go to college.
- How do you think math will be important to you when you're an adult?

- Reading and writing well are two of the most important skills you can have when you're in your career.

Words, Phrases, and Actions to Use

- ... the big picture ...
- ... efficiency ...
- ... routine schedule ...
- ... quiet ...
- ... cool ...
- ... strengths and weaknesses ...
- ... likes and dislikes ...
- Study hard.
- Move around when you need to.
- Do a little each day.
- Make good study notes.
- Help a friend and let a friend help you.

Things Not to Say and Do

Don't ignore your boy's study habits. Don't say such things as:

- School is your responsibility.
- I don't care if you study or not. It's your life.
- Do what you like.

Don't refuse to help your boy with his studying. Don't say such things as:

- I'm not going to help you.
- You have to do it on your own.
- It's not my job.

Don't refuse to give your boy a good place to study. Don't say such things as:

- You can just do it here in the dining room. It's noisy, but so what.
- I'm not giving you a special place to study.

Don't ignore your boy's strengths and weaknesses. Don't say such things as:

- You should be good in every subject.
- If you're stupid it's not my fault.
- You'll just have to figure it out for yourself.

Words, Phrases, and Actions to Avoid

- You're stupid.
- Do it on your own.
- You'll have to work it out.
- I won't help.
- Do what you like.
- It's your responsibility.
- Don't ask me for help.

Yes/No

◈

Even though your boy is now a teenager you still bear moral responsibility for his welfare. You still need to provide rules and discipline and tell him what he can and can't do even though you are not with him for most of his day. Saying yes, he can do this, and no, he cannot do that, means showing him what your values are by applying them to specific situations. When he wants to go out with his friends you must say yes or no. When he wants to have a party at your house you must say yes or no. When he says he's finished his homework and studying and wants to surf the Internet you must say yes or no. When he wants to stay out late on Saturday night to be with his friends you must say yes or no. When he wants to have his friends sleep over you must say yes or no. When he wants to go to a movie and needs you to drive him you must say yes or no. The list goes on. Each time you make the yes or no decision you are telling your boy what you think about him, how much you trust him, and what you think about what he wants to do. You are determined to consider your decisions carefully and do what's best for your boy, not just what's easiest for you.

Things to Consider

When my wife and I began to reflect on when to say yes and when to say no to our kids' requests we realized that we wanted to do what was best for our children, not simply what was easiest for us. We decided that our approach would be to say yes, unless we had a good reason to say no. We noticed that this seemed to be the opposite of many parents who automatically said no, unless they had a good reason to say yes. It seemed that they were making decisions based on what was easiest for them rather than what was best for their children. We didn't want to be like that.

Because we lived in the country where there was no public transportation our kids couldn't go anywhere without us driving them, at least until they were sixteen and could drive themselves. It meant a lot of driving for us, but looking back on it, it was certainly worth it. We never deprived our kids of the companionship of their friends simply because we couldn't be bothered to drive them. We also made it clear that all their friends were welcome at our house because they were nice kids and it made it easier for us to keep track of what our children were doing.

When we decided that we would say yes unless we had good reason to say no we realized that we were putting a lot of trust in our children to do the right thing. They had earned that trust over the years and we were never disappointed in them, even though one of our boys was a very difficult child who managed to get himself into trouble on many occasions. In effect saying yes was our way of giving our children increasing control over their own lives as they grew up. It made them more responsible for their own actions, even though our own responsibility was always there.

As I said before we rejected saying no. This is a route many parents seem to take because it seems the easy way out. Saying yes means making arrangements, perhaps inconveniencing themselves, having a bit of a mess in the home, trusting their kids to do the right thing, and trusting their kid's friends to behave themselves. Saying no solves the problem because it keeps the kids under their parents' control. But it also creates a problem: very unhappy teenagers.

The theme of this book has been that girls and boys are different and must be treated differently in many situations. My wife and I found this to be true in issues of yes/no. We had two boys and a girl, only three years separating the three of them, so they were all teens together. We sometimes found good reason to say no to our daughter when we would have said yes to our boys. Keeping our daughter safe was more of an issue than protecting our sons. We believed, rightly or wrongly, that they could take care of themselves in situations that would be dangerous for our daughter. It's a sad fact, but true, that boys are less at risk from sexual predators, even though they are more at risk of violence from other boys. However, we expect our sons to look after themselves better than our daughters.

In our quest to be good, loving parents we had a few rules that went along with our giving our children more freedom. These rules were our way of keeping control while giving it up at the same time. They didn't change until our kids left home, although some were obviously modified when they were able to drive themselves.

- We will always drive you where you want to go and we will pick you up.
- We must always know where you are, whom you are with, and what you're doing.
- You can call us any time of the day or night to let us know where you are.
- Your friends are always welcome at our house.
- If you are going to be late getting home you must call us regardless of the time.
- You must never ride in anyone's car if he or she has been drinking.
- No smoking!
- No drugs!
- No drinking, except for a small glass of wine or champagne under our supervision on special occasions!

Raising newly pubescent boys means making yes/no decisions about many things, including money, sports equipment, tattoos and body piercing, clothes, vacations, school trips, friends, curfews, and so on. I have discussed many of these topics in other chapters and hope this discussion has given you some good ideas of when and how to say yes or no.

Three Things You Must Do

1. Know that saying yes or no tells your boy what you think of him.
2. Make the choice for your boy's sake, not yours.
3. Say yes unless you have good reason to say no.

Things to Say and Do

Talk to your boy about issues of yes and no in general. Let him know your philosophy and approach. Say such things as:

- I want to talk to you about what you can and can't do.
- Let's talk about your independence and control over your own life.
- Let me explain why I will generally say yes to your requests unless I have good reason to say no.

Talk about specific areas in which your boy has the responsibility to follow some rules if he wants the kind of freedom you're prepared to give him. Say such things as:

- I think you should be able to spend lots of time with your friends.
- I expect you to observe the curfew we agree on.
- I must always know where you are, whom you're with, and what you're doing.
- You can call me any time of the day or night to let me know where you are and what's happening.

Talk about why you're giving your boy this kind of freedom. Say such things as:

- Over the years you've shown that you're a nice, trustworthy boy.
- I know I can trust you. That's why you're getting this freedom.
- As long as you continue to show you can be trusted to do the right thing you'll continue to have this independence.

Words, Phrases, and Actions to Use

- ... trust ...
- ... freedom ...
- ... independence ...
- ... self-control ...
- ... yes, rather than no ...
- ... your responsibilities ...
- ... sensible ...
- ... more freedom as you get older ...
- Here are some rules to follow.

Things Not to Say and Do

Don't say no to all, or almost all, of your boy's requests. Don't say such things as:

- No, you can't do that.
- No, I don't have time to drive you.
- No, it's too much trouble.

Don't try to control every aspect of your boy's life. Don't say such things as:

- You can only do what I say is okay.
- I'm in control here.
- Don't do anything without asking me first.

Don't disparage your boy's ability to look after himself. Don't say such things as:

- You're still too young.
- I'm your parent and it's my responsibility to look after you until you can look after yourself, which isn't yet.
- You're just a kid who needs to be protected from yourself and the world.

On the other hand don't abrogate your responsibility to look after your boy. Don't say such things as:

- You can do whatever you like.
- I don't care what you do.
- You're not my responsibility anymore.

Words, Phrases, and Actions to Avoid

- You stupid kid.
- I can never trust you.
- You're on your own.
- Do whatever you like.
- No! No! No!
- I don't care.
- Make up your own rules.
- I don't care where you are, whom you're with, or what you're doing.

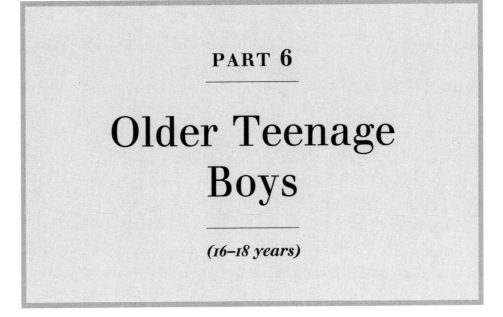

PART 6

Older Teenage Boys

(16–18 years)

ALCOHOL, DRUGS, AND CIGARETTES

◆

You have a boy who's almost a man, yet often seems a young boy. You remember when he was just a toddler, when he reached puberty, when he had his first crush, and when he dated his first girl. Now he's in the last years of high school, looking forward to going to college. You know he's been exposed to drinking, smoking marijuana, and smoking regular cigarettes. You don't know if he's done any of these things but you think he probably has. What you want to know is what you should say to him, how to get it across that you have certain values and expectations for him, and how to make certain he listens to your rules and yet has enough self-discipline to do what's good for himself. You want to trust him, yet you know that he's still a crazy teenage boy who thinks he's immortal, that nothing can really hurt him, that he needs to be one of the guys, and that he also needs to impress the girls. You know you probably should have broached the subject earlier but better late than never. You decide you need to have a good talk about alcohol, drugs, and smoking so he knows where you stand on these things.

Things to Consider

He's a teenage boy! Boys are programmed to be risk-takers. Drinking, doing drugs, and smoking are all high-risk activities that almost every teenage boy is tempted to do. It's certainly worth talking about these things with your boy if you haven't done so already.

Actually, the best time would have been when he was thirteen or fourteen since research has shown that that's the age during which he would be most tempted to try one or all of these things. At that age he will most likely know other boys who drink, do drugs, or smoke. He will probably know how to get hold of any of these things.

Now that your boy is sixteen, or older, he almost certainly has tried alcohol, taken some kind of drug, and smoked a cigarette or two. If your boy is eighteen you may not be able to control his habits, especially smoking, which is legal in many states at this age. But it might still be worth a try.

It's generally easy to find out if your boy takes drugs. Hard drugs will leave their mark on him, not only physically but also emotionally and psychologically. You'll see it in his eyes, his complexion, his appetite, his temperament, and his mood swings. You may also notice things going missing to pay for his habit. The only solution to the problem of drug addiction is putting him into a treatment center.

Smoking is also easy to spot because your teen's breath, hair, and clothes will smell of smoke. So will any room or car in which he smokes. He will also need money to support his habit. Drinking is harder to catch because, unless your boy is an alcoholic, it may not show up in his behavior.

What do you do about any of these habits? Here's my advice for what it's worth. Doing drugs and smoking are unequivocally unacceptable. Drugs are also against the law. But both are terrible for your boy's health. I suggest you make your views about these things known to him without any apologies. Of course, it's imperative that you neither smoke nor do drugs yourself. You must be a model for him.

Drinking, I believe, is a different matter. It is legal, socially acceptable, and may even be healthy for you, as long as it is done in moderation and never before driving or doing any kind of activity requiring clear thinking and quick reflexes. You may want to introduce your boy to wine and beer before he's legally able to drink so that his first drinking is under your control, and so it's not forbidden fruit. You can help him understand his limits and how to drink responsibly.

Three Things You Must Do

1. Find out if your boy drinks, does drugs, or smokes.
2. Let him know your views on each of these things.
3. If he does drugs or smokes get him into treatment if you can.

Things to Say and Do

Talk to your boy about drinking. See what his experience has been and tell him yours. Hopefully he will be honest with you because he trusts you to react reasonably. Say such things as:

- Does a lot of drinking go on at the parties you go to? Do you join in?
- Do you and your friends drink a lot of beer? How do you get it?
- Why don't we have a glass of wine together?
- I think you need to know how to drink responsibly. Let's talk about what that means.

Offer your boy some wine or beer on special occasions. Talk to your boy about drugs. If you've ever done any drugs tell him about your experience and why you would never do it again. Say such things as:

- I smoked marijuana when I was in college. I hated the smell and it made me sick. If you ever do it let me know and we can compare notes. However, I hope you never do.
- Hard drugs are deadly! Please don't ever try them.
- I don't need their names but do you know anyone who does hard drugs?

Talk to your boy about smoking cigarettes. If he smokes say such things as:

- I know you smoke, which really disappoints me.
- It's very expensive and very, very bad for you. Why is that okay with you?
- As far as I'm concerned smoking is only for dopes. It makes your breath smell evil, it ruins your clothes, it stains your teeth and fingers, and gives you cancer or heart disease. It also makes people look stupid. Can you tell me anything good about smoking, other than it makes you feel good when you do it?

If your boy doesn't smoke simply tell him your views and ask him for his. Say such things as:

- I hope you never decide to smoke. It's expensive and dangerous.
- Do you think you'd ever start smoking?
- Did you ever kiss a girl who smokes? It's awful.

Words, Phrases, and Actions to Use

- . . . addictive . . .
- . . . evil . . .
- . . . dangerous . . .
- . . . death . . .
- . . . moderation . . .
- . . . treatment . . .
- Drinking is pleasant when done responsibly.
- Never drink and drive.
- Never drink and do anything that could be dangerous.
- Smoking looks stupid.
- Doing drugs is against the law as well as stupid.
- That's unacceptable.

Things Not to Say and Do

Don't ignore any signs of drug taking. Don't say things like:

- I know you've never done drugs.
- If you ever do drugs I don't want to know about it.
- You can't afford to do drugs.

Don't ever make it seem like drugs are acceptable. Don't say such things as:

- Some drugs are okay. They're nonaddictive and harmless.
- I did drugs when I was your age and I'm all right.
- This drug thing really isn't a problem as long as you don't have an addictive personality.

Don't smoke. Don't condone your boy smoking. Don't say such things as:

- Smoking a few cigarettes a day is safe enough.
- I like a cigarette now and again, especially after meals.
- There's nothing like your first cigarette of the day.

Don't allow your boy to drink too much. Don't say such things as:

- Drinking in moderation is for sissies.
- I can hold my liquor and I'll teach you to hold yours.

Don't ignore any problems your boy may have with drinking, doing drugs, or smoking. Don't say such things as:

- If you have a problem that's too bad. You'll just have to deal with it. I'm not interested.
- I warned you but you didn't listen. Now you have to deal with it on your own.
- You're just a juvenile delinquent. That's your problem, not mine.

Words, Phrases, and Actions to Avoid

- It's not a problem.
- Drink as much as you want.

- Some drugs are good for you.
- You can handle it.
- Only sissies don't drink or smoke.
- I love a cigarette.
- It's not my problem.

BODY PIERCING AND TATTOOS

◆

It's the fashion. And your boy wants to join in. He'd love a chain tattoo around his bicep. He's already got a diamond stud in his left earlobe and talks about getting a ring in his navel. You wonder where it will all end. Personally, you find tattoos quite ugly and would never willingly give your consent for your boy to get one. The earring doesn't bother you quite so much, although you like earrings on girls much more than on boys. You've learned over the years to pick your battles wisely and you wonder whether the tattoo battle is worth fighting. It depends, you realize, on the type, location, and size of the tattoo. You would never agree to what you've seen on some boys—large serpents across their backs, tattoos all over and up and down their arms. You've even seen some older boys at the beach with their whole bodies seemingly covered in tattoos. The thought of your boy piercing his body doesn't please you either when the piercing involves the more sensitive parts of the body like his tongue, nipples, or eyebrow. In all of this are issues of health and safety. What you agree to and what you oppose will ultimately be decided in conversations with your boy and how you come to some agreement and maybe compromise.

Things to Consider

Tattoos and body piercing can be important to boys because they send a strong social message. They show membership in a club, group, or gang. They express independence from parents and other adults. They can convey contempt for traditional social values. They can also express a spirit of rebellion.

In most states, if he is under eighteen, your boy must have your permission for legal tattooing and piercing. You can simply say no and that will be the end of it unless he can find someone willing to flout the law. Many parents prefer to reach a compromise with their boy rather than simply say no because they realize how important this issue can be for their teen, even if its importance is lost on them.

In order to deal with your boy's request there are a number of issues you need to discuss. If you already have a good communicative relationship with your boy through years of open discussion of things and if your boy likes and trusts you, then you can probably reach a conclusion on this issue that is acceptable to both of you.

First, let your boy talk about what he wants. Ask him to tell you why he wants the tattoo or the piercing, or both. Find out what it involves, what kind of thing he wants, where it will be on his body, who can do it, and what he knows about the process and its risks. Listen without judging him. Don't interrupt. Don't make rude or disparaging remarks about his plans.

Once he has finished ask him to listen to your concern. You must put your position in the context of who your boy is. Does he want this for positive reasons—he thinks it will look "cool," his friends have them, or he needs it to "fit in"? Or for negative reasons—he wants to be different, or he rejects normal society and wants that to be obvious?

Tell your boy what you think about these things, and why. Ask him if he's ever seen these things done. Suggest you both visit an establishment and watch the procedure if possible. Arrange for your boy to talk to your physician about the procedures and their possible complications.

Here are some of the issues you can raise. Some of these need to be investigated by you so you know what you're talking about because your boy will probably have done his homework on it.

You can talk about both the short-term and long-term issues involved. These are the short-term issues:

- Healing may take a long time and affect things like sleeping, eating, and speaking.
- Physical activities like swimming and contact sports may be curtailed during the healing process.
- Healing may prohibit exposure to the sun for two to four weeks.
- There is a risk of infection.
- There is pain.
- There is the risk of HIV and hepatitis.
- An employer may prohibit workers having tattoos or piercing in open view.

These are the long-term issues:

- Fashions and tastes change.
- Life circumstances change.
- It may prevent you from finding a regular job.
- You will be scarred for life.
- It may impair sexual functioning.

- Tattoos fade.
- Your skin may eventually become old and flabby.
- The removal procedure is painful and expensive.
- You may tattoo something that you would later regret.

Having said all this, here are some options you can give your boy:

- A removable tattoo that can last up to four weeks.
- Clip-on magnetic rings for the lip, nose, or navel.
- Studs that can be glued on the nose.

If, after all your talk and weighing the pros and cons, you decide to let your boy have a small, tasteful tattoo or pierced earlobe, then visit the place at which it will be done, make sure that it is licensed (where required), and check its premises and procedures for cleanliness and the quality of its materials. Do this incognito, or your embarrassed son will go elsewhere.

Three Things You Must Do

1. Listen to your boy's reasons for wanting tattoos or piercing.
2. Explain your position to your boy.
3. Make sure your boy knows all the short- and long-term considerations, as well as the options.

Things to Say and Do

Talk about your boy's reasons for wanting a tattoo or piercing. Say such things as:

- Tell me why you want to do this.
- Do any of your friends have tattoos or studs that I can't see?
- What do you find attractive about tattoos and body piercing?

Ask your boy what he knows about the procedures. Say such things as:

- Do you know how this is done?
- Have you ever seen this done?
- Do you know the risks of this kind of procedure?

Talk to your boy about your own thoughts and feelings. Say such things as:

- Let me tell you what I think about this.
- I know you've thought about this a lot, but let me tell you all the things I've found out about the procedures and the problems that can arise.
- I have strong feelings about this procedure that I'd like to share with you.

Talk about the short-term considerations. Say such things as:

- Here are some of the things about the procedure and healing process that I've found out.
- Have you thought about the things you can't do while this heals?
- I hear that tattooing can be quite painful. Is that okay with you?

Talk about the long-term considerations. Say such things as:

- Do you know what's involved if you ever decide you don't like the tattoo?
- How do you think an employer might react?
- What if you tattoo your girlfriend's name on your body and then you change girlfriends?

Talk about the options. Say such things as:

- Let's talk about options to this that are not permanent.
- I've found out that there are tattoos and studs that you can wear that only last a month or that can be held on by glue or magnets.
- Why not try these temporary ones before you go for the real thing?

Words, Phrases, and Actions to Use

- . . . permanent . . .
- . . . temporary . . .
- . . . scarring . . .
- . . . painful . . .
- . . . disfiguring . . .

- . . . difficult to remove . . .
- . . . affects your life . . .
- . . . healing process . . .
- . . . health risks . . .
- Tastes and fashions change.

Things Not to Say and Do

Don't dismiss your boy's needs as trivial or stupid. Don't say such things as:

- That's the dumbest thing I've ever heard.
- Only a fool would want to get a tattoo or have their body pierced.
- Boys don't wear studs and earrings.

Don't withdraw from the situation. Don't say such things as:

- Do what you like. I don't care.
- If you want to disfigure yourself, go ahead.
- I don't care what you do with your own body.

Don't ignore the important issues involved. Don't say such things as:

- Lots of boys do it so I guess it's safe.
- It probably doesn't matter where you get it done.
- You don't need my help. Just find a place yourself.

Don't make it a life-and-death issue. Don't say such things as:

- If you do this you're not my son anymore.
- I forbid you to do this. If you go ahead don't bother coming home.
- I can't believe a son of mine would want to do a thing like this.

Words, Phrases, and Actions to Avoid

- . . . never . . .
- . . . no risk . . .
- That's forbidden.
- No problem.

- It's not worth discussing.
- I'll disown you.
- Don't bother coming home.

CAREERS

◆

You want your boy to be happy and successful. He's sixteen and he still doesn't seem to know what he'd like to do with his life. You would like your boy to have a career that he really likes, has some security and prestige, offers a good income, and offers good chances for advancement. You've been paying particular attention to his work in school, the kinds of things he likes doing in his free time, the kinds of friends he has, what he likes watching on television, his preferences on the Internet, and the things he likes to read. In all of these you're looking for clues to his abilities, preferences, and likes and dislikes. Now you'd like to have a good talk with him about a possible career.

Things to Consider

Many boys, myself included, had no idea what they wanted to do until they were finished with college, and some not even then. For many boys it's not so much what they want to do but what they don't want to do. There have always been the lucky few who have known since they were ten that they wanted to be an architect, mechanic, lawyer, electrician, or computer programmer. Most boys are not like that. They discover their likes and dislikes through summer jobs while they're in college, or by trying a number of jobs after high school or university. In some cases that means more study; in other cases that means an apprenticeship of sorts.

The best help you can give your boy in his pursuit of a career is to be there for him when he needs advice, moral and financial support, or someone to use as a sounding board against which he can throw ideas. You are his support group, cheerleader, critic, and banker. Talk to your boy and spend time with him. See what he likes, what his choices are, whom he admires, and what he reads in magazines, in newspapers, and on the Internet. Talk to him about what he likes and doesn't like in school. Know if he's prepared to go to college for four to eight years after he finishes high school. See if you can tell how important material possessions are to him. Will he need to make lots of money to be happy? How hard a worker is he? Does he like working with his hands, or is he mainly a thinker? You can tell him what you think he's best suited for given what you know of his personality, talents, interests, and academic record. You can do this even if he doesn't ask.

Be realistic about your boy's abilities. Don't try to fulfill your own career dreams through him. Don't think of him someday as a professional athlete if he doesn't have the talent or the desire. Don't push him toward university and ultimately medical school if he doesn't like blood and can't stand biology. Don't expect him to go to MIT or Cal Tech and become a physicist, engineer, or computer geek if he hates math.

One of the best things you can do for your boy is let him work some summer or part-time jobs. Those experiences will often point him in the right direction, or at least point him away from the wrong direction.

All of these steps will help you, and him, start thinking in the right direction about possible careers.

Three Things You Must Do

1. Give your boy advice on possible careers, but remember that the final choice will be his.
2. Accept your boy for whom he is, not for whom you want him to be.
3. Realize that many boys will not choose a career, rather, a career will choose them.

Things to Say and Do

Talk to your boy about any thoughts he might have about what he'd like to do after high school and/or college. Say such things as:

- Any ideas of what kind of career you'd like to have?
- What would you like to do with your life?
- If you had to draw up a list of occupations that you'd like to do what would be on the list?

Give your boy your impression of him and what he might be good at. Say such things as:

- Let me tell you what I think you'd be good at.
- I think you'd enjoy doing this.
- When I think of the things you seem to like doing the most I think of this kind of career for you.

Make sure your boy understands that you're behind him, whatever kind of career he might like to pursue. Say such things as:

- Don't think I'm pushing you in some specific direction. I'm happy with whatever you want to do.

- I think the most important thing is to know what you want to do and to do it.
- I want to see you happy in whatever you do.

Talk about the kind of boy he is and tell him that at his age he doesn't have to know what he wants to do with the rest of his life. He only has to know whether or not he wants to go to college or go to work after high school. Say such things as:

- I know that many boys don't know what they want to do until after college, which is quite okay. It's probably going to be that way with you, isn't it?
- I think you're one of those boys who will suddenly realize what he wants to do later in life.
- These days people have lots of different careers so you may choose one, find out it doesn't suit you, and then choose another.
- I think you have the ability and desire to go to college. What about it?

Words, Phrases, and Actions to Use

- . . . career . . .
- . . . choices . . .
- . . . talents . . .
- . . . abilities . . .
- . . . desires . . .
- . . . goals . . .
- . . . realistic . . .
- . . . multiple careers . . .
- . . . too soon . . .
- . . . college . . .
- What do you most like doing?

Things Not to Say and Do

Don't try to force your boy into making career decisions at such a young age if he's not ready to do so. Don't say such things as:

- You're sixteen years old. You should know what you want to do with your life.
- If you don't have a plan you're not going to get anywhere.
- You have to choose a college based on the career you want to follow.

Don't belittle your boy's career plans if he has them already. Don't say such things as:

- That's a stupid career.
- How can you want to do that? You don't have the talent or the brains.
- You better choose something better to do than that.

Don't refuse to talk to your boy about what he might be good at. Don't say such things as:

- I don't want to talk about it. It's totally up to you.
- I'm not interested in talking about you and your career. You're too young to know what you want.
- I'm too busy. We can talk about it when you're in college.

Don't be unrealistic about your boy's career possibilities. Don't say such things as:

- You can do anything you want to do.
- If you want to do that you just have to try harder.
- I want you to be _____. That's what I would have become if I had had the opportunities you've had.

Words, Phrases, and Actions to Avoid

- That's stupid.
- That's useless.
- That's a waste of time and effort.
- You're not talented enough.
- That's a rotten career.
- How can you want to be that?
- That's not good enough for my boy.

CLOTHES

◆

Your boy wants to dress the same way his group of friends dresses. You often wonder why he doesn't realize how ugly these clothes are. But he doesn't and you're not going to fight this battle. The biggest problem is the cost of these clothes. Another is the fact that he's still growing and you can't see spending so much money on things he'll grow out of in a year. Still another thing that bothers you is how quickly fashions change. Once things are out of style your boy refuses to wear them. You have no alternative but to tell your boy that you are happy to pay for his clothes but only for the things he really needs, like underwear, socks, reasonably priced jeans, shirts, jackets, shoes, sports shoes, and so on. If he wants designer clothes that cost way beyond your normal budget you will give him what you would have spent and he will have to find the rest out of his allowance, the money he earns from doing special jobs around the home, or from any part-time job he has. You think that this is a reasonable approach. Your boy does too, although, like all teenagers, he sometimes complains that his friends' parents buy them the latest and greatest fashions. Your reply is simple: "Get them to adopt you."

Things to Consider

Your boy has fashion needs just like you do. You may think of a girl's need to dress fashionably but not your boy's. However, today boys are quite as fashion conscious as girls, sometimes even more so. Of course, boys and men have always been fashion conscious. We just seem to be more aware of it with our own boys because in today's world clothing manufacturers, advertisers, and the media make boys' fashions a prominent thing.

Don't be surprised when your boy talks about his need to dress like his friends. Even if you think his clothes are ugly, outlandish, provocative, and hopelessly unflattering he thinks they are cool, sexy, perfect, and make just the kind of statement he wants to make. Of course your boy may be a jock or a preppy, in which case you may even like what he wears. On the other hand he may want to dress like a goth, geek, grunge, punk, or any of the other new and old groups you can find in high schools these days.

In any case his fashion statement is as important to him as yours is to you. You wouldn't go to work in inappropriate clothes. If you find the need to dress to suit the expectations of your colleagues, boss, clients, and job why should you expect anything less from your boy?

My advice is to go with the need your boy has to dress like his friends. Make the cost the big issue, not the fashion. Believe me, the need to wear clothes like one's friends is one battle you don't want to fight. Your position should be to find the best way to finance your boy's clothing needs. As I said earlier you should be able to work out an arrangement that you pay the basic cost of necessities and he uses his own resources to buy the fashionable designer clothes.

One issue you should insist on is that he dress appropriately for the occasion. You need to draw the line here. When he's at school or out with his friends he can dress as they do. When he's going out with you to a restaurant, a concert, your place of worship, a wedding, a funeral, or a family celebration you can insist that he dress properly. The same applies to going for a job interview.

The other rule I would suggest you have is that whatever he wears must be clean, reasonably modest, and safe. You have already conceded that he can wear the styles he wants and that you'll make a substantial contribution toward their cost. The least he can do is dress in clothes that won't reflect badly on you because they are unwashed, torn, too revealing, or too large or small.

Three Things You Must Do

1. Accept that your boy needs to dress in the fashions of his group.
2. Work out a means for him to make a good contribution to the cost of expensive clothes.
3. Insist that he wear clothes appropriate to the occasion and that are clean, modest, and safe.

Things to Say and Do

Talk to your boy about his needs and his wants in clothes. Work out with him what are necessities and what are luxuries. You write out a list if that would help. Say such things as:

- We need to talk about your clothing and about the difference between what you need and what you want.
- Let's make a list of the kinds of clothes you need and the kinds of clothes you would like to have, and then we can talk about how you can get them.
- How much of what you wear has to be fashionable and expensive, and how much can just be generic clothes?

Talk about costs and ways to pay for your boy's wants and needs. Say such things as:

- My problem is how to pay for the expensive stuff you want. Do you have any suggestions?
- I'm willing to pay for your basic clothing needs. What are you willing to do to pay for the fashionable clothes you want?
- How much are you willing to contribute to the cost of your style needs?

Talk about your need to have him dress appropriately for different occasions and to wear clothes that are clean, in good repair, and modest. Say such things as:

- Your idea of nice clothes and mine are different, but that's not necessarily bad.
- I have only two real concerns. The first is this: I expect you to wear clothes that fit the occasion. If you're going out with the family to some place special, like a restaurant, the theater, or some holiday party, I want you to dress appropriately. It's all right to dress like your friends when you're out with them, but when you're out with me I'd like you to dress differently. The second is this: you can wear clothes that you think are fashionable at school and with your friends as long as they are clean, with no huge tears or holes, and as long as they don't show too much of you in the wrong places. Do you have any problem with these concerns of mine? Because if you do, then we need to talk it out and to resolve the problem.

Words, Phrases, and Actions to Use

- . . . fashion . . .
- . . . clothing needs . . .
- . . . clothing wants . . .
- . . . clean . . .
- . . . neat . . .

- . . . in good repair . . .
- . . . modest . . .
- . . . too expensive . . .
- . . . your contribution . . .
- . . . compromise . . .

Things Not to Say and Do

Don't ignore your boy's clothing needs. Don't think they are unimportant. Don't say such things as:

- You'll wear what I tell you.
- As long as I'm paying I'm saying what you can and cannot wear.
- What you wear doesn't matter. It's who you are underneath the clothes that counts. (This may be true, but your boy won't understand.)

Don't simply give your boy everything he wants. Even if you can afford it, it is probably better for him to have to make a contribution. Don't say such things as:

- You go down to the store and buy whatever you like. I'll pay.
- I want you to dress as well as your friends. I'll pay for it all.
- Money is no object.

Don't ridicule your boy for the clothes he wears. Don't say such things as:

- You look awful/ridiculous.
- That's incredibly ugly.
- Those clothes don't suit you at all. How could you wear such terrible clothes?

Don't threaten your boy. Don't say such things as:

- If you're going to live in my house you're going to dress as I tell you.

Don't let your boy wear anything he wants. Don't say such things as:

- I don't care what you wear.
- It doesn't matter to me.
- Wear whatever you like.

Words, Phrases, and Actions to Avoid

- That's ugly.
- That's stupid.
- That's unnecessary.
- That's too extreme.
- You don't need fashionable clothes.
- Get out.
- Who cares?
- Wear whatever you like.

COLLEGE

◆

Will your boy go to college, or not? For you this has never been a question. You expect your boy to go to college and have been encouraging him to do well in high school so that he can go to the college of his choice, and maybe even get a scholarship. You have talked to your boy about college a lot and you think you know his views. Even though he doesn't know what kind of a career he'd like to pursue he does know that going to college will give him options that he won't have if he goes to work right out of high school. On the other hand your boy has also talked on occasion of spending a few years working after high school. This would accomplish a couple of important things, he says. First, it would help him clarify what he might want to do with his life and that would point him in the direction of the right college and the right major. Second, it would give him a chance to earn some money to buy a car and to put some aside to help pay for college. You're quite open to this idea since you think that boys who have a little real-world work experience before going to college do better because they are more focused, realistic, mature, and aware of how limited the options are for someone without a college degree.

Things to Consider

By the time they're sixteen boys seem to have regained some of the academic ground they lost to girls in elementary, middle, and junior high school. They have the chance, if they want to take it, of doing very well in school in preparation for college entrance tests and applications. If, in addition, they are high school athletes their chances of getting good grades and going to college increase even more.

Older high school boys seem to more naturally think about career options than girls do. In spite of the increasing opportunities for girls in the workplace boys still feel the obligation to get ahead in the world through going to college and having a successful career, even though some statistics show that girls outnumber boys in college these days. Research suggests that postpubescent boys have an academic advantage over girls the same age whose high estrogen levels interfere with intellectual processes. Boys' performances in written examinations improves in late adolescence more than that of girls, whose work can be affected by their menstrual cycle.

You've been encouraging your boy all his young life to do well in school because you know from experience how important it is to get good grades and have a wide choice of options after graduation, whether your boy wants to work, join the armed forces, or go to a technical school, community college, or university. Often you feel that your advice has fallen on deaf ears. But now that your boy is a junior or senior in high school you'll find him more likely to listen to you for a number of reasons. He hears his friends talking about their postgraduation plans. His teachers and the school guidance counselors have talked to him about his options for college, making sure he has taken the right classes. His girlfriend has told him of her plans and they talk secretly about going to the same college. And he knows that his SAT scores will be important so he's talking to you about doing the SAT preparation course. So you know he's serious at last, at least as serious as a seventeen year old can be.

As I've said in *How to Say It to Teens* I believe that almost everyone can benefit from a college education that teaches him or her to think critically about the world. Whether they major in education, engineering, English literature, mathematics, or philosophy is a matter of personality, aptitude, and personal choice. But in whatever they do and whatever knowledge and skills they need to acquire they should take the opportunity college gives them to talk to people of very different backgrounds, ideas, and beliefs; read widely and deeply; and think about the validity and reliability of what they are taught, what they read on the Internet, in newspapers, and in magazines, and what they hear about the world through the media.

College should present your boy with the opportunity to learn to think and reflect on life as well as give him what he needs to have a successful and happy career. Talk to your boy's teachers and counselors about colleges that they think might best suit him. Look at the various college guides available in bookstores and on the Internet. Spend the summer between his junior and senior years visiting some potential college choices. Talk to the admissions officers there.

The following things should govern your boy's choice of college:

- His academic ability and interests
- Admission requirements
- Courses of study
- Family circumstances
- Costs and financial aid available
- His desire to live away from or at home

Three Things You Must Do

1. Encourage your boy to do well in school to increase his options upon graduation.
2. Be realistic about your boy's talents, interests, and ambitions.
3. Research the best college for his goals and abilities and your family circumstances.

Things to Say and Do

Talk to your boy about his own thoughts about college. Know as well as you can what he would like to do. Don't leave it to the last moment. Say such things as:

- What kind of thoughts have you given to going to college?
- It's not too early to be thinking about college. Do you have any preferences for where you'd like to go?
- What do you think you would like to study?

Let your boy know about your own opinions about his going to college. Say such things as:

- You know I'd love you to go to the college I went to.
- You know I want you to go to college. That's why I've always been after you to get good grades so you can get into a good college.
- I want you to go to college but I don't want to force you to do something you're not ready to do. So if you'd rather work for a year or so after high school that's all right with me.

Talk about the value of college. Listen to your boy's thoughts on this and give him yours. Say such things as:

- Let's talk about why college is a good thing.
- Why do you want to go to college? Is it just to get a good job afterward?
- I think a good college is important because of whom you meet there as well as what you learn.
- I don't think of college as a trade school just for job preparation. It's a place to go to learn how to think critically about things.

Talk about majors. Let your boy tell you what he thinks he'd most like to study. Say such things as:

- Do you have any idea what you'd like to study?
- Even if you don't know what you'd like to major in what subject would you most like to study?
- Have you any ambitions to be a lawyer or doctor? You know that requires lots of school and good grades.

Talk about finances if they are an issue. Say such things as:

- We'd like you to be able to go to any college you want but we can't afford the Ivy League schools unless you can get financial aid. Why don't you write to them to see what's available?
- Whatever school you go to you'll probably need to work part-time to help us with the finances.
- If you can get a scholarship that would really help us out a lot, but if you don't we'll see what we can manage.

Words, Phrases, and Actions to Use

- . . . admission policies . . .
- . . . early admission . . .
- . . . your likes and dislikes . . .
- . . . your favorite subject . . .
- . . . your choice of a good school . . .
- Get good grades.

Things Not to Say and Do

Don't try to impose your dreams on your boy. You can have dreams for him but let him make his own choices. Don't say such things as:

- I'm paying so you'll go to the college I choose.
- I'm not sending you to college to study philosophy. You're going into engineering or business.
- College is about getting a good job after graduation. Nothing else really matters.

Don't be hard on your boy if he doesn't want to go to college right away, or at all. Don't say such things as:

- I want you to go right into college and not waste your time hanging out doing nothing.
- There'll be plenty of time for you to work after college. Right now the important thing is to go to college and finish as quickly as you can.
- You're going to go to college whether you like it or not.

Don't take the other position, refusing to let your boy go to college if that's what he wants to do. Don't say things like:

- You don't need to go to college. It's a waste of time and money.
- College is no good unless it trains you for a good job. You're better off going to a technical college or trade school.
- I didn't go to college and I'm doing fine.

Don't refuse to help your boy find the right college for him. Don't say such things as:

- You'll have to find your own information about college. I don't have the time to help you.
- You don't need my help.
- I can't help you look at colleges. Ask your friends.

Words, Phrases, and Actions to Avoid

- College is a waste of money.
- College is to train you to get a good job.
- You're too stupid.
- You can't go.
- You'll have to find a way to pay for it yourself.
- You're going to college whether you want to or not.
- My choice of college is the only option.

DATING

◆

You've discouraged your boy from going out on single dates with girls because you wanted him to wait until he was sixteen and he's listened to you. He's gone out with boys and girls as a group, but no single dates. Now he is sixteen and he has a girl he'd like to take out, just her and him. You're ready for this and you'd like to talk to your boy about things that you think it's important for him to think about. You want to talk about girls, about how they should be treated, about relationships, about love and sex (not the mechanics but the dangers and precautions), and about the consequences of moving too fast or being too serious in a relationship at his age. You also want to know more about the girl he wants to take out. You think you've seen her and he talks about her a lot. But you'd like to meet her and get to know her, not because you think your boy is too serious about her but just because you want to know what kind of girl your boy is attracted to her. But even though you'd like to talk to your boy about all these things you don't know how to go about doing it. Where do you begin, what do you say, what do you expect your boy to say in reply? Or is it his job to simply listen and learn?

Things to Consider

In one research study on teen sexual behavior more than half of the sixteen-year-old boys surveyed reported that they had had sexual intercourse. You must help your boy understand and control his sexual needs and desires and channel them into appropriate dating behavior. You don't have to discuss his urges with him. He knows all about them and so do you. You need to talk about proper moral and social behavior toward his date. Here are some of the things about dating you might want to say to your boy in conversation, not as a lecture:

- Your sexual impulses are natural but you have to control them.
- Your male hormones push you toward risk-taking, but your date's female hormones may not push her the same way.
- You need to respect your date's privacy.
- Your date's body is her own and you must not touch her inappropriately.
- You must never physically or verbally abuse your date.

- Sexual pleasure lasts for seconds but its consequences can last a lifetime.
- Remember that unprotected intercourse can result in pregnancy and/or sexually transmitted disease.
- There is no such thing as totally safe sex.
- I recognize your strong feelings for your date.
- There are many acceptable ways to show your feelings toward your date.
- Love, sex, and commitment should go together, but only at a later age.
- You and your date can express your feelings for each through talking, kissing, hugging, and appropriate touching, but not through sexual intercourse.
- You must never force your date to do anything she doesn't want to do.
- No means no!
- When you're out on a date you must never drink and drive.
- Your first responsibility is the comfort and safety of your date.
- You should never put your date into a situation in which she feels anxious, uncomfortable, or unsafe.
- You must be sure to meet your date's family.
- I must always know where you and your date are going and if you change your plans.

Your boy is at an age during which his sexual feelings are strongest and he lives in a society that stimulates these feelings in movies, TV, magazines, and music. Yet he also lives in a society that offers little good advice on how to control or satisfy these feelings. Your job is to help your boy understand how dating can do this morally with total respect for his date.

Three Things You Must Do

1. Recognize that age sixteen is a good time to let your boy start to single date.
2. Talk to your boy about proper dating attitudes and behavior toward his date.
3. Encourage your boy to talk about his dates and his feelings.

Things to Say and Do

Talk to your boy about dating and about what he thinks about love and relationships. Say such things as:

- Dating is a good way to test your feelings about a girl.
- Tell me about your idea of a good date.
- You know the most important thing is to treat your date with respect?
- What are your obligations to your date?

Talk about meeting his date's family. Say such things as:

- I think it's a good idea to meet your date's family, as long as she wants you to.
- What do you think of your date's mom and dad?
- Tell me about your date's family. Do you like them?

Talk about sex on a date, specifically about the temptations and dangers. Say such things as:

- You know my attitude toward having sex at your age. Intercourse can lead to all kinds of emotional and health problems, as well as pregnancy. It's just not a good idea for you or the girl.
- Do you know what kinds of sex are safe and what are not?
- You can do a lot of kissing, holding, and touching without going too far.
- What are your feelings about sex with your date? What do your friends, boys and girls, think? What do they say?

Talk about your boy's responsibility to his date. Say such things as:

- Don't forget that you have certain responsibilities toward your date.
- Try to remember never to put your date in an uncomfortable situation, take her someplace inappropriate, or do something that she doesn't like.
- Would you agree that your first responsibility is to keep your date safe and secure?

Talk in general terms about self-control and morality in dating. Say such things as:

- Talk to me about what you think are the most important things for boys to think about when they take a girl out.
- Do you think it's a good idea to have sex before marriage, or not? Would your friends agree?
- I expect you've heard the expression "No means no!" What does it mean to you?

Talk about the practical aspects of dating. Say such things as:

- You know that I always need to know where you are with your date. The same rules apply to your dating as when you're out on your own.
- If in spite of everything I've said you do have sex make sure you use protection.

Words, Phrases, and Actions to Use

- ... love ...
- ... respect ...
- ... relationships ...
- ... safety ...
- ... sex ...

- ... privacy ...
- ... consequences ...
- ... impulses ...
- ... abuse ...
- ... consideration ...

Things Not to Say and Do

Don't ignore the possibility that your boy may misbehave toward his date. Don't say such things as:

- I know you're not just interested in sex.
- I don't think boys abuse their dates. Girls just want to get boys into trouble.

Don't encourage your boy to be disrespectful of his date's privacy and independence. Don't say such things as:

- All girls want the same thing as boys.
- Girls really want sex even when they say they don't.
- When a girl says no she really means yes.

Don't encourage your boy to have intercourse with his date. Don't say such things as:

- If you ever get a girl in trouble I don't want to hear about it.
- Remember, if you get in trouble you're on your own.
- If something happens keep it to yourself.

Don't ignore your boy's desire to talk about dating. Don't say such things as:

- Dating is a natural thing. You don't need to talk about it.
- I'm not interested. It's up to you.
- Don't talk to me about your problems.

Words, Phrases, and Actions to Avoid

- You can't trust girls.
- Girls don't know what they want.
- Don't expect me to help you.
- You're on your own.
- How can they expect you to deny your instincts?
- As long as you use protection sex is okay.

DISCIPLINE

◆

Your boy still needs your love and caring and he still depends on you financially. He still gets into trouble at school and around the house on occasion and expects you to understand and help him out. One moment he talks and behaves like a man and the next moment he seems like he's no more than ten years old. He still needs disciplining from you even though you have tried over the years to teach him right and wrong so he could develop a good sense of self-discipline. At the root of most of his problems seems to be an impulsiveness that he can't always control. You recognize this as one more way in which boys and girls are different. You've had arguments with your daughter about issues but usually your fights are about attitudes and words rather than deeds. Your boy gets into trouble for doing things on impulse, things that are dangerous to him or to others. He sometimes forgets to think first and then act. He just does what he feels like doing and it comes back to haunt him. You wonder how you can best help him work through his male need for instant action, his feelings of tension, and his ability to release it in socially acceptable ways. You realize that he still needs your reminders of discipline in order for him to remember to discipline himself.

Things to Consider

Teenage boys often send conflicting messages about discipline. On the one hand they want to be treated as independent, self-disciplining adults. On the other hand they want you to give them strict guidelines, sometimes even ultimatums, that say, "Do this in this way by this time, or else face the consequences."

Why the mixed messages? Because your boy thinks that you don't have enough time for him if you don't give him rules, even if he rebels against them. And he equates this with a lack of love. His thinking tells him that if you care about him then you'll take the time to discipline him. And he needs you to care about him because that caring, that discipline, gives a structure to his life.

Your boy wants to be responsible for disciplining himself but self-discipline and the independence that goes along with it can be frightening for a sixteen-year-old boy. Even though you're happy to let him grow increasingly independent of you, you have to remember that he still needs some of the parental concern and guidance that he needed when he was ten. He needs rules to show that you care, even though he rejects the rules you make.

Although you want to encourage his self-discipline, you need to continue to provide him with rules and consequences for violating the rules. But you can enlist his help in creating those rules and deciding on the consequences for breaking them. This will surely make him feel wanted and involved. It will also help him develop an even better sense of self-discipline because he's responsible for both his behavior and for the rules governing that behavior. If he violates the rules he's violating his own rules. And he's the author of the consequences.

Here then are some tips for disciplining your sixteen- to eighteen-year-old boy:

- You and your boy together sit down and create the rules that he needs to follow. They should cover things like school grades, homework, money given and money earned, jobs around the house, curfews, politeness in the family and to others, use of the car, bedtime, getting-up time, food, loud music, behavior that disturbs others, respect for property, tidiness in his room and around the house, part-time work, and practice times for sports or music.
- Make it clear that you won't bail your boy out of trouble right away. If he breaks the rules he's going to suffer some consequences.
- You and your boy should both agree that you don't expect him to be perfect. No one's perfect. He's entitled to make mistakes. The important thing is for him to learn from those mistakes.
- Show your boy you applaud him when he shows good self-discipline. Reward him verbally and perhaps with some more tangible token of appreciation like giving him the use of the car more often.
- Work with your boy to make the punishment fit the crime. When he breaks a rule you have jointly created he should know more or less what the consequences are and they should follow immediately.
- Finally, be a model of good self-discipline for your boy. Show him that you too have rules you need to follow. Be honest with him when you break them and show him that you have faced the consequences.

Three Things You Must Do

1. Give your boy rules and consequences.
2. Jointly create these with your boy.
3. Never let him think you don't care.

Things to Say and Do

Let your boy know that you want him to have good self-discipline but that you still care about him enough that you expect him to obey your rules as well. Say such things as:

- You're old enough to decide for yourself what's right and what's wrong.
- If you like, I'm happy to go over what the rules are and what will happen if you break them.
- Although you should be self-disciplining, you still need to obey my rules.

Suggest that you and your boy sit down and set out what the rules are for him and what the consequences will be if he breaks them. Say such things as:

- What would you think of the idea that you and I together work out the rules that you need to follow if you and I are going to get along? We can also work out what the consequences should be when you break a rule.
- Let's compare rules. You tell me what rules you think you need to have and I'll tell you what I think the rules are that you need to have. Let's talk about the consequences of breaking the rules also.

Talk to your boy about the areas of his life that he thinks he needs rules for. Say such things as:

- Can you tell me where you think you need rules?
- What kind of discipline works best for you in the different parts of your life?
- Let me give you a list of areas in which I think rules would help.

Talk to your boy about the basic principles that underlie the kind of self-discipline you expect from him. Say such things as:

- Let's talk about the reasons why you need to be self-disciplined.
- What do you see might be the basic rules for people to use to get along? What makes you do what you do and not do? Do you think it is just your parents' set of rules, or the rules in school, or the law? Maybe it goes deeper than that. I'm thinking of things like The Golden Rule.

Be a model of self-discipline for your boy.

Words, Phrases, and Actions to Use

- . . . rules . . .
- . . . discipline . . .
- . . . self-discipline . . .
- . . . love . . .

- . . . The Golden Rule . . .
- . . . consequences . . .
- . . . punishment . . .
- Respect others.

- Do the right thing.
- Control your impulses.
- Show courtesy.
- Show politeness.
- Have consideration of others.

Things Not to Say and Do

Don't let your boy think you're ignoring him. Don't say such things as:

- You can do what you like. I'm not interested.
- You're old enough to take care of yourself.
- I don't care what you do.

On the other hand don't be too rigid in your rule making for him. Don't say such things as:

- I make the rules, you follow them.
- You'll do as I say.
- You're not old enough to make your own rules.

Make the punishment fit the crime. Don't say such things as:

- You broke a rule. I don't care if it was an accident or not. You're grounded.
- Maybe this punishment will make you think twice about breaking one of my rules again.

Don't expect your boy to be self-disciplined if you are not. Don't say such things as:

- I expect you to do as I say, not as I do.
- I'm the adult, you're the child. I can do what I like.
- I make the rules so I can break any of them I want to.

Words, Phrases, and Actions to Avoid

- You're totally irresponsible.
- I don't care about you.
- My rules must never be broken.
- You are so stupid.

INDEPENDENCE

◆

Your boy is seventeen, really almost an adult, and you want to arrive at a good balance between treating him as your child and treating him as you would treat a friend. You want to be the parent and the authority figure but you also want to be able to talk to your boy as you might to an equal. You wonder if you can manage to do both. In the back of your mind you realize that you probably can but that you have to be careful. If you treat your boy too much as a friend you threaten his needing you as a parent, providing the stable base from which he can venture forth on his own. You also take away some of his need to rebel against you, an important part of testing his independence and self-discipline. However, if you only relate to your boy as your child and not as a friend you miss the chance to deepen the bond between you. This bond can include both his need for the security you give him and the love you have for him as your child, as well as the love and sharing you can have with a friend. It's a tough balancing act and you need to talk to your boy about it so he will understand that you're encouraging him to become more independent while, at the same time, you don't want to lose him to adulthood.

Things to Consider

Boys seek independence from parents and other males earlier and more aggressively than girls do. This seems to be true in every culture on earth, thus it's a biological rather than a social fact of life. Michael Gurian in *The Good Son* lists four important facts about boys' need for independence:

1. Boys have that familiar hormone, testosterone, which results in male aggression, competitiveness, and risk-taking behavior.
2. Boys seek separation as an aggressive response to the process of growing up.
3. Boys feel they are competing with other boys to show that they can successfully stand on their own two feet.
4. Boys see other males exhibiting far more independence than females, who seem to remain bonded to parents and other females physically through hugging, kissing, and touching, and psychologically through talking and sharing.

Boys, although there are exceptions, are more aggressively independent than girls and give parents a tough time throughout adolescence. You may have noticed your boy is hard to talk to, hard to reason with, resentful of advice or explicit or implied criticism you may give him, uncooperative just when you need him to cooperate with you the most, moody, touchy, and defensive about everything, including his appearance, his schoolwork, his friends, and his ideas of fun and relaxation. This is normal.

Your boy needs your views, opinions, rules, and simple presence in his life as something important to react against. If you didn't continue to parent him and react to his moves toward independence he would think you didn't care about him anymore. It's the classic push-pull, love-hate relationship, although hate is really too strong a word. He's caught between his need to reject you as a parent and resisting this rejection. He wants you to let him go but be there to catch him if he falls.

You want to let him go but you recognize that he still needs you. You're still his main life-support system and without you he'd be truly on his own. Some boys of sixteen or seventeen can survive without their parents, and some actually choose to do so. But most older teenage boys still need Mom and Dad as a security blanket. This security lies in your caring and in showing that you care through commenting on and criticizing his behavior, his schoolwork, his appearance, his friends, his eating habits, his lack of ambition, and everything about him. It's not what you say that's really important. Whatever you say shows that you care and that he's not really alone.

Three Things You Must Do

1. Recognize his need for independence as biological as well as social.
2. Recognize that he must reject you as parents but still needs you to show that you care.
3. Help him on his way by keeping your rules and discipline in place.

Things to Say and Do

Encourage your boy to think for himself about his life, his choices, and the consequences of his actions. Say such things as:

- How are you doing in school? Do you think you're doing your best?
- What do you want to do after high school? Have you given it much thought?
- Your actions have consequences. Do you ever think about what you do in terms of what effect it might have on your life?

Talk to your boy about ways that he can be more independent of you. Ask him what he would like to be able to decide for himself. Say such things as:

- Over the years I've tried to give you more responsibility. Are there still things that you'd like to be able to decide for yourself that we haven't thought of?
- I think you're ready to handle things like deciding your study times, your bedtime, your weekend curfew, and the jobs you do for me around the house.
- What rules do you want me to give you and what rules do you have for yourself?

Tell your boy that you are still his parent and still have responsibility for him until he's eighteen so you are not going to stop disciplining him. Say such things as:

- I still have responsibility for you so you still need to follow the rules for living here. I think that's fair, don't you?
- I'm not going to stop telling you what I think is right and wrong. Are you okay with that?
- I think you still need my advice on some things so I'm going to give it and you can tell me what you think.

Let your boy know that you will always love him and care for him and that he will always be your son, no matter how independent he becomes. Say such things as:

- You're my son and you will always be my son.
- You're almost a man now, but no matter how old and independent you are, you will still be my boy.
- You're never going to get rid of me, no matter how old and independent you are. I love you too much.

Words, Phrases, and Actions to Use

- ... independence ...
- ... caring ...
- ... rebellion ...
- ... rules ...
- ... discipline ...
- ... responsibility ...
- ... need ...
- ... love ...
- ... separation ...
- I'll always be there for you.

Things Not to Say and Do

Don't take your boy's need for independence as a personal rejection of you. Don't say such things as:

- You think you don't need me anymore so you're rejecting me.
- That's a fine thank-you for all the years of love and caring I've given you.
- Now you think you're all grown up and don't need me anymore.

Don't overreact to your boy's need to separate from you. Don't say such things as:

- If you don't like it here you can leave.
- Any more behavior like that and I'll throw you out of here.
- If you don't want to be part of the family anymore why don't you leave home?

Don't stop giving your boy the discipline, rules, and supervision he still needs. Don't say such things as:

- Do what you like. I don't care.
- I'm not going to worry about you anymore. You can do what you like and suffer the consequences.
- If you get into trouble don't expect me to help you out.
- I don't care what you do, when you do it, who you do it with, or what happens to you.

Don't desert your boy. Don't tell him he's truly on his own. Don't say such things as:

- I resign as your parent.
- Don't expect me to help you anymore. You're on your own.
- Today you're a man and you don't need parents anymore. You can do everything for yourself.

Words, Phrases, and Actions to Avoid

- Get out of here.
- I'm through with you.
- I've had enough.
- Don't come to me for help.
- You're on your own.
- You're not my son anymore.
- Leave and don't come back.
- I'm sick of your criticism.
- Go live on your own.

MONEY

◆

You want your boy to have a good sense of the value of a dollar and you've been helping him develop that over the years. He's almost eighteen and has been working a part-time job, full-time in the summers and on holidays, for two years. You've worked out an arrangement that he can keep half of the money he earns in cash but you insist that he put the other half into a savings account, stocks, bonds, or mutual funds. He resisted this to some extent because he wants to buy a car. But you've said he can use the savings to buy the car and that you'll pay for half of it. You've shown him how important it is to have money in reserve. You've talked to him about how much his car insurance will cost, even with you again paying half. You think you've done a pretty good job getting him to think about money for immediate and future needs and to make money grow for him. This hasn't been easy because your boy isn't the frugal type and would just as soon give money to a friend who needs it than spend it on himself.

Things to Consider

If there's one thing that's true about most of our lives it's that we never have enough money. There are a few lucky people who seem to be satisfied with whatever they have, but most of us are not among that group. For example, your boy probably talks a lot about the new jeans he must have, the new snowboard that he can't live without, the car that will make his life complete, and the inadequate amount of money he has that makes all these needs unattainable without your help.

Although for him it is still a number of years in the future, your boy will need to become responsibile for his money. What are the most important things you can teach your boy about money? Here is a short list:

- Never spend more than you have.
- Save some for a rainy day.
- Don't put all your eggs in one basket.
- Never count other people's money.
- Live within your means.
- Make the miracle of compound interest work for you.
- Save a set amount each month.

- Be patient.
- Don't be greedy.
- Never put money you can't afford to lose into speculative investments.
- Buying lottery tickets is not a good way to plan for retirement.
- The tax man cometh!

All of this advice has some truth to it. It's also true that none of us live up to all of them, but knowing them helps us reflect on what we're doing with our money before we spend or invest it.

Your boy is still too young to appreciate how important it is to discipline himself when it comes to money. He's at an age during which he thinks he will live forever and thinks he'll someday have a job that will let him afford all the luxuries he can't afford now. And he may be right, at least about the job.

But you can help him develop a good, healthy respect for the value of a dollar by working with him from his point of view, understanding his strengths and weaknesses about money, giving him practical experience in saving, investing, and budgeting whatever money he has coming in, and being a good role model for him in your financial dealings, showing him what you do with your money and how and why you do it.

At his age you don't want to preach to him about money. You want to give him real-life experience in earning it, spending it, saving it, investing it, and even losing and wasting it. For example, since most of us live on credit by using our credit card you might want him to have a credit card on your account that he can use in emergencies. You certainly want him to see the outrageous interest he would pay on any unpaid monthly balance.

You want to discuss these experiences with him. Each experience can be a case study of what went right and wrong. You want to talk about the value of money in the context of the things and opportunities it brings with it, as well as the dangers it presents. Above all you need to talk about money in the context of your boy's value system. Money, after all, is not an end in itself. We use it to tell others who we are and what we value. Use the issue of money to talk about who he is and what he values and what role money plays in all of that. And talk about money and careers. Discuss the relationship of the kind of work he does with the kind of money he can earn.

Three Things You Must Do

1. Make sure he has control over some money.
2. Talk about the value of earning, spending, saving, investing, winning, and losing.
3. Talk about your boy's values as expressed in his attitude toward and need for money.

Things to Say and Do

Talk about your boy's need for money. Let him tell you how important money is to him and why. Say such things as:

- How important is money to you?
- What do you need money for? Could you live without it?
- How much money would make you happy?

Talk about the relationship between careers and earning power. Discuss the kind of work he thinks he might like to do and how much money he can earn doing it. Say such things as:

- Do you know what careers would allow you to earn the most money?
- If you had to choose between being happy in your job and looking forward to going to work each day, or being unhappy in your job but making a lot of money doing it, which would you choose?
- If you're very good at any job you can probably earn a good living, but in some jobs the chances are much higher. I expect you've already thought about that.

Discuss the importance of saving money. Talk about what you do and what you've encouraged him to do. Say such things as:

- I try to put a regular amount in my savings account every month. When I have enough I put it into something that pays good interest.
- If you save a set amount of money each month and put it into something that pays good interest and if you let it sit there for years, it will grow very nicely.
- It's a good idea to save for emergencies.

Talk about other kinds of investments that you make. Say such things as:

- I get advice on good investments from my broker but I also do my own research into stocks, bonds, and mutual funds. Why don't you and I go and talk to my investment advisor about what you might want to do with some of the money you're earning?
- I try to spread out my investments to minimize the risk.

- Most investments outside of savings accounts and government bonds have some risk that goes with them. The higher the risk the better the interest rate.

Talk about money and values. Say such things as:

- You need money for food, shelter, and clothing. But these things come in lots of different shapes and forms. How important is it to you that you eat the most expensive food, wear the most expensive clothes, and live in the most expensive house?
- When you're married and have children how much money do you think you'll need for you and them to be happy?
- How important is money for happiness?

Words, Phrases, and Actions to Use

- . . . earn . . .
- . . . save . . .
- . . . invest . . .
- . . . risk . . .
- . . . values . . .
- . . . buy . . .
- . . . need . . .

- . . . want . . .
- . . . the best . . .
- . . . adequate . . .
- . . . enough . . .
- . . . greed . . .
- . . . happiness . . .

Things Not to Say and Do

Don't refuse to give your boy any experience with or control over money. Don't say such things as:

- As long as you live here I control all your money.
- You're too young to make any decisions.
- I'll give you money when you need it.

Don't be a bad example for your boy. Don't waste money, don't be greedy. Don't say such things as:

- When I want something I buy it.
- I use my credit card to its limit.
- I never pay off my credit card at the end of the month. I don't care about the interest.

- I could never have enough money.
- If you want to get rich you have to take risks.

Don't encourage your boy to waste his money. Don't say such things as:

- If you want it buy it. You could be dead tomorrow.
- I never save anything. I can't afford to.

Don't discourage your boy from saving and investing. Don't say such things as:

- I'd rather keep all my money in cash in a jar than put it into one of those blood-sucking banks.
- I don't trust banks. They just want to use my money and pay me almost nothing for it.
- Investment advisors are all crooks; they make money whether you do or not. You're better off spending your money and having something to show for it.

Words, Phrases, and Actions to Avoid

- Spend, spend, spend.
- There's never enough money.
- Buy now, pay later.
- I know I'm greedy.
- Get rich quick.
- Buy on credit.
- Money is the most important thing in life.

MUSIC, ART, DANCE, AND DRAMA

◆

You want your boy to love the arts. You love going to all kinds of music concerts, visiting museums and art galleries, and going to the theater. You've taken your boy along on many occasions, hoping that he would enjoy it, if not now, then when he's older. He certainly likes music. He's had piano and guitar lessons. He listens to his CD player constantly. Sometimes you think those headphones are growing out of his ears. He downloads music from the Internet. He loves going to concerts with his friends and he watches music television more than any other programs. He's not quite so keen on art. You've taken him to painting and sculpture exhibits you thought he might enjoy. But he has gone only reluctantly. You think maybe he has a real talent for drawing from the doodles and little pictures he does in the margins of his school notebooks. Maybe you'll try to get him to do some classes in life drawing or painting. You're sure that actually doing art will get him interested. Dance is something he likes doing at parties but you've never been able to get him to go with you to see a ballet or even jazz or modern dance. You hope when he's in college he'll come around. You've taken him to the theater, straight drama as well as musical theater and opera. He seems to like some of it, although not opera. Maybe you've taken him to the wrong opera. Overall, you've worked hard at introducing your boy to the arts and you're sure that when he's older he'll go to concerts, exhibits, and shows because he wants to.

Things to Consider

Boys seem generally to be much less interested in the arts than girls. Why is this the case? I know of no simple answer. Nevertheless, the truth is that many more girls than boys have music lessons, dance lessons, singing lessons, and join theatrical societies.

Giving your boy an appreciation of the arts, or, even better, giving him the skills and encouraging him to participate in them, is one of the greatest gifts you can give to him. The arts separate us from other animals more than anything else I can think of. Other species can communicate, use tools, and solve problems but they don't sing, play instruments, dance, or act simply for the pleasure of doing so. Even the most isolated people in the world do these things for each other.

Here are some of the very practical things you can do for your boy that will, at least, let him enjoy all the different forms of music, art, dance, and drama.

MUSIC:

- From an early age encourage him to listen to music, to play music, and to take music lessons.
- If you can, have a piano in the home, or at least a guitar or recorder.
- Don't censor his music. Let him listen to whatever he wants.
- Take him to concerts when he is old enough to sit still and not disturb those around him.
- Sing to him and encourage him to sing. Even eighteen-month-old boys can carry a tune.
- When he is a teen, if he doesn't already take lessons, encourage him to study an instrument, any instrument.
- Take him to see musical theater productions. Show videos of Broadway shows and Hollywood musicals.
- Buy your boy tickets to concerts for his birthday.
- Take him to see popular operas like *Porgy and Bess*, *La Bohème*, and *Carmen*.
- Above all, know that your boy is an older teen and talk to him about music, what he loves, what you love, and why you love it.

ART:

- Encourage him from an early age to draw, paint, and sculpt.
- Visit galleries, public art spaces, and museums.
- Make a space in your house for doing arts and crafts.
- Give your boy the tools to do art.
- Now that he's an older teen, talk to your boy about the art he sees in the community.

DANCE:

- Because this is the toughest sell of all for boys take it gently.
- Hopefully you encouraged him when he was a little boy to express his joy with life by dancing.
- Encourage him to see the kind of dance that he would enjoy, particularly jazz and tap.
- Point out the superb conditioning required of male ballet dancers.
- Watch old movies like *Grease* and *Saturday Night Fever*.

DRAMA:

- Talk about movies as theater.
- Encourage him to get involved in amateur community theater or in his high school drama club.
- Talk to him about how many more girls than boys there are in drama societies.
- Give him tickets to the theater for his birthday, Christmas or Hanukah, or any other gift-giving occasion.

While your boy is still a teen your best hope of getting him involved in the arts might be to show him how many girls he can meet by playing music, dancing, or acting. If this doesn't work don't despair or give up. Your encouragement might seem to be falling on deaf ears while your boy is still in high school, but as he grows older he will very likely remember those early experiences in the arts that you provided and thank you for them.

Three Things You Must Do

1. Realize that you cannot force your boy to enjoy all these things.
2. Take him to performances, galleries, and museums and encourage him to go on his own.
3. Talk about your love of the arts and give him the opportunity to love them too.

Things to Say and Do

Now that he is an older teen talk about his feelings for the arts. Ask him what he enjoys and why he enjoys it. Say such things as:

- Who's your favorite singer and band?
- Tell me something about that show you went to last night with your friends?
- I can tell your favorite kind of music from the CDs you play. What do you particularly like about it?

Offer to take your boy to concerts and shows with you. Say such things as:

- I'm getting tickets for the opera next month. Would you like to go with me?
- There's a great dance company coming to town this year. If I get tickets will you go with me?
- I'm going to see the show *Les Misérables* when it comes to town. It's a wonderful musical. Will you come with me?

Ask him about the opportunities he has for getting involved in theater. See if he's at all interested. Say such things as:

- Do you have a drama club at school? Are any of your friends involved?
- We have lots of community theater groups. Would you ever audition for them, or even work backstage?
- I think you'd be a great actor. Ever think you'd like to try?

Words, Phrases, and Actions to Use

- . . . art . . .
- . . . music . . .
- . . . drama . . .
- . . . dance . . .
- Play an instrument.
- Sing.

- Act.
- Meet lots of girls.
- Performing can give you a real high.
- It's beautiful.
- It's exciting.

Things Not to Say and Do

Don't try to force your boy to start music lessons, dance, or sing. You can ask him if he's interested but don't say such things as:

- You're going to learn how to play the piano whether you want to or not.
- I want you to take dance lessons. And think of all the girls you'd meet.
- You must start singing lessons now!

Don't discourage your boy if he shows an interest in any of the arts. Don't say such things as:

- Music lessons are for sissies.
- What makes you think you can dance?
- If you get a part in that play it'll take too much time away from your studies.

Don't refuse to help your boy with lessons if he wants them. Don't say such things as:

- It's too late for lessons now.
- If you want music lessons you'll have to pay for them yourself.
- I'm not paying for any son of mine to study ballet.
- I won't pay for voice lessons.

Don't pass on any dislike of the arts you may have to your boy. Don't say such things as:

- I've never understood these modern paintings. I think they're a lot of nonsense.
- Opera is just for snooty types.
- Ballet leaves me cold.

Don't criticize your boy's tastes in music, art, dance, or drama. Be thankful that he likes these things at all. Don't say such things as:

- Your taste in music stinks.
- I don't want you listening to that noise in my house.
- That art you like is really ugly.
- I don't know how you can listen to that stuff.

Words, Phrases, and Actions to Avoid

- That's sissy stuff.
- That's not worth it.
- That's just noise.
- That's meaningless.
- That's a waste of time and money.
- I can't waste my money on lessons.

PRIVACY

◆

You recognize your boy's increasing need for privacy. It's all part of his need for independence from you. Now that he's sixteen you don't really want him to have to share a room with his younger brother. You think giving him his own space in the basement is the best solution. You also recognize another aspect to privacy besides giving him his own physical space. He needs mental privacy as well. He needs the right to his own thoughts and feelings, his own goals and desires, his own beliefs about what is right and wrong, and his own chance to make mistakes. As he grows up you see in him the need for separation, both physical and mental, yet you also recognize that he still needs your guidance, support, and attention. It's a very hard time for both of you. You have arguments and disagreements about almost everything as he tests you and himself against his own ideas, interests, and actions. He wants you to include him in the family but he wants the right to exclude you from his life. He's like the young buck deer that wants to be included in the herd, but at the same time recognizes that it has no choice but to leave the safety and security it gives him. He is literally forced to strike out on his own, ultimately to form his own herd around him.

Things to Consider

Your boy has reached the age during which he must find himself and his place among other boys his age and he recognizes that he must do it alone, without much help from you. He needs to complete this search for identity and his personal sense of self-worth in the privacy of his own room, his own thoughts and feelings, and his own journey inward and outward.

Girls at this age seem quite different. Their need for privacy comes much earlier when they reach puberty, but even then their needs differ from boys. Physical privacy is the main issue. Relationships within the family are still very important for girls. They still share more of themselves with the family, especially with their moms. They do not need to withdraw from their family as boys seem to need to do. The girls remain within the group, boys must withdraw from it.

Your boy uses his time apart from the group to look inside himself to see what's there and how it compares to his friends and neighbors at school, as well as the young men he reads about and sees in the media. He's also looking outside himself to see what other young men say and do, what their thoughts and feelings are, what they have accomplished in school, sports, and relationships, and what they hope to accomplish in the future.

You can help him in his search by giving him room to try things, say things, and think things that are experiments in living. He's learning what works for him and what doesn't. One moment he's still your little boy, looking to you for attention, advice, comfort, and help; the next moment he's withdrawn from you, telling you that you don't understand him and you never will, that your values are corrupt, and that you are a hypocrite.

Can you live with this? Hopefully you realize you have no choice. You either live with it or you throw him out of the house, if not physically then symbolically. But this is not a good option. Even if he doesn't realize it, you are there to protect him from others and from himself. You give him his privacy because you are relieved for the moment from having to talk to him about stressful things like school, manners, curfews, drinking, drugs, and respect for others. Your boy may be a good son, but even the best boys at this age have their extreme moods. At times you're not even sure if you know who your son really is.

Privacy works for him and you. It gives him the isolation he needs to mull things over. It gives you a time-out from working through these problems with him. But there is another aspect to privacy that you should recognize. Privacy for your boy means the right to hold his own opinions without you telling him he doesn't know what he's talking about, he's too young to know about these things, or he's being selfish, misguided, pigheaded, stubborn, or just plain wrong.

When you talk to your boy you need to recognize when he's in his public mode—being open to you, sensitive and caring, loving and attentive, and the boy you think you know—and when he's in his private mode—being closed to you, inward-looking, searching, criticizing, inattentive, self-centered, and uncaring about others. Both modes are necessary for him at this age and you can help him on his road to manhood by working with him, whatever mode he happens to be in at the time.

Three Things You Must Do

1. Recognize your boy's need for physical and mental privacy.
2. Give your boy the privacy he needs.
3. Work with your boy whether he's in his public mode or private mode.

Things to Say and Do

Tell your boy you understand that he needs his private space, both physical and mental. Say such things as:

- I know you need time by yourself and I respect that.
- I don't need to know everything that's going on in your life, only the things you want to talk to me about.
- Let's talk about whatever you want to talk about.

If you have a physical space problem talk to your boy about his feelings about it and possible ways to solve it. See how much of an issue it is for him. Say such things as:

- I would love you to have your own room but we just don't have the space just now. Any ideas about what we can do?
- Let's talk about your need for a private space of your own. Let's see what we can come up with that will work for you and me.
- I think we can take part of the basement and make it into a room for you.

Talk about your boy's different moods and how you and he think you should handle them. Say such things as:

- I must be honest, I find it hard to cope sometimes with your different moods. Do you realize that I'm never sure which you I'll be talking to?
- Tell me about your feelings about how we should communicate with each other when you criticize everything I say and do.
- Sometimes I think you're crazy and sometimes I think I'm crazy when we talk to each other, and you and I seem to be coming from totally different places.

Make sure your boy knows that you will never give up on him no matter how withdrawn and critical of you he may become. Say such things as:

- I'm always going to be here for you because you're my son.
- I know we may argue and disagree on lots of things sometimes but I will always be here to listen to you and react to what you say.
- I don't mind when we argue about things. I don't expect you always to agree with me and I hope you don't want me to always agree with you.

Words, Phrases, and Actions to Use

- . . . independence . . .
- . . . private mode . . .
- . . . public mode . . .
- . . . moody . . .
- . . . erratic . . .
- . . . alone . . .
- . . . your space . . .
- . . . respect . . .

- ... value ...
- Your need your privacy.

- It's okay.

Things Not to Say and Do

Don't demand your boy's constant attention. Understand his times of withdrawal. Don't say such things as:

- You're a member of this family and I expect you to behave like one.
- Listen to me when I'm talking to you!
- I want to talk to you NOW!

Don't refuse to give your boy the physical privacy he needs if it's available. Don't say such things as:

- I shared a room when I was your age and it didn't bother me.
- You can have privacy when you have your own apartment.

Don't refuse to give your boy the mental privacy he needs. Don't expect him to share all his thoughts with you. Don't say such things as:

- I demand to know what you're thinking.
- I don't expect you to have any secrets from me.
- I'm your parent and I have a right to know what you're thinking.

Don't withdraw from your boy. Don't say such things as:

- If you won't talk to me I won't talk to you.
- I'm fed up with you. I wish you'd just go away.
- I feel like you're not my boy anymore.

Words, Phrases, and Actions to Avoid

- Tell me, or else ...
- You don't need your own space.
- Privacy in a family like ours is unnecessary.
- Go away.
- You're like a stranger to me.

Rights and
Responsibilities

◆

As your boy has grown older you've given him more rights and responsibilities. You want to make sure that he understands that he doesn't get one without the other. It's important, you realize, to guard against him taking things for granted, including the privileges he's been given now that he's almost eighteen. You've had long talks with him about what it means to mature, to be more responsible for himself, to use this responsibility wisely, and to show that he's able to handle these responsibilities. You've emphasized that the freedoms he wants—his "rights" as he calls them—have strings attached. Although he's almost finished with high school he still needs to depend on you for most of the essentials of life. You're responsible for his food, shelter, clothing, spending money, and many other things too numerous to mention. He contributes to these things also by working during the summer. You discourage him from working too much during the school year because school is, in fact, his most important work. His responsibility is to do his best in school. Your responsibility is to do everything you can to help him. He, in return, has the right to make decisions about lots of things in his life, from the kinds of clothes he wears to when he'll do his studying and what he'll do on the weekends.

Things to Consider

At age sixteen your boy has begun the last years of his childhood. By the time he's finished with high school he will be legally and physically a man. Although he may remain dependent on you for many things after the age of eighteen, he is legally responsible for himself. He can drive a car and may be able to get a drink in a bar in your state or a neighboring one.

You may decide to give him more responsibilities in conjunction with his need for more freedom to make his own decisions. If you let him borrow the family car for his own use you may want him to drive some of his younger siblings to their appointments. If he has the right to spend his weekend skiing with friends you might expect him to do some grocery shopping during the week to help you out when you're too busy to do it yourself. If he has the right to privacy and to have his own room you may give him the responsibility for keeping it neat and clean.

In other words you're showing him that rights and responsibilities are a trade-off. The more rights and freedom he has the more responsibilities he needs to take on, not just for himself but for the family. He may complain that you're not being fair, but that's okay. It gives you the opportunity to talk to him about what rights and responsibilities as an adult really mean. Talk to him about his views of the things you've given him, and give him yours. Make sure you listen patiently as, for example, he details the injustice of having so many new duties piled on him just when he's working so hard at school to get good grades so he can get into a good college. "You're not being fair," he says.

But of course you are being fair. You're teaching your boy that rights and freedoms have a price tag. That price is responsibility. As a boy, your son wants his independence from you. He needs it. He needs to measure himself against his friends who are also getting their first real taste of independence and responsibility for their own actions. He's concerned with his identity as an individual, his new relationships with other boys and girls, his path toward financial independence, which in most cases is still many years in the future, and his need to separate himself from his family and to make his own decisions. He measures himself against his friends using them as a standard, not necessarily a standard you would endorse.

Your work as a parent has changed from being your boy's main guardian and caregiver to giving your boy ever-increasing responsibility for himself as a kind of test of his readiness to take on the role of adult. You are involved in his rite of passage from being a boy to being a man.

Three Things You Must Do

1. Give your boy increased rights over his life.
2. Tie his increased rights to increased responsibilities.
3. Talk about any concerns that he may have with his new responsibilities.

Things to Say and Do

Your boy certainly wants more rights and privileges but he might not want the responsibilities that go along with them. This is your chance to talk about why the two have to go together. Say such things as:

- You know that everyone who wants more freedom has to pay for that freedom by taking on more responsibilities.

- Do you think rights and responsibilities go together? How?
- Does it seem reasonable that you should have more rights to run your own life without also having more responsibility for how you run it?

Discuss the need for your boy to be increasingly independent of the family. At the same time talk about the need for him to have more responsibilities within the family. The two need to go together. Say such things as:

- Now that you're using the car there are certain driving responsibilities I need you to help me with.
- I am happy for you to have more freedom to run your life as you want to. But you realize that the family needs your help more than ever to be responsible for things around the house.
- You are almost ready to leave the home and be out on your own, responsible for yourself. Until you do, we need you to be responsible for certain jobs here at home.

Your boy may complain that he needs more freedom, more rights, but not more responsibility. He'll tell you he has too much else to do. You can sympathize but tell him that he needs to learn to balance his rights with his obligations. It's part of being a man. Say such things as:

- I hear what you're saying. We all have too much to do but we learn to cope with it.
- Part of being an adult is learning to fulfill one's responsibilities while enjoying the rights and privileges that being an adult brings.
- You may think you have too many responsibilities already. I know what you mean. But you're a reasonable person and I know you'll cope.

Your boy wants to distance himself from the family. It's his way of becoming an adult. Talk to him about this process, showing you understand and support him in this. Say such things as:

- I know you need to make your own decisions.
- I understand what you're doing. It's part of growing up. But remember that I'll always be here for you.

Words, Phrases, and Actions to Use

- ... responsibility ...
- ... freedom ...
- ... rights ...
- ... independence ...
- ... growing up ...

- ... being an adult ...
- ... cutting the ties ...
- I need your help.
- You're a member of the family.
- I'll always be here for you.

Things Not to Say and Do

Don't refuse to acknowledge your boy's need for more rights and freedom. Don't say such things as:

- You're still a child.
- Just because you have a driver's license you think you're a man but you're still a little boy to me.
- Don't get too big for your boots.

Don't forget to give your boy increasing responsibility for himself as well as for family obligations. Don't say such things as:

- You're not old enough to take care of yourself.
- You can't do that. You don't know how because you're too young and inexperienced.
- You have too much to do already. Don't worry about doing things for me.
- I can promise you responsibilities only get worse as you get older. It's the price you pay for independence.

Don't refuse to give your boy new rights as he gets older. Don't say such things as:

- You can't get a learner's permit. You're not responsible enough to drive.
- You're not the best judge of what you can and cannot be responsible for.
- You'll do what I say as long as you live under my roof.

Words, Phrases, and Actions to Avoid

- You're too young.
- You're too immature.

- You're still a child.
- You've got no sense of responsibility.
- You'll do what I say.
- It's my way or the highway.
- No!
- I'll do everything for you but you don't have to do anything for me.
- You're still my little boy.

Safe Sex

◆

Your boy is almost seventeen and you think he's been sexually active already, although you're not completely sure. He has a steady girlfriend. They've been seeing each other for four months and he seems quite smitten with her and she with him. She's a nice girl from a nice family. You've met her parents and like them. You guess that they are as concerned as you are about the possibility that your children are having sex. Of course you think it's a bad idea but you realize that hormones are raging and the power of your boy's sexual urges has never been greater. He's a responsible boy and he would never intentionally do anything to hurt a girl. So there's no danger that they would have sex if she were unwilling. You know that girls have strong sexual urges too, although not as strong as boys. Girls remain the sexual gatekeepers. Yet you think that your boy's strong feelings for her and hers for him might easily have led them to intercourse. As they say in the murder mysteries you read, they have the motive, the time, and the opportunity. So, to err on the side of caution you decide you need to talk to your boy about the importance of safe sex.

Things to Consider

Your boy is programmed by nature to be the sexual aggressor. Testosterone makes the male sexually aggressive, competitive, and a risk-taker. Sexual intercourse with a girl is for many, if not most boys, a teenage holy grail. The drive to attain it is not easily denied. And statistics support this. Although percentages differ marginally in different reports, about 73 percent of boys report having had sexual intercourse by the time they reach the age of eighteen, compared with 56 percent of girls. Ninety-three percent of American males report having had sexual intercourse before marriage.

Boys need sex to prove they are men and having sex with a girl is the ultimate proof. Sex proves masculinity. Sex, for girls, seems to have a very different meaning. They see it as an act of love and connection.

However, like all things in life, it's not really that simple. Boys are often confused about sex. They know they want it but they know also that they must respect girls, their bodies, and their feelings. Boys are taught that sex before marriage is wrong yet their bodies and popular culture tell them that sex is one of their reasons for living.

Let's assume that you've talked to your boy about sex a long time ago, when he was a pubescent young teen. He knows your values and he's been taught to explore his own. You've taught him that sex is about more than satisfying his biological urges. And you've emphasized respect for girls and women.

But now you must deal with the very real possibility that your boy is having sex. So safe sex must be the most important thing on your mind. Here are the things you must discuss with your boy:

- The only really safe sex is no sex at all.
- If this is unrealistic then any sex must be protected sex.
- The birth control pill will prevent pregnancy but it will not prevent sexually transmitted diseases.
- AIDS (acquired immune deficiency syndrome) is one of the most serious diseases that can result from unprotected sex.
- AIDS is caused by the HIV virus, which is transmitted through the exchange of body fluids.
- HIV affects both the homosexual and heterosexual population.
- AIDS is the second leading cause of death among people twenty-five to forty-four in the United States.
- HIV infection can take up to ten years to turn into AIDS.
- Other sexually transmitted diseases include syphilis, gonorrhea, chlamydia, genital warts, herpes, and hepatitis B and C.
- Masturbation is a safe substitute for intercourse.
- Latex condoms are the best protection against pregnancy and disease during intercourse but they are not a hundred percent effective.

Three Things You Must Do

1. Recognize that abstinence may be an unrealistic expectation for your boy.
2. Talk to your boy about the dangers of unprotected sexual intercourse, and using condoms.
3. Make sure your boy knows he can always come to you for support if things go wrong.

Things to Say and Do

You have talked to your boy about sex when he was younger and it has sometimes come up in conversation during his teen years. But it never hurts to make your views about sex before marriage known to him. Say such things as:

- You know that I think sex before marriage is not a great idea for anybody, but especially for teens.
- I know you're in a good relationship with your girlfriend. I know you'll remember all the things we've talked about regarding sex and respect for her person.
- Sexual intercourse can cause an untold number of problems ranging from pregnancy to disease. That's why I'm against it for kids your age.

Assuming that your boy is one of the 73 percent of boys who have reported having sexual intercourse by age eighteen you need to talk about the consequences of sex. Say such things as:

- You know that you need never be afraid to come to talk to me if something happens and your girlfriend gets pregnant.
- You'd never have to face anything alone. I'm always here to help.

Talk about the feelings you know your boy must be having. Let him tell you what he feels and how he's coping with it. Say such things as:

- You're a virile, teenage boy and I know you feel certain things about girls. Would you like to talk about it?
- I know it's hard to talk about sex with your parent but are there any things you'd like to discuss?
- If you need to talk about your urges with anyone I can arrange for you to talk to our doctor about it. He's a good guy to talk to.

Words, Phrases, and Actions to Use

- . . . STDs . . .
- . . . condoms . . .
- . . . safe sex . . .
- . . . abstinence . . .
- Find a good Website that talks about STDs.
- Talk to our doctor.
- Don't be afraid to talk to me.

Things Not to Say and Do

Don't pretend your boy doesn't want sex. Don't say such things as:

- Don't come to me if anything ever goes wrong.
- You know I don't approve of sex before marriage so don't tell me things I don't want to hear.

Don't give your boy the impression that AIDS is a homosexual disease. Don't say such things as:

- It's only gays who get AIDS.
- AIDS is God's way of punishing gays for their sins.
- Normal people like us don't get things like AIDS.

You may have strong principles about using contraceptive devices like condoms. You must ask yourself if your boy's, or his partner's, health is more or less important than your principles. My position is that it isn't. So I would urge that you don't say such things as:

- You must either abstain or take the risks. Condoms are forbidden.
- Sexual intercourse outside of marriage is a sin. Contraception is a sin.
- If you sin you must accept the consequences.

Words, Phrases, and Actions to Avoid

- AIDS is God's punishment.
- You're a sinner.
- No contraception.
- Abstinence is the only way.
- Don't come crying to me.
- You get what you deserve.
- You're evil.
- You'll regret it.

SUCCESS

◆

You want your boy to succeed in everything he does: school, sports, relationships, and later college, marriage, and career. You've spent hours thinking about your boy and what would be best for him. In your more vulnerable moments you've thought about your financial circumstances and agonized over the possibility that you haven't been able to provide your boy with all the material advantages and opportunities he needs to become a successful man. But in your more lucid moments you've realized that you've done your very best and the rest is up to him. The best thing you think you've done is to talk to him about what success means to you and what you hope it will mean to him. You have tried to impress upon him the fact that success is a relative term. It means very different things to different people and also different things to the same people at different stages of their lives. You've told him the truth about your own experiences in life thus far and what have turned out to be the most important successes and failures for you. You hope he's taken in and understood some of what you said but you realize that your experiences can't be his and much of what he finally thinks about success he will have to learn for himself.

Things to Consider

Boys are programmed to compete with other boys for prizes. Prizes can come in many shapes and forms. The prize can be a higher grade than his friend's or girlfriend's, it can be higher status among the boys in his group, it can be a date with the girl he has a crush on, it can be a place on the starting team, or it can be a reputation as a "cool dude." These are some of the more positive prizes in their lives. They can also compete for negative prizes like having sex with a girl against her will, joining the toughest gang, shoplifting an expensive item, or getting expelled from school.

As boys compete they experience successes and failures and learn that they need to direct their energy where success is a possibility and not where failure is most likely. You don't have to teach most boys about this. It comes to them naturally. But there is some useful advice you can give them. You can talk to your boy about his personality, the kind of person you see in him, and, in your judgment, the kind of life and career he seems most suited for. He may not agree with you and he may not take your advice, but it's worth a try.

I firmly believe that the happiest people and, in that sense, the most successful are those whose work best suits their personality. As a teacher of teachers I have had many students who will spend their lives as teachers, underpaid and unappreciated by parents, school boards, and governments, working in overcrowded classrooms, with students whose parents and communities talk about doing their best for them but then chronically underfund education. Most of my students could have done anything with their lives—law, medicine, engineering, business, trades, or the arts—and been successful at it. And some will leave teaching after a while and pursue these other careers. But most will stay as teachers and thoroughly enjoy their careers in teaching because it suits their personalities. They will succeed in spite of all the negative things in teaching because they enjoy the interaction with young minds, the relative autonomy of the classroom, and the freedom to work out creative solutions to students' learning problems.

You can give your boy a great gift if you can convince him to listen to his innermost feelings about who he is, what kinds of activities he most enjoys doing, what kinds of people he likes to be around, and how important material things are to him. Help him see what he values and why. Talk to him about the choices you've seen him make in his young life. What kinds of friends does he have, how does he like to spend his free time, how much does he really like school, what subjects are his favorites, does he like sports, and how does he interact with you and other adults? Helping him to answer these questions honestly can give him insights into what kind of life choices he might make in the future that would bring him the greatest chances of success.

Three Things You Must Do

1. Let your boy know what you think most matters in a successful life.
2. Help your boy understand the pattern of his own life choices.
3. Teach your boy about the importance of personality as a factor in a successful life.

Things to Say and Do

Talk to your boy about how you see success and what it means to you. You can use yourself as an example, as well as others. Say such things as:

- We all want to succeed in life. The important question is, what counts as success?
- I think I've been quite successful in my career, even though I'm not making a fortune. Money is important but not as important as happiness in your work.
- I think money becomes the most important measure of success for most people

because they find little meaning or happiness in their work other than that. Take
Mr. _____, for example.

Help your boy gain insights into his personality. Talk about its importance in choosing
a career in which he has the best chance of success. Say such things as:

- Let's talk about what you're like, the choices you've made in friends, schoolwork, girlfriends, summer jobs, leisure activities, sports, music. All the things
  you find most important to you.
- What kind of person do you think you are? Where do you find the greatest
  pleasure and happiness?
- I think I've learned a lot about what you're like from what I know about you as
  my son, as well as from what others say about you.

If your boy is feeling that everything he does is unsuccessful sit down with him and
take an inventory of his successes and failures and see if there are any patterns that
appear. Talk about the reasons behind these successes and failures. Say such things as:

- It might be interesting to make two lists. The first one is all the things you think
  you've succeeded at and the second is the things you've failed at. Both are
  important experiences for you and you can learn a lot.
- Let's talk about what might be the reasons for your successes.
- Let's talk about what might be the reasons for your failures and how to avoid
  them in the future.

Words, Phrases, and Actions to Use

- . . . success . . .
- . . . happiness . . .
- . . . failure . . .
- . . . personality . . .
- . . . competition . . .
- . . . winners . . .
- . . . losers . . .
- . . . money . . .
- . . . family . . .
- . . . independence . . .
- What's most important in life?
- Be yourself.
- Know yourself.

Things Not to Say and Do

Don't try to impose your definition of success on your boy, especially if you see it solely
in terms of money. Don't say such things as:

- Money is the measure of all things.
- There's nothing more important than making a pile of money.
- If you don't make a lot of money in whatever you do you're a failure.

Don't ignore your boy's views on what matters to him. Don't say such things as:

- You're not old enough yet to know what real success is.
- You can talk about happiness all you like but real success is making lots of money.
- Your idea of success is too idealistic. Success is money and power.

Don't ignore your boy's successes and dwell on his failures. Don't say such things as:

- Boy, you really failed at that.
- I don't care about your successes; people only remember your failures.
- You must succeed at everything you try.

Don't dismiss your boy's chances of success in life. Don't say such things as:

- You'll never amount to anything.
- You'll never succeed at anything you do.
- You're a total failure and you always will be.

Words, Phrases, and Actions to Avoid

- You're a failure.
- You'll never succeed.
- Success and money are the same thing.
- You're a fool if you think that.
- You don't know what success is.

VALUES

◆

There's nothing more important to you than that your boy have good values. You want him to know what's right and wrong, good and bad, worth having and doing, and not worth having and doing. Your own value system has come from the religious teachings you were taught as a child but even more from your general experiences in life. You've learned what you really value and what you don't. When it comes down to your real value system you would say you didn't know what it was until you had to test it in some real-life situation. You've realized that you can claim that you value love, truth, honesty, compassion, caring, selflessness, and hard work but you didn't know what these really meant or how you would live them until you were in a situation in which you had to make decisions and take some kind of action. You know that your boy is quite idealistic and has a romantic notion of values. He's a good boy and you don't want to disillusion him by telling him what you think. On the other hand you want him to be prepared for the realities of life and how they can wreck a young man's idealistic view of the world. Most of all you want to make sure he understands the difference between claiming a certain set of values and putting those values into practice. You don't want him to think that most people are hypocrites simply because they seem to be saying one thing and doing another. You want your boy to realize that real life is much more complicated than that.

Things to Consider

What do you think are the core values that your teenage boy should live by? Love, respect, honesty, compassion, self-control? Your boy is physically a man but what is he emotionally? He has the muscles, strength, and stamina of a man. But that combined with the competitive and aggressive instincts and emotional immaturity of a boy can be a lethal combination. As I've noted elsewhere in this book boys give teachers most of the discipline problems, the roads are littered with the wreckage of cars crashed by teenage boys, and the newspapers and TV are filled with reports of violent acts committed by young men. It's not by accident that the ranks of armies are mainly filled by men between the ages of eighteen and thirty. They can become expert killing machines.

Where does this leave the value question for you and your boy? It makes it very real because you know that your boy is often close to the edge of aggression, either by him or by another boy. This makes the issue of values even more important because it is a good value system that can work to inhibit unthinking acts of aggression. It goes beyond that as well. Good values in a boy mean the promise of a good man. Good boys value:

- School
- Homework
- Parents' wishes
- The rights of girls and women
- Honesty
- Love
- Friendship
- Talking through problems

- Compromise
- Tolerance
- Forgiveness
- A sense of humor
- Sportsmanship
- Respect
- Giving to others

Good boys also value:

- Winning
- Competition
- Rough-and-tumble sports
- Sex
- Winning a girl's affection
- Loud music

- Independence
- Privacy
- A car of one's own
- Beating the other guys
- Being cool
- Being right

You have to work with your boy when these values conflict to make sure he sees the conflict and tries to make the right choice. Expect him to be imperfect, as you are. Expect him to make mistakes, as you do. Expect him to need help, as you might. Expect him to have to learn most of his values from his own experience, as you have.

Three Things You Must Do

1. Be realistic about the values you teach your boy.
2. Expect him to learn most of his values through a combination of what you've taught him and his own experiences.
3. Teach that value conflicts are a normal part of life.

Things to Say and Do

Talk about values based on everyday issues and experience. Specific examples help make values real. Say such things as:

- Did you hear about those kids cheating on a test at school? What was your reaction?
- I read recently about a couple of boys who killed a student just because he was homosexual. I can't understand why anyone would do that, can you?
- I often see athletes cheat in football games, saying they caught the ball when it's clear on the replay that it hit the ground first. I think doing a thing like that just to help your team win is wrong, don't you?

Talk about your boy's values. Ask him what he thinks are the most important values a boy his age should have in specific cases. Say such things as:

- If you had to list the things that a boy should use to guide his behavior toward his girlfriend, what would you say?
- Are marks more important than anything? Would you ever cheat to get a good grade?
- If you found a bag of money, what would you do with it?

Talk to your boy about your values. Be realistic and honest. You can use stories to illustrate your points. Say such things as:

- I think capital punishment is wrong for all sorts of reasons. What do you think?
- I've always thought that a good sense of humor was an important thing to value, don't you?
- Love and compassion are at the top of my list of values. What's at the top of your list?

Talk about situations, very real, in which values come into conflict with each other. Say such things as:

- Value decisions aren't always easy or clear-cut. In real life things are too complicated.
- I can think of lots of times when I held two values that were in conflict with each other. Have you ever had that happen? Like when you wanted to do something good for someone and you could get to do it by lying. What's the more important value—doing good or complete honesty?
- Did you ever tell someone they looked good when you really thought they looked awful? You don't want to hurt someone's feelings so you lie. Is that the right thing to do? That's the kind of value judgment we often have to make.

Words, Phrases, and Actions to Use

- . . . honesty . . .
- . . . compassion . . .
- . . . love . . .
- . . . respect . . .
- . . . friendship . . .
- . . . sense of humor . . .

- . . . choices . . .
- . . . a complex world . . .
- . . . not clear-cut . . .
- . . . confused . . .
- . . . difficult . . .

Things Not to Say and Do

Don't be a poor role model for your boy. Don't say such things as:

- Whatever you do make sure it's in your best interests. That's what I do.
- I don't think values matter. Just do what feels right.
- You have to look out for yourself. No one else will if you don't. So do what's good for you.

Don't give your boy the wrong values. Don't say such things as:

- It's the law of the jungle, kill or be killed, eat them before they eat you.
- I don't think anyone's value system makes much sense. You just have to do what you feel like doing.
- I don't see any sense in having a value system in today's world. It seems like anything goes.

Don't expect your boy to be perfect. Don't say such things as:

- You have terrible values.
- You never do what you ought to do.
- You're an evil person.

Don't pretend to be perfect yourself. Don't say such things as:

- Someday you might be able to live up to my standards.
- You'll never be as good as I am.
- You're a dead loss. I give up on you.

Words, Phrases, and Actions to Avoid

- You're a loser.
- That's immoral.
- You have no values.
- You're evil.

- You're a sinner.
- You're a bad boy.
- I don't want to know you.
- You're not my boy.

REFERENCES

Here are some books that I read in my search for important information about boys and the important differences between boys and girls. These books range from personal accounts of boys, and parents of boys, to psychological, medical, and pediatric discussions of brain and hormonal differences between the sexes and how these differences influence and shape social and cultural norms.

Bassoff, Evelyn. *Between Mothers and Sons: The Making of Vital and Loving Men* (Plume/ Penguin, 1995). A psychologist draws on research, myths, legends, and experience to advise mothers on how to raise sons to become vital, loving men.

Boyd-Franklin, Nancy, and A. J. Franklin. *Boys into Men: Raising Our African-American Teenage Sons* (Dutton, 2000). A husband and wife psychologist team discuss the issues involved in raising African-American teenage boys, giving advice on how to deal with such topics as violence, drugs, peers, gangs, sex, and racism, among others, and offering parents effective problem-solving strategies.

Glennon, Will. *200 Ways to Raise a Boy's Emotional Intelligence* (Conari Press, 2000). This book offers specific advice on how to free boys/men from their stereotypical roles and behavior. It gives practical suggestions but stops short of telling parents what to say to their boys.

Gurian, Michael. *Boys and Girls Learn Differently! A Guide for Teachers and Parents* (Jossey-Bass, 2001). Gurian, a therapist and educator, takes a comprehensive look at the brain differences in boys and girls and the implications of those differences for teaching and learning.

Gurian, Michael. *The Good Son* (Tarcher/Putnam, 2000). One of three books specifically on boys written by Gurian. This book provides quite a comprehensive discussion of the problem of moral decay among boys and young men, and specific advice on what to do about it.

Gurian, Michael. *What Stories Does My Son Need?* (Tarcher/Putnam, 2000). A guide to two hundred movies and books that will build character in boys. This book is an annotated catalogue of films and books categorized by appropriate age and school grade.

Gurian, Michael. *The Wonder of Boys: What Parents, Mentors, and Educators Can Do to Shape Boys into Exceptional Men* (Tarcher/Putnam, 1997). This focuses its advice on what to do to make boys strong, responsible, sensitive men by channeling boys' natural propensities for competition and aggression. He emphasizes the importance of adult and community role models and support groups.

Moore, Sheila, and Roon Frost. *The Little Boy Book* (Ballantine, 1987). These two writers have written a parents' guide to the first eight years of a boy's life. It's designed to answer parents' questions about boys' growth and development, and parenting practices in light of what boys are like.

Newberger, Eli H. *The Men They Will Become: The Nature and Nurture of Male Character* (Perseus Books, 1999). Written by a Harvard pediatrician, this book discusses parenting practices that will help a boy become a secure, competent, ethical, loving man. It illustrates its ideas with interesting stories and anecdotes.

Pollack, William S. *Real Boys: Rescuing Our Sons from the Myths of Boyhood* (Henry Holt, 1999). A *New York Times* bestseller written by a clinical psychologist at Harvard, this book explains what adults can do to help boys deal with very real issues that are often masked or ignored in our stereotypical raising of boys. It illustrates its argument with many stories and anecdotes.

Pollack, William S. *Real Boys' Voices: Boys Speak Out about Drugs, Sex, Violence, Bullying, Sports, School, Parents, and So Much More* (Random House, 2000). A collection of anecdotes from boys about their experiences growing up as boys in a society that ignores male problems by assuming that boys are the chosen gender.

Sommers, Christina Hoff. *The War Against Boys: How Misguided Feminism Is Harming Our Young Men* (Simon & Schuster, 2000). Written by a former philosophy professor at Clark University and current fellow at the conservative think tank the American Enterprise Institute, this book argues that boys are at risk because of the attention being given to girls at boys' expense. Boys need academic help, love, discipline, respect, and moral guidance. "They do not need to be rescued from masculinity."

Stevens, Patricia (ed). *Between Mothers and Sons: Women Writers Talk about Having Sons and Raising Men* (Scribner, 1999). A series of personal stories about the raising of boys edited by a writer on women's experiences.

Thompson, Michael. *Speaking of Boys: Answers to the Most-Asked Questions about Raising Sons* (Ballantine, 2000). By the psychologist author of the bestseller *Raising Caine*, this book gives parents advice on a wide range of topics, using a question/answer format.

Williams, Gregalan. *Boys to Men: Maps for the Journey* (Doubleday, 1997). Written by an African-American actor and author, this book is an autobiographical account of how he survived his boyhood by overcoming many external and self-created obstacles to become a successful man.

INDEX